LATINO
IN AMERICA

A CELEBRA BOOK

SOLEDAD O'BRIEN

with rose marie arce

LATINO

CELEBRA
Published by New American Library, a division of Penguin Group (USA) Inc., 375 Hudson Street, New York, New York 10014, USA • Penguin Group (Canada), 90 Eglinton Avenue East, Suite 700, Toronto, Ontario M4P 2Y3, Canada (a division of Pearson Penguin Canada Inc.) • Penguin Books Ltd., 80 Strand, London WC2R 0RL, England • Penguin Ireland, 25 St. Stephen's Green, Dublin 2, Ireland (a division of Penguin Books Ltd.) • Penguin Group (Australia), 250 Camberwell Road, Camberwell, Victoria 3124, Australia (a division of Pearson Australia Group Pty. Ltd.) • Penguin Books India Pvt. Ltd., 11 Community Centre, Panchsheel Park, New Delhi - 110 017, India • Penguin Group (NZ), 67 Apollo Drive, Rosedale, North Shore 0632, New Zealand (a division of Pearson New Zealand Ltd.) • Penguin Books (South Africa) (Pty.) Ltd., 24 Sturdee Avenue, Rosebank, Johannesburg 2196, South Africa

Penguin Books Ltd., Registered Offices:
80 Strand, London WC2R 0RL, England

First published by Celebra,
a division of Penguin Group (USA) Inc.

First Printing, October 2009
10 9 8 7 6 5 4 3 2

Cover photo credits: A member of Together Car Club (Kyle Christy/CNN), Lupe Ontiveros with Rose Arce and Soledad O'Brien (Mathieu Young/CNN), Eva Longoria Parker (Kyle Christy/CNN), Soledad O'Brien at a parade (Rose Arce/CNN), George Lopez (Edward M. Pio Roda/CNN), Soledad O'Brien reporting (Jensen Walker/Getty Images for CNN), Edward James Olmos (Edward M. Pio Roda/CNN), Erica Sparks (Kyle Christy/CNN), Senator Mel Martinez (Mark Hill/CNN), "Marta"(Mark Hill/CNN)

CELEBRA and logo are trademarks of Penguin Group (USA) Inc.

Library of Congress Cataloging-in-Publication Data

O'Brien, Soledad, 1966-
   Latino in America/Soledad O'Brien with Rose Marie Arce.
   p. cm.
   ISBN 978-0-451-22946-5
   1. Latin Americans—United States-History. 2. Latin Americans—United
States—Social conditions. 3. Cuban Americans—History. 4. Cuban Americans—
Social conditions. I. Arce, Rose Marie. II. Title.
   E184.S75O276 2009
   973'.00468—dc22   2009025838

Set in Sabon
Designed by Pauline Neuwirth

Printed in the United States of America

contents

introduction   1

1 ▪ my life in black and white   7

2 ▪ children of the revolution   32

3 ▪ have a magical day   73

4 ▪ the mexican in town   97

5 ▪ eva and lupe   132

6 ▪ morir soñando   158

7 ▪ lowriders in mayberry   186

8 ▪ the graduation of cindy garcia   216

epilogue   245

acknowledgments   249

WHEN YOU HAVE a name like María de la Soledad Teresa O'Brien, you have a lot of explaining to do. My mother is black and also Latina, more specifically Cuban. She is a devout Catholic who credits the Virgin Mary with any success she's had in this country. But it was my father, a man who spoke no Spanish, who chose the name María de la Soledad to honor the Blessed Virgin Mary of Solitude ("solitude" in Spanish is *soledad*).

My name is altogether too long for Americans, who've always struggled with it. It's even too long for a driver's license. African-Americans assume I'm named after the notorious Soledad prison or Mount Soledad in California. Latinos want to know if I'm lonely. That doesn't fit because I grew up with five siblings and I have four kids of my own, so I'm not lonely at all, though I do often seek solitude, the actual meaning of my name.

My father was Irish and Scottish, but from Australia, and my parents added Teresa when I was confirmed. My parents named all their children after people they loved and admired, and when it got to me it was the Virgin Mary's turn. When I married I thought about taking my husband's name (Raymond), but I realized that, odd as it is, the name I have works. I have a mass of kinky hair, light brown skin, and lots of freckles. I'm black and Cuban, Australian and Irish, and like most people in America, I'm someone whose roots come from somewhere else. I'm a mixed race, first-generation American.

My ethnic roots are relevant when you look at the broader picture of who brings us the news. Who you are matters oh so very much when, according to the National Association of Hispanic Journalists (NAHJ), just 6 percent of the people working in TV news and 4 percent of the newspaper reporters in this country are Latinos. The NAHJ presents a report on media diversity called the "Brownout Report" and it determined that less than 1 percent of the stories aired by the networks include Latinos, and that tiny amount is heavily concentrated on immigration, crime, and drugs.

It's hard to be the lone ethnic face in the room. People look to me to explain a community that is diverse and ever-changing, a community with which sometimes I don't have a great deal in common. There is so little in-depth reporting on people of color that I set the bar high for myself and the people around me. I see the job I have now as my opportunity to get good reporting about black and brown people on TV, as a chance to bring people together, and to tell a fair and accurate story of communities of color, not just rehash stereotypes for the sake of drama.

More than anything, the stories have to be good, the story lines compelling, and the people in them interesting. If no one watches, then I've accomplished nothing.

The communities I cover have their own high expectations. People see this as a rare chance for good reporting about their communities to make it to television and they expect a lot. It can be exhausting to be reduced to your race and ethnicity. You can be made to feel bad about where you come from or feel bad about succeeding or feel like you're not a part of a community because your experience is different. My Cuban-born mother is wonderful on this topic. This woman who didn't teach her children Spanish did teach us pride. "Don't let them tell you you're not black," she tells me. "Don't let them tell you you're not Hispanic or not Cuban." And I don't.

The fact that I work for CNN has fostered my commitment to telling great stories about people of color. CNN, a part of the Time Warner company, lives for news about everything and anyone. In the office, the bosses openly discuss the need for a diverse staff and diverse stories, and each time we draw new viewers, the effort intensifies. There is an active diversity council, aggressive diversity training, regular speeches from the highest officers of the company about how our country is changing and CNN has to be a part of that change. They see the demographics of the future and know they have to look at their hiring and reporting practices so that they appeal to the widest possible audience.

As CNN saw our growth in African-American viewership, they affirmed a fundamental truth of news coverage—people will watch you if they see themselves in what you report. It doesn't hurt if the people doing the reporting look like them, too.

In 2007, CNN's coverage was altered dramatically by the launch of a series called *Uncovering America*, and the entire staff was asked to find compelling stories about the broadest range of people possible, not just people of color but folks of every race and ethnicity from all walks of life. That series was followed by the launch of a documentary project called *Black in America* and I was tapped to be the correspondent.

The yearlong effort of *Black in America* was exhausting for me. I was one of a handful of black voices on the staff and each day was a meshing of ideas and backgrounds and cultures. In other words, we argued a lot. I compiled everything. I learned new things about the black community that I'd lived in and covered my entire life. The result was a four-hour documentary that earned terrific reviews, got more viewers than almost any CNN documentary, and started a discussion about the community of which I continue to be proud.

Not everything was perfect. It's critical in covering a community well to report both the good and the bad. I learned so much about reporting on race and some unexpected lessons about the stress of being a woman of color in the media. But by the time the project ended I felt like I had started an important conversation about the struggles and the successes of the African-American community.

It became time to bring the same focus to bear on Latinos. So CNN began reporting *Latino in America* in the fall of 2008 with the goal of showing a community that was changing the United States even as the United States was changing them. I was tapped to be the correspondent once again.

My first thought was what a terrific opportunity this was for me! After so many years of fighting for fair and accurate coverage of people of color, I finally had a chance to work on a wide-ranging project that could show all Americans a fuller picture of who Latinos are and what they mean to this country. I vowed to give voice to the part of the community I knew, an optimistic, family-centered people who infuse U.S. culture with the warmth of their humanity.

My community embraced this project from the outset with an enthusiasm I'd not expected. Total strangers approached me with advice and assistance. Over and over, I was asked to please report on the people who are so often ignored, the Latinos who do not reflect the "illegal alien" who crosses the border "to steal American jobs." People, many of them my own coworkers, asked me to push past the rancor of the immigration debate, which has strayed from being a discussion of policy and law enforcement to one that demonizes and stereotypes and hurts people whether they are illegal immigrants or not.

Latinos saw this documentary as a wonderful opportunity to showcase the cultural struggles and contributions of Latinos; to focus on education, community, and faith and show the broader public a more complete picture of how we live. It was clear that the community felt starved for good solid coverage. No one asked me to do a snow job. Just please don't reduce us to crime, immigration, and racial conflicts, they asked. Folks just didn't want to see their community hurt anymore and were very blunt about it. One afternoon I had lunch with Lupe Ontiveros in Los Angeles. She is a beloved Latina actor who has been reduced to the role of the maid or the nanny in scores of movies. I asked Lupe to be a major character in our documentary and she offered an enormous amount of assistance. When I left the table she turned to my producer and said bluntly in Spanish, "Please, just don't f— us."

In the end, that wasn't hard because there are so many great untold stories to tell about Latinos that I knew would interest an audience of any racial or ethnic origin. The numbers of Latinos are exploding and spanning out into places where Latinos have never been seen before. Their impact on the United States is awesome. I knew from the outset I had to have as broad a focus as possible to cover such a large story. My team of producers, photographers, and editors had to look at the Latino community through many sets of eyes. I urged our team to break new ground, to not end up rehashing the same old story told of any minority community, that there are Anglos unhappy they've arrived. That is not what it means to be Latino in America. We had to step back and watch a more complex human story unfold.

As we did our reporting, I realized quickly how challenging this was going to be. Latinos are an extremely diverse ethnicity that can be of any race and have many different origins, history, and traditions. You can't easily group people who come from as far away as Buenos Aires and Rio with people of Mayan, Inca, and Taino descent who have mixed with Spaniards, Africans, and Jews. We are about so much more than where we came from or how we look.

The essential point is that we don't come together in a real way until we set foot on U.S. soil. That's when our "Latino" experience begins. Latino is an American identity. It is a word to describe Americans who are drawn to each other by this intangible cultural link, the similarity of the way we run our families, our devotion to faith, and the warmth of our personalities, our connection to a history that recognizes no border to the south. Latinos are a people who celebrate the new culture they've created in the United States while struggling each day with whether we need to assimilate or integrate into this new society. We ask ourselves what good things we want to preserve from our culture and what American values we want or need to adopt. And that question never goes away, not one, two, or three generations beyond immigration.

That is the major reason I was compelled to take my project further, to write this book and crisscross this country speaking publicly about my community.

I truly believe more Latino journalists need to be talking about the future, about what will happen if this nation does not embrace the biggest cultural change of its lifetime and to educate people about it. I feel I am up to the task.

If I had any unease defining who I am, reporting this story has shown me my place in this Latino community. That place is as the Latina journalist charged with telling the story of the culture my mother gave me, the culture that is changing America and being changed by America. I need to show America the beauty of my culture, the work ethic of my people, and their unflagging faith. I need to introduce America to the wonderful music, food, and sport our culture has brought to the American mix, just as previous immigrant groups—the Germans, Jews, or Irish—did before Latinos. I need to be the one who explains that our American Dream is not the same as those of other immigrant groups because our journey to the United States, back and forth across the border, predates the journeys of all those immigrant groups and will obviously continue into the future regardless of what happens. Latinos have a plan, not a dream, and it is to mix the best of ourselves with the best of this country.

I want to talk about a people who hold fast to familiar roots however distant they are from immigration, who believe that humility and pride can come together, that resentment and fear are a toxic mix, that you have to have a bit of fight in you to get ahead but cherish the ability to smile at yourself at the end of the day. I have never wanted to be defined by the color of my skin, my funny freckles, or my mother's obvious accent. But I am happy to let it determine how I stand in the world.

Latinos are already the majority minority in the United States and their numbers are so great that they will be the future of this country even if immigration stops tomorrow. The number of Latinos who are U.S.-born now surpasses the number of immigrant Latinos. The average age is in the teens. This young population wants to identify as Latino, they want to speak the Spanish of their ancestors no matter how many generations they are removed from immigration. They are proud of who they are, just as I am.

I worry about our future if the current young Latino generation feel like strangers in the land where they were born or end up resentful because they have seen their parents and their culture demonized by the people around them. I came to love who I am because I had parents who allowed their kids to prosper as individuals. I was well educated in a community that valued difference. I have a high investment in the future. One of four children in this country is Latino, and four of them are mine. So I will tell the story of Latinos the way I know it should be told. Starting with my own.

1

my life in black and white

MY FAMILY WAS born of flight. My mom and dad hit it off in part because they were both people who had left their childhood homes and set off on their own. They are united by something stronger than the racial divisions that surround them. They came to this country to start life anew, to write a new history.

My dad, Edward Ephram O'Brien, always spells out his life in simple facts. He was raised in a rural town called Toowoomba in Queensland, Australia. His folks had a giant family tree that traced their roots to Brian Boru, High King of Ireland a thousand years ago (hence the O'Brien). It was the same line, my aunt used to tell us, as Ronald Reagan's. He rode an old broken-down horse to his private boys' school and had a stocky build from playing rugby. His family ran a bakery and milling company that did very well and they became wealthy when it went public ten years ago.

My father received a B.S. from Queensland University in Brisbane in 1955. There was a job waiting for him as a chemical engineer in the family mill when he graduated. But he wanted to study mechanical engineering and be on his own, so he left for the United States. He came to study at Purdue University, where he remained until he received an M.S. in 1957. I always thought of him as the opposite of my mother, quiet where she was assertive, mellow where she was intense. As a teenager I thought they were a terrible mismatch. They celebrated their fiftieth anniversary last year, so clearly I was wrong.

My mother's history is harder to pin down. Her name is Estela Lucrecia Marquetti y Mendieta. Her father, Nicolás Alberto, and her mother, Luz, were very poor. My cousins told me she was raised on the same street where the singer Celia Cruz had lived. Nicolás Mendieta was a gambler, which meant good times when he was lucky and struggle when he was not. In the 1940s, being black and poor guaranteed a terrible existence.

"In Cuba the whites had more money, more contacts, many had American friends who were very racist. We didn't have to discuss it. It just existed. We all knew who had more, who had less. It wasn't often that a black family would have more. In general, white families had more," my mother remembers. "Having a job in Cuba was a big deal. Even a little job because there were so few jobs and whoever had one, had more possibilities. It was a big deal to your family. One job in Cuba would feed a whole family. It was crucial. The people were very hardworking. They worked and they earned their money. That's the way I remember them."

My mother didn't see her life going anywhere. White folks hid their black friends and being black was not a plus. This was before Castro; before politics changed the island's relationship with the United States. If you wanted to come to the United States you could. My mother had a friend who could speak English and she wanted to learn it, too. She told her parents she wanted out.

Her departure was simple. She was fourteen and her father took her to meet the Oblate Sisters, who operated several missions in Cuba until Fidel Castro's revolution closed them down. The Oblate Sisters claim to be the first Roman Catholic female religious order of African descent. In addition to Cuba, they had sisters in several U.S. cities, Costa Rica, the Dominican Republic, and in Africa, and had devoted themselves to educating the black poor. They ran a school for girls in Baltimore, where they were established.

"We went to the sisters in Havana to talk about what it was like in the United States. Was it possible for me to go? They explored the possibility of me going to the United States for one year to learn English. That's when we decided," my mother said.

Was she nervous about leaving her family behind? "Hate to say this, but no," she said. It was 1947.

The Oblate Sisters were devoted to the Virgin Mary and my mother clearly embraced their religiosity with vigor. Their symbol is a white cross dividing a blue shield. The cross reflects their humility. There is also a lily and an anchor to represent purity and trust in God and a lily and a heart to represent love of children and oblation to God.

At first, they took my mother to St. Frances Academy in Baltimore. She was smart, ambitious, and hardworking and ended up at the College of Notre Dame of Baltimore. Her siblings stayed behind in Cuba. She liked life at the boarding school. There was a routine. They would say Mass every morning at 6:30, and there were rules and uniforms so you didn't have to worry about something to wear. She was there for four years, then four more because she couldn't afford a place to live while she went to college and they let her stay. This was back when people from Cuba could travel freely. She went back to visit her family after the first year; then her father came for graduation. Her mother came to visit when she graduated from college. She always intended to go back, but that's not how things turned out.

Finding out about this period in my mother's life and how it affected her was very challenging. I have no real sense of how she went from being a Cuban teenager to an immigrant Latina because it is not something she likes to discuss. She doesn't willingly talk about Cuba or the past. She knew her family was back there working and that she had more opportunities than they did. I know she kept in touch. But one of the things that distinguishes Cuban immigrants from other Latinos is that we can't just go back and touch home base whenever we want. So at whatever point the country closed down, my mother did too. The Ecuadorians can visit distant cousins and understand so much about their family life in the United States. The Cubans are left to build their identity on U.S. soil and many of them group together and preserve their traditions.

My mother didn't even do that. Once she married my father, our family became her community. When I began to write this book, she did agree to talk about her past, but her memories were selective. She talked a lot about her embrace of Catholicism, how her experience living with the nuns wiped away so much else about her life and ushered in a new reality. She talked a little about the life she'd left behind. She recalled her family's devotion to Santería, a Caribbean religion that is sometimes derided as voodoo but holds a sacred place in Cuban culture, particularly for black people. The word "Santería" means someone who has the spirit. She remembers her cousins shutting her out because she walked away from the religion, with its drumming and rituals, high priests and priestesses. It was a link she severed when she left Cuba.

As little as she personally embraced Santería, she insisted that I include it in the story of her childhood in Cuba.

"I think I hurt my mother's feelings when I came to this country because I wasn't doing it. My mother was slighted because I had been to college and university. I didn't want to get together with it. It didn't have a place with me. I have never used it. But as you get older you begin to see the value of it. You can see it more clearly," she said.

"When we were children we used to go to a town where they used to have a date in September when people would come [and] they had rituals at various houses. They would dance and play drums at the house of a big person. At the end of the day there were twenty women cooking all kinds of chickens and pigs and this, that, and the other. A chance for people who didn't have a chance to eat to eat. Then they would end up by the drums dancing. My nieces and nephews don't want to have me over because they felt that because I am Catholic that I don't go to these things. It's not that cut and dried."

She did bring her "spirit" with her to the United States, she insists, this girl they nicknamed "Cuchi," which doesn't sound pious at all. But it is the solitary spirit of the religious young woman I see in black-and-white photos from that convent school long ago. My mother with her thick black hair standing alongside these very serious nuns, her pocket eyes and full lips swollen with a girl's smile. At that age she looks a bit like I do now, a little bit of this, a little bit of that.

As my mother's memory fades along with the memories of all the people from that era, I feel my history being lost. I was able to extract the tiniest portion of hard information from my mother, the contact details for Sister Alice Chineworth, who had been one of the Oblate nuns she knew in school. When I got the address I took the first flight I could out of New York to Washington, D.C., to meet a woman who promised to open the doors to my mother's history.

Sister Alice Chineworth is ninety-two and still lives at the convent on Gun Road in Baltimore. I confess that I made this appointment to meet her because I knew she was getting older and was likely the only person who could answer the questions my mother wouldn't answer. I thought I had to interview her before she died, but when I met her I saw I needn't have worried. In person, she seems barely sixty. Even though she uses a walker, she gives the impression of being strong, sturdy, and of sharp mind.

"The worst thing about getting old," she tells me as we walk the halls of the motherhouse of the Oblate Sisters of Providence in Baltimore, "is you have no one to share things with."

We have breakfast downstairs in the convent, which has this feel of a school from the seventies. Black-and-white pictures of the order from its founding in the 1800s line the walls. Later I had breakfast with about twenty-five nuns, including one who knew my mother from Cuba. They all hugged me and said my mother had sent them tapes of me on TV, my mother who never discusses my work and keeps us all humble and sane. As the stories came out I wrote furiously to keep up, surrounded by all these aging women with their walkers and canes.

But sadly many of the stories she tells me send my mother's eyebrows air bound when I recount them. They are false recollections. The only thing my mother confirms is that the Oblates were fiercely devoted to educating black children, and they had burned in my mother a pride and a consciousness about being black that explains why she walks with her head so high. I also learned that at a very young age my mother was on her own.

The only conversation my mother and I ever had about her time living in a convent was when I was a frustrated sixteen-year-old, bristling under strict household rules and desperate to leave Long Island for college. I was practically spitting at what I saw as rank hypocrisy.

"You moved on your own to another country at fourteen and I can't stay out until ten o'clock?" My mother's answer was equally snitty.

"Go to a convent and you can stay out," she said. End of conversation.

At the convent, I kiss the sister good-bye and make promises. I will help with the fund-raising for the new building that sits half finished on a plot among their many acres of land. I promise to help host their next banquet. While the sister is fuzzy on the details, I do feel I have tapped into a part of my family history that no one else will share with me. I have a better understanding of my mother's absolute determination to keep her children near her. "I love you too much to send you to camp," she would say. But I don't know if my mother will ever answer the questions I have. Does she appreciate that her parents saved her from poverty? That she avoided sharing the fate of her siblings and nieces and nephews stuck in Cuba to this day when she was shipped off to a foreign land to be raised by a nun? Does she resent the decision? I can't even imagine what it must have felt like when she realized there was no going back.

My mother's adult history as a Latina is much easier to trace because it involves my father, whom she called Ted. In 1958, she was working at Johns Hopkins University in Baltimore in a science lab. My father was there pursuing his Ph.D. in mechanical engineering and they met. For many weeks he offered her a ride to a nearby Catholic church and she said no. Then one day she said yes.

My black mother and my white father couldn't legally marry in their church in Maryland. The ban on interracial marriage was being challenged by civil rights activists and a lawyer suggested they become a test case. Instead, on December 26, 1959, they decided to drive to Washington, D.C., where they could get a license. Castro had come to power the previous February, kicking out the Oblates and other religious orders, and ending up in a tense stalemate with the United States that stopped easy travel. As one chapter of my mother's life closed, she opened a new one on U.S. soil.

Their marriage situation was similar to that of Mildred Jeter, a black woman, and Richard Loving, a white man, who couldn't marry in Virginia. They also drove to Washington, D.C., to wed in 1958, but one night after they returned home, police officers burst into their bedroom and arrested them. They were convicted of violating the antimiscegenation statute, the Racial Integrity Act of 1924, and had to leave town. What Virginia Judge Leon Bazile ruled in their case speaks volumes about the atmosphere that surrounded couples like my parents:

"Almighty God created the races white, black, yellow, Malay and red, and he placed them on separate continents. And but for the interference with his arrangement there would be no cause for such marriages. The fact that he separated the races shows that he did not intend for the races to mix."

The Lovings became the test case. In 1967, in a case called *Loving v. Virginia*, the U.S. Supreme Court ended all race-based legal restrictions on marriage in the United States. But the last state to do so, Alabama, did not remove the statutes from its books until the year 2000. For someone like me who is the product of a marriage like that, this is astounding. It puts into sharp focus how untraditional our childhoods must have seemed to the people around us.

"Blacks have had one long affair," my mother told me of that era, meaning it's been a long and difficult struggle. "What makes me laugh about children today is that they don't know that there were times when you couldn't go into the store and try on a dress, go to a restaurant and sit down. Ted and I didn't have a restaurant where we could sit down. So blacks have persevered."

After my father received his Ph.D. at Johns Hopkins in 1960, my parents had three children and left Baltimore. The names they chose for us reflect how their faith united them and the degree to which the Oblate Sisters had become my mother's family. Everyone was named for a religious or family figure or someone who qualified as both. Maria Consuelo was named for Mary Mother of Good Counsel, who had all but adopted my mother as a teenager. Cecilia Augustin drew her name from my father's sister, another nun. Tony (Anthony Nicolás) was named after my father's twin brother, who is a priest, and my mother's father, Nicolás Alberto.

My family moved to Smithtown on the North Shore of Long Island when my father began teaching fluid mechanics in the Mechanical Engineering Department at the State University of New York at Stony Brook. My sister Estela Valerian was born there, named for my mother and my father's sister Valerian, who was also a nun (Aunty Bernadette). I came next.

We grew up among well-educated white kids, with a nice home and good schools, and pursued a life that seemed limitless. My parents hoped that the fact that one of them was white and the other black would not define us. They believed that time would change the way people viewed our family. But our new history was being written in a town that today is 95 percent white, has roughly 100,000 residents, and a median household income of about $100,000. That is a whole lot of rich white people.

When I was growing up, I'm sure it was not as large or as wealthy as it is today, but it was just as white. I felt out of place at times. In my baby pictures I'm a mass of dark curly hair and have a seriously intense look. In my childhood pictures I have brown skin with freckles across my nose and a broad smile. I never thought of my parents as immigrants. They seemed like everyone else's parents, only stricter. I never referred to myself as a first-generation American until I was a teenager and figured out I didn't quite fit in. I was barely aware of the efforts my parents made to fight for our place in Smithtown.

"Truth of it is, as the political movement escalated and the children were at an age where you wanted them to see other blacks, we started a group called Black Families," my mother recalls.

"We had this group of people from all over because in order to have Black Families we had to go pick them up. Many of us started to walk the streets of Smithtown trying to get open housing. We had some friends we met at the church, leaders [in the fight for] open housing, some of them very well known. We'd walk the streets and we'd sing. We didn't really do much other than make people aware. One of the problems was that it was only from me. The black men wanted Ted to be very involved. Ted is not involved in political things. He will do what is necessary but he won't take a leadership position. I think some of the guys didn't think Ted was involved enough so we lost contact because they were not satisfied. . . . The group fell apart. Open housing came through and became part of the law but we did very little."

My dad told me that he would have been willing to lead the group but that it was falling apart from racial mistrust. He recalls that a "talkative white lawyer" took over but the group broke up anyway.

While she dug into her new community, my mother didn't put her past totally behind her. When her sixth child, my younger brother, Orestes, was born on a trip to Australia, she named him after one of her siblings who had passed away. He is living evidence that she lived her life here with Cuba someplace in her mind. When my *abuelita* Luz came to live with us in the 1980s, my mother would watch her painting her perfect long fingernails with red nail polish and not say a word while she kept her own nails unadorned. She kept her hair simple, a short-cut Afro that was actually very modern at the time. Then she let it go gray on its own. She couldn't have looked more regular. She would watch her mother at the table and say to me, "Ah, your grandmother always liked the fancy things. You're just like her."

My mother had hoped that my grandmother would stay with us. They had been apart for so long and her father had died. But there was no one at home to speak Spanish to her.

"It is very much part of the culture to spend time with people and to talk, and where we lived it was not possible," my mother said. "We had kept in touch before by telephone and we did write letters and there were lots of phone calls, which was easy. But by the time she came I was married. Children come and take over your life."

My grandmother increasingly spent her time in Union City, New Jersey, a thriving place with a large Cuban population. Eventually, she just moved there. I got to see the inside of an apartment for the first time. It seemed incomprehensible to me that people could fit all their stuff—their whole lives—into a four-room apartment. Stranger still was Union City, the exact opposite of my home on Long Island. Where my neighborhood was quiet and leafy, Union City was full of noise and laughter. Neighbors called to each other, shouting at times. And the smells! Union City was a pot of black beans always simmering on the four-burner stove. My grandmother, like my mother, roasted green peppers on an open flame to make *sofrito*. I had never seen anything like it in anyone else's house.

Here I was visiting my grandmother in the heart of Cuban New Jersey and I was a stranger in a strange land. My mother was the language teacher in one of my local high schools, Smithtown High School–East, but she didn't teach either the French or Spanish she taught other kids to her own children. Her decision not to teach us Spanish, which she later regretted, didn't seem contradictory at the time since we thought of ourselves as Americans.

My mother had enough to navigate in her new country without worrying about preserving vestiges of the old one.

"There are so many things to do when you arrive in a country," she said. "You have to decide what you are actually going to work on. The parents have to get a job, the kids have to go to school. It's a lot."

The little Spanish we heard she reserved for curses, lullabies or prayers. Meanwhile, my grandmother spoke two words of English: "hello" and "bye-bye." She had absolutely no interest in learning English and no practical need to. She was living in Union City, a Cuban town.

As much as my grandmother was comfortable in Union City, my large black Latino Australian family stuck out like a sore thumb in suburban Long Island. Had it not been for my five siblings, I would have felt like a freak of nature. We were tight. There were enough O'Briens to field a ratty baseball team on the front lawn or have even sides for pretty much any game we wanted to play. I look at photos of us in the 1970s and we all have giant Afros, except my dad, as we lean casually against our VW bus dressed in bright stripes. The photo makes me laugh now, but as a teenager I always felt aware of our big hair, brown skin, and freckles.

If our looks didn't betray us, my mother's accent betrayed her roots. Even though she didn't discuss Cuba or talk much about being Latino, what she taught us seemed obviously formed by her Cuban/Latino experience, even if we only realized it years later. She insisted that we strive, even compete, in that aggressive way American children are expected to be competitive.

When I've asked her since whether she was aware how much we stuck out, she says that seems totally ridiculous to her.

"It never occurred to me they would look different. After a while I started to teach at the school. We found that if the children were smart and did their homework it was a real plus. If children were dumb that would be harder. I don't remember if we had any racial incidents. It's possible but I don't remember. People do racial things constantly. You have to live with it. You have to know it will happen. You have to learn to live with it. It's easy to [stand up for yourself] if you're willing to be alone because you will stick out like a sore finger. But you had to be willing to be alone."

As much as we appeared black to the people around us, our traditions remained classically Latino. She demanded we maintain a profound sense of humility but be proud of who we were. She required a devotion to our family and a strong immigrant work ethic. She always worked; we always worked. She cooked; we ate. She focused on us; we *focused*. My parents were not radicals as individuals but their way of life was radical by definition. They were a mixed family in a single-race town. There was a lot of racial self-discovery going around in American society, but not in my household. My mother and father had studied and studied and when we were born, we studied, too.

We had plenty of time to study since we didn't exactly connect with our neighbors, who were mostly white, Jewish, Irish, and Italian. It was clear to me I wouldn't ever date as long as I stayed in Long Island. First of all my parents would never allow it, and, truth be told, there were no potential suitors. I was also brainy and that didn't help. There were no notable racial incidents but there wasn't a critical mass of minorities. There was a handful of families—the Loos, who were Chinese, the Pengs from Korea. The Onleys from Bermuda were, for most of my childhood, the only other black family in my town. Their daughter, Shevoy, was my best friend through elementary school. There were the Cinqumanis, whom I occasionally passed in the hallway and assumed must be the only other Latinos. We rarely spoke for reasons only available to the teenage mind. We were it.

In middle school when I was thirteen, I'd be stopped in the hallway, with a question. "If you're a nigger, why don't you have big lips?" I was often asked. "Why is your name so weird?" People would apologize for asking me if I was black. I didn't know how to take the apology. I just ignored them and pushed forward with a quest to become a typical Long Island teenager. I chopped off the end of my name and had people call me Solie, which I spelled with a heart over the "i" in true Long Island high school–girl fashion. But my hair would never "wing" like Farrah Fawcett's. In a small town, we were an aberration, the unfamiliar brown face in the sea of white.

Although my mother taught at Smithtown High School–West I was destined to go to Smithtown High School–East across town. I thought I'd escaped her walking around in this gigantic purple hat with two white skunk stripes, as she was fond of doing. Then my senior year she transferred to my school. She was utterly comfortable with herself even as we remained these caught-in-the-middle kids, children with no particularly obvious race to claim. Latino didn't feel like an identity to me; it was a condition, a situation that needed occasional handling after my mother had embarrassed us in some way.

Then came the day I was visiting my old school after I'd gone off to college. My mom and I were marching down the halls, her this extraordinarily proud woman, an immigrant who carefully preserved her black Cuban identity regardless of where she walked. That afternoon an adolescent black boy was running madly through the hallways of a school that was nearly all white, with the exception of my mother, Estela Lucrecia Marquetti y Mendieta O'Brien. A group of administrators caught up to him about mid-hall and the boy just stared at them with this startled look, fully aware he'd just been caught where he didn't belong. I wanted to keep walking. This was not our business and it was all a bit embarrassing. I was in a rush. One of the men was my former principal and my mother's boss. But my mother stopped. "It's okay, Mrs. O'Brien," they told her. "We have it under control."

"That's okay," she said. "I'm just going to stay here for a while." And the power dynamic shifted like the San Andreas fault. She was there just to watch, clutching the macramé handbag she always carried around, fulfilling an unspoken obligation to watch over her tiny number of folks in this foreign land. I went from being impatient to being entranced by her quiet power. She waited them out while the men grew uncomfortable.

The boy glanced from my mother to the three tall administrators, shifting back and forth on his heels. He was obviously not sure what was happening but was fully relieved that this black lady with the short Afro had stopped. The discomfort everyone felt broke when the principal patted the boy on the back and sent him on his way with an admonition to not run in the halls. My mother just turned with me and we walked away. I took with me her refusal to move, her power of being an observer and recorder of moments like these. It was almost a thrilling spot to be in and one I slowly began to covet.

The world opened up with possibilities after I left for college. I started at Harvard in 1984. I was very sheltered. I remember venturing out of Harvard Yard one evening and being scared to cross the street to make a phone call. I'd never lived in a big city; I'd never been away from home for more than a few days at a time.

After a while, being in college gave me an enormous sense of freedom. What was a burden in Long Island became instantly interesting on campus. I reclaimed Soledad and studied Spanish. I made friends of all races and socioeconomic classes. My sophomore rooming group was an Asian girl from Michigan, a wealthy Tex-Mex girl from Laredo, a lawyer's daughter from Scarsdale, New York, a girl from Berkeley, and me. We were the United Nations and I fit right in. I dated for the first time—white guys, Asian guys, Puerto Rican and black guys. I felt comfortable. My siblings also went to

Harvard, and now my sister Maria is a law professor, Cecilia is a corporate lawyer, Tony heads a documents company, Estela is an eye surgeon, and Orestes is an anesthesiologist. We may have not blended into Long Island, but when it came to academic achievement we didn't struggle. This ragtag, multiracial gang from Smithtown did all right.

Starting work was a different story. I went to work as an associate producer and news writer for WBZ, the NBC affiliate in Boston. My job was standard bottom-of-the-ladder production assistant work: running errands, fetching coffee, opening the mail. Some Harvard kids might have felt underwhelmed by the opportunity but I had grown up accustomed to the benefits of hard work. I was promoted to minority writer trainee, a job that paid $19,000 but gave me skills that distinguished me from my colleagues.

As a TV writer, I was the "other," the person consistently being tapped to cover the "community" (read black and Latino) stories. These were never the most important stories and were often relegated to the back of the local news lineup. My story would emerge after the weather as a thirty-second snippet—a community center has opened in Roxbury! I had to fight to get to produce the "A-Block stories," the ones that lead the newscast. I was torn. I knew that covering the community stories, no matter how well you did them, wouldn't get you promoted. But I did those stories well. I spoke enough Spanish to do short interviews and I was familiar with the folks in the community. Poverty didn't scare me. I fit right in.

But it was clear that my ethnicity rubbed two ways. I applied for a job in Connecticut and the news director asked me if I'd consider changing my name. "María de la Soledad? I'm going to change the name of the Virgin Mary? I'll go to hell," I told him, laughing. But I got the point. I was impossible to categorize. I didn't get the job.

I moved up to NBC News in New York in 1991 as a field producer for *Nightly News* and *Today*. Then, I finally got my chance to be an on-air reporter at the San Francisco affiliate, KRON, in 1993. Soon after I arrived, I walked past a group of coworkers gossiping in the hallway and stopped to say hello. They were talking about the affirmative action employee who'd been hired and didn't deserve the job. Their faces tightened with embarrassment. I realized the person they were discussing was me.

I had met my future husband, Brad Raymond, at Harvard. We lived in the same house and I was trolling for votes to be class president. He didn't vote for me. He didn't vote at all. But he belonged to a very cute rooming group so I kept in touch. We worked in New York at the same time and in Boston at the same time. By the time I moved to San Francisco to work for KRON in 1993, he was one of my best friends. He had moved out there to start a small business and I was heading for a great reporting job and to be with him.

While Brad was studying for an MBA at the Haas School of Business at UC Berkeley, I was bureau chief (and the only reporter) in KRON's Oakland office. So we were both very busy, but Brad had a car and we explored Northern California's mountains and beaches together on the weekends. He was ambitious, like me, and hardworking, but also kind, generous, and compassionate to others. He was also the son of teachers who valued their family and people over possessions and, just like me, he loved people. By 1993 we were spending every day together, and in August 1995 we got married.

In 1996, I got a shot at anchoring for a program called *The Site*, a technology show on the fledgling MSNBC network. It was the first time I realized how much of a plus it could be to your reporting to be ethnically diverse. Critics talked about how the show was more interesting and distinguished itself from all the other shows doing the same thing. I came back to New York in 1997 when I was offered an opportunity to anchor MSNBC's weekend morning show. By then, the fact that I'd grown up with this indistinguishable racial identity began carrying a certain allure in an industry reaching for the broadest of audiences. I became a familiar face around the country. I began anchoring *Weekend Today* with David Bloom in July 1999 and got to work big stories like the space shuttle *Columbia* disaster and the war in Iraq.

Brad and I started a family when Sofia was born in 2000, a blue-eyed girl who looks exactly like her father. Seventeen months later we had Cecilia. In our quest for a third child we were doubly blessed by twins, Jackson and Charlie, who came in 2004. They are fraternal twins, just like my father and his brother, Tony, born seventy years earlier.

I left NBC to anchor *American Morning* for CNN in 2003, just months after David died covering the war in Iraq. By then the show had changed and the sadness there was palpable. I was ready to move on. I wanted to tackle more hard news and travel the globe and eventually start covering the story that I realized had defined my life, the story of race in this country. That mission became clear to me as I stood in the hideous silence and sweltering heat of New Orleans after the storms of Katrina had knocked a predominantly black population off its feet. I felt like this was what I was meant to do as a reporter. My stories on the deaths, the destruction, the agony of what had happened left me angry and questioning why there is a disparity in the way people of color are treated in this country.

The toilet in our RV died early on and there were no showers so I felt and looked almost as filthy as the people I was interviewing. On little sleep, we'd awake early each morning and freshen up with baby wipes I'd brought from New York and begin our day anew. I pulled back my uncombable hair and buried it beneath a CNN cap. We told this troubling story with a nuance and depth I'd never been able to muster on the short, day-of-air stories I was used to doing, and we did it under tough circumstances. But I was totally energized by the need to record the desperation of the folks around me.

After two months rotating in and out of New Orleans, I marched with my team through the New Orleans airport in our CNN clothes to leave. I was winding through the crowds of relief workers and newly homeless NOLA residents coming and going from the disaster zone when suddenly a wave of clapping ripped through the terminal. I was stunned. They were applauding us. I have never felt so proud of the work I do and the place I work as I did that day. Usually at the end of a story tainted by death and disaster, the people of the community are dying for you to leave in just a few days. These people wanted us to stay. I learned once again that my job as a journalist was to speak up and make things happen. Nothing was happening for these poor folks stuck in the filth and mud. I knew all I could do was keep talking.

In April of 2007 I became an anchor and special correspondent for CNN Productions, which produces documentaries and long-form reporting and allows me to step in for major news events, like the presidential elections. I was one of just two documentary reporters for CNN and the other was Christiane Amanpour so it was quite an honor. I produced a documentary called *Children of the Storm* and returned over and over again to New Orleans to remind folks that the suffering continued even as the political debate raged. Since then, I have been given opportunities to anchor political coverage of Barack Obama's presidential campaign with Anderson Cooper and investigate the assassination of Dr. Martin Luther King Jr. Race—my race and ethnicity—matter, and how I incorporate it into my work matters now more than ever. I am getting an opportunity to do what my mother did in that hallway at my high school that day long ago, to use my presence as an observer to make a difference.

When I was asked by CNN to report a documentary on Latinos, it was my chance to record what was happening in my own community. Until then, what I'd known about being Latino were boiling pots of black beans and white rice, wistful tropical ballads, memories of relatives left behind, and outbursts of Spanish directed at wayward children. I absorbed a few more things from the many Latinos I met along the way. But basically I didn't fully comprehend what it all meant.

It wasn't hard to figure out why I would be the face of our documentaries. I am just one of two correspondents who report for our documentary unit and I had broken some ground reporting on Katrina. I have always embraced my multiracial identity at a time people are having conversations about race. It seemed like the timing was perfect. *Latino in America* was to be the second documentary I had reported that focused on a minority group.

The first had been *Black in America*. The goal was to tell the story of African-Americans forty years after the assassination of Martin Luther King Jr., how far we had come and how far we still have to go. I wanted the documentary to provoke conversations about race and racism, skin color and educational and economic opportunity. I wanted to show the struggles and the successes of black people, to do more than just an analysis of high incarceration rates and school dropout figures. As we were reporting, Barack Obama was taking steps toward becoming the first African-American president. But this was far from a perfect process, even within CNN. Our editorial meetings were uncomfortable and sometimes even unpleasant, as everyone hesitated to have frank discussions about race.

In the community outside my office, I found myself constantly questioned about my own race. Was I black? Latino? White pretending to not be white? Black pretending to not be black? I had a conversation with a Dominican woman who insisted she was not black even though she was as dark as my mother. "I'm Dominican," she kept saying. Yeah, and I am Cuban, I figured, but so what?

Race is a complicated topic in this country and it is even more complicated when people come from other countries with their unique race issues. Latinos aren't even a race. We're an ethnicity. This feeling of having my identity challenged was in no way new to me, and I was grateful to my parents, who had drilled into my head who I am and where I came from.

My husband, Brad, is cohead of an investment banking firm, a white guy who shares my love of family and respects my identity. I came from a family of six kids and wanted lots of kids. He had just his sister but immediately understood and respected my need to form our own little gang. He listens, thinks before he talks; he has patience, says what he means. He is everything my father is, everything my father was to my mother. Where I am hyper, he is calm. He knows when to hide his intensity. I definitely don't. Those are the things I notice about him, not the color of his skin.

My kids all look a little like him and a little like me, save Cecilia, who has my face but a head full of blond ringlets. Brad and I work hard to teach our children about their ethnic and racial identity— we talk about skin color and race. My first daughter, Sofia, has this profound awareness of who we are and where we came from that has to do with something deep inside. It's just who she is, and now she's learning Spanish in school, as are all of her siblings. I really want her to be fluent even though neither Brad nor I speak Spanish, and I think she wants that enough to get there. She is very smart and went with me on some of my *Black in America* shoots. At eight, she is wise enough to know that if you sit her next to me with my brown skin and curly hair and her grandmother with her black skin and tight Afro, we are going to look "different," as she put it. But we actually look a lot alike. I hope as she gets older she's proud of being Latina, black, Cuban, and Australian.

Where we fit into this picture of Latino in America is really something each of us will have to decide on our own. I know, however, that there will always be a place for us. One wonderful thing about the Latinos is that they love to claim people. Latinos can be black or white, even Chinese, like one aunt I discovered in Cuba! We are a mix of so many things. What matters to us is what's inside.

Latinos get a little prickly about the quality of your Spanish and can be troublingly aware of skin color, but if you have so much as a "Maria" sandwiched anywhere in your name, they exclaim that you are all theirs. I went to the Latino Inaugural Ball this year and smiled on the red carpet right behind J.Lo and George Lopez. And when I entered the big hall full of ladies in sparkly gowns, the cameras popped as people stepped forward to embrace me. *"¡Es Soledad!"* they screamed and a torrent of Spanish would follow.

Over the course of this documentary I have come to understand why Latinos like to play this numbers game. We have a deeply vested interest in being many. If we can prove that we are many then it gives us inevitability as part of "American" culture. Our growing numbers count. We are the majority minority now and all minorities combined will comprise the majority by 2032. The United States is about to undertake the 2010 census, which harvests data that businesses use to market and Congress uses to divvy up money for hospitals, schools, and roads. The numbers are what ensure we are represented.

The census worries a lot of Latino leaders. As much as Latinos want to be counted, it's hard to find us. We don't get our news in the typical places or hang out where everybody hangs out. We come from places where you don't necessarily respond to a total stranger in a suit asking about your family or a government letter prying about your finances. There are a lot of people like my mother who keep their past in some little box of their own. It is very hard to define who and what we are. In reporting this documentary, I got a taste of how hard it will be for those census takers. It is not easy to tell the story of a community that defies an easy definition.

In early research, one of the producers assigned to the project, Emily Probst, suggested we work on something around the name Garcia. Garcia stands at number eight in the list of top-ten last names in the United States, so being a Garcia is like being one of the Joneses. Or another way of putting it is that 15 percent of the Joneses are actually Garcias, and by 2050 that number will rise to 30 percent. In not long, this country will no longer be majority white, according to U.S. census projections. In 2007, the number of new U.S.-born Latinos outpaced those immigrating into the United States.

This boom of Latinos is a U.S. phenomenon now.

The Garcias are mostly Mexican, about 28 million of them, followed by nearly 4 million Puerto Ricans before you even get to my 1.5 million Cubans or the Dominicans and El Salvadorians who are numerically right behind them. Puerto Ricans are born U.S. citizens. The other groups are not an ocean away, like European immigrants, so it's easy for them to come and go. Cubans get work papers just for stepping on dry ground, followed by economic assistance and a fast track to residency and citizenship. Depending on the country of origin and the circumstances, the United States has made all sorts of government allowances for immigration, because of everything from hurricanes to wars to an acceptance of a tide of immigration as part of our economic engine.

The first Garcia I met reporting the documentary was not a Mexican. He was a Puerto Rican guy named Bill Garcia and was working for the U.S. census in Charlotte, North Carolina, where he provided technical support to the people who go out in the field to account for this complicated population. Bill and his wife, Betty, had moved from New York City to Charlotte for reasons that become obvious when you stare out their kitchen window at the tulip beds and honest-to-God white picket fences. Their housing development is repetitious in a good way; every house has an identically manicured lawn and smiling youngsters out front.

Bill is a handsome Puerto Rican with brown skin who resembles my little brother, Orestes. Betty looks like my mom. Her skin is dark and her hair loses ground to the humidity a bit like mine. Back in New York, she lived in the northern part of Washington Heights, *Santo Dominiquito*, a little Dominican Republic where she remembers fondly how folks used to scream *Hola* to each other on the street. Bill had lived on the Upper West Side of Manhattan, where it was cool to be a Nuyorican even if you didn't speak a word of Spanish without a little pressure. People understood them, shared their values, celebrated the happy, pulsating music of the Caribbean and the seasoning of their food. Latinos drink and dance, and include the kids and the grandparents. Their parties are cross-generational, with a lot of food and laughter and silly talk. Everyone feels like a cousin, if they aren't already.

Charlotte has given them a lovely life but they fear they have left something intangible behind. The ease with which they walked around Manhattan has been replaced with awareness that folks look at them and see a biracial couple. They are not Latin here; they are black with white. Their sons identify with black kids at school and want to play black music. If Betty turns up the merengue in the car, the boys want her to keep the windows rolled up so their friends won't hear. The boys tell folks they're from Charlotte, and it means something more profound than just a location.

Betty says it's getting better as Charlotte changes.

"When we came here they were trying to categorize us, that was weird. We weren't used to that . . . when we first got here they didn't know where to place me. I spoke Spanish so I'm not black, but I speak good English, but I'm not American . . . or they thought that I was biracial or from India or some mixture, but now people are more accepting. I think they are more aware of the differences."

Both Bill and Betty regret not teaching their sons to speak Spanish because they worry they won't be proud of who they are. Betty looks at Bill and remembers what it was like when her boys were little.

"It was hard and he would speak mostly English and our younger son was two years old and he wasn't uttering any words, so we were getting concerned, and I thought, 'Well, maybe if we speak one language he'll start talking,' and since Bill didn't know how to speak Spanish fluently, I said, you know what, everyday life is too hard, let's just go with it. This happened because we were here. If we were in New York around our family, they would have learned from just being around our families, because you know if Ti Ti Silvia says, 'Pasa me un vaso de agua' ['give me a glass of water'] they would have to know what she's saying."

I feel their sadness and I think of my own little girl picking up her first words of Spanish in her elementary school without the benefit of her mother speaking it to her at home. I know it's not that Bill and Betty have an issue with their boys being black or with being seen as mixed race any more than I care how other folks define me or my children. It really is about what's happening for them inside. It's that in their own eyes they are Latino and that means something good to them that they want to pass along. "Being Latino in New York is like being a blade of grass in a field," I tell Betty, and her face lights up with recognition.

These parents, so much like my own, will tell you that if you just succumb to assimilation you lose something of enormous value for the sake of gaining a sense of comfort. It's not really a trade-off you need to make. As soon as they say it, I know exactly what they're talking about and I flash back to something my mother used to say when we got sassy: "Where did I get all these little Americans?" And I'd think to myself, "You and Dad made them by moving here."

Bill and I both share the regret that we don't speak stronger Spanish. A woman named María de la Soledad Teresa O'Brien should speak Spanish! When folks walk up to me and begin talking in Spanish I always take a deep breath. I know Spanish, but I don't have that fluency you need to meet people where they are. It's such a gift to be able to speak to someone in their own language. For me, it also opens up a world of culture that I love.

Bill tells me something about his limited Spanish that leaves me nodding in recognition:

"Some people might question my authenticity because I'm not speaking the language, and while I can make an attempt and say a few phrases here or there, I really can't carry a full conversation in Spanish, and so it's unfortunate that [people] might take that as an opportunity to have a disconnect with me, but I'm certainly fully Latin. I'm one hundred percent Puerto Rican so the music, the food, the dance, the elements of the culture I have in me and beyond that. I have a passion and a love for my people so I do my work in terms of community organizing or sitting on boards, things of that nature, with a love for the Latin people. So whether or not I speak the language I'm doing good things that help to promote that whole community, our community to move forward."

Spanish is one of the few things a lot of Latinos have in common and I think a lot of non-Latino folks see it as something that defines us. But sitting there with Bill I know that I'm not defined by what I think or how I look. Just like them, I know I can hold on to my roots wherever I may travel. That's what Bill and Betty Garcia have done. He knows how to find his Latinos. He knows they won't get lost in the Charlotte that's around them.

One Saturday morning I accompany them to a Unity Summit seeking to build bridges between African-Americans and Latinos. The organizer is a Mexican woman married to an African-American. She received some nasty e-mails about the event but she's pretty pleased to see about eighty folks sitting in a room willing to speak honestly about race. Some of the black folks are frustrated that some Latinos seem to run from their black roots, but what stands out is how much they want to understand each other.

An African-American woman talks about how she'd really like to get to know her Mexican neighbors. They have these really adorable children and they seem very nice. But she doesn't speak any Spanish and all the nodding and smiling hits a quick dead end. A Latina schoolteacher talks about her commitment to one African-American student whom she will not let fail. Her determination is intense and I smile at this full-headed Latina who is doing this as much for herself as for the girl. Several folks are upset about allegations that Latinos are ruining the schools. Fifty percent of the blacks aren't graduating from high school, either, and they don't speak a word of Spanish. The fact that we need to fix the schools for everyone is the headline in this room.

Walking out of the event, I feel like I've known Bill and Betty all my life. We don't come from the same places but we totally get each other. I feel upbeat when people in the room recognize me and claim me as one of their own. I understand the conversation in the room; empathize with the confusion of trying to figure out where to fit in when people see your race but you feel your ethnicity. It's an odd thing to be discussing unity between two groups of people who represent parts of you.

Betty came to this country when she was twelve and, like my mom, she does not think that either her skin color or her language is what makes her Latina. When people ask her why she doesn't identify as black, she just says, "I'm Dominican, it's not that I'm not black, it's that I *am* Dominican."

My mother came here at a time when it was all about black and white. She didn't get to sit at restaurants because she was black, not because she was Cuban. But she was still Cuban. Bill isn't sure what to think. He never quite thought of himself as white. He was Puerto Rican, which means something. He is not an immigrant from anywhere. Puerto Ricans are U.S. citizens and he was born in New York, where saying you are Puerto Rican means something, while in Charlotte, you are just black or white.

Bill lost his job with the U.S. census two months after starting it and is struggling to find work. While he's searching, he helps out at the Museum of the New South with an exhibit that explores how population shifts are changing the South.

"We as a country are in a changing demographic where we have this newly emerging dominant minority group and there is a history and powerful institutions in the old minority group, traditions that tie back to their old country, and we need to explore how these new groups that are migrating to parts of the country, as we have, are going to mix," he says.

"How does culture and tradition and language and music get preserved in this new environment? At what point do we form a new society and new coalitions? At what point do we go from having our own parades and own chambers of commerce to being part of everything else?"

As he looks for a job to replace the one he lost at the U.S. census, he says his priority is clear. "I want to work in an environment that's inclusive and appreciates diversity." That may mean going back to New York. He really isn't yet sure.

I ask both of them if they feel biracial. Bill launches into this:

"Well, my mother is very light-skinned and my father was the same complexion as me, a little darker, so my father's origin had to come from somewhere and he would always emphasize his Taino, Indian ancestry, and so that was something we heard a lot about in our life coming up, so in that sense, sure."

Betty immediately perks up when he says that. "You think we're biracial?"

Bill looks at her, surprised. "Well, I mean, think about where did the Cuban, Puerto Rican, Dominican folks get their dark skin, well, those three islands. It was slave trades as you know, but there were also Spaniards and you also have to bring into the conversation, you know, colonialism. Let me remind you all that Puerto Rico is still a colony of the United States, so therefore all of those factors over time in history have created people that look like us. We're all different shades, and so naturally I think at some point we have to recognize that we are biracial."

They look at each other and pause. I was actually asking if they felt like a biracial couple because of the way folks look at them. He is fairer and she is black. But they see the world through different eyes, so they took the question differently, and right then we are all smiling and realizing our eyes see ourselves in a way that few others see us.

This is where it becomes hard to write our own history the way my parents tried to do so long ago when they joined forces in this new land and tried to raise their mixed-raced brood in suburban Long Island. Outsiders try to get in your children's heads. You have to keep affirming that life is not about how we look but about how we look at our world.

Bill and Betty can't write out of their children's lives that they are now brown kids living in Charlotte, North Carolina, who don't speak a word of Spanish. But they can keep insisting that it means something to be Dominican and Puerto Rican from New York. The residents of a new geography can't take that away from you. They have plans to take their kids to a big New York family reunion this summer. It's their way of touching home base, of taking their kids to the last place where they felt totally at home so they do not lose touch with their culture. I often want to do the same, but it is very hard when your past is rooted in Cuba, this tropical forbidden zone.

When I began to write this book and produce this documentary I felt this urge to reconnect, but I'm not sure what or where I'm reconnecting to. When the census takers come knocking on my door, I wonder what box I'll check. Where do I go visit when I choose to travel home?

2

children of the revolution

I TRAVELED TO Cuba for the first time in January 1998 to cover Pope John Paul II's visit for NBC. I thought I was going to report on all these grand stories. Then the press found out that an intern named Monica Lewinsky had had sex with the president and suddenly I couldn't get on the air. So instead, I got a chance to explore a bit of my mother's country.

It was an odd experience. In Cuba everyone assumed I was Cuban and started chatting with me. I fit right in but I was a visiting journalist with limited Spanish, so I really didn't. As an American reporter I was under very tight restrictions and I assumed I'd be watched all the time. The food was awful, unless it was great. There was terrible street pizza with fake cheese. Then there were beautiful private homes that doubled as restaurants serving the most wonderful food, black beans even better than my mother's. I envied other Latinos who could spend their summers back home. This kind of trip must feel so warm and familiar to them. I walked around in awe of the amazing architecture, as if I was looking for an address.

I ditched the journalists' hotel and hired a car to see if I could meet the cousins I'd heard so much about.

What I knew of my mother's family, I knew mostly from pictures. In one of them, my mother is smiling in her white girlish sweater and tiny earrings. In another, her mother drapes her arms around my mother and an uncle. My grandfather is shown in big prescription glasses and a thin mustache. Mom once told me that her father nicknamed her "Russa" because her hair turned a shade of red in the summer. You can't tell from the black-and-white photos, but

TOP: "Marta," age fifteen, at the modern Boystown/Children's Village.

BOTTOM: Sen. Mel Martinez (R-Florida) at the site of the old boys' Boystown, then known as Camp Matacumbe, where he was sent alone at age fifteen in 1962.

the story always made me smile because my hair does the very same thing. The red in my hair made me feel connected to things from back then. My grandfather died in 1960 before he had a chance to meet any of his six American grandchildren, so stories like that are all I had of him. My grandmother joined us in New York so I knew her better, but that tie to Cuba was also severed. After she arrived, she never wanted to talk about Cuba.

The members of my family left in Cuba seemed distant from us, characters in family stories, faraway voices my mother spoke to on the phone in a language I didn't understand. When I meet them, they don't even look like their photos, in which they're dressed up, smiling, and trying to look their best. I visit during *"la crisis,"* when everything is in short supply and prices in the markets are soaring beyond reach. The withdrawal of Soviet support (there is no more Soviet Union by this point) and the continuing U.S. embargo have crippled the economy.

I get directions from my mother and ride over with my team from NBC, including my translator. When I get there it's exactly as my mother described it. My uncle Jose owns the house but there are multiple families living there and the place has been divided into several rooms to accommodate everyone. One of my uncles has passed away so his wife, Marta, lives there. There are family members at every turn.

My Cuban family lives in a very nice home, which, like a lot of homes in Havana, is deteriorating. The stairs are buckling and the outside is falling apart. My cousin Aquiles offers to translate because they feel uncomfortable using a stranger. They tell me they are reliant on all the resources of the revolution to survive, like rations of food, universal day care, and a free education. I sit in their home with its white walls and linoleum floors and I feel very happy and welcome. But I'm frustrated that we can't communicate directly and curse myself for not having learned to speak better Spanish. I'm surrounded by people who look vaguely like me, though everyone is two shades darker black than I am. We have the same hair, the same eyes, the same tight nose and freckly features, the same toothy smile. My cousin Denice has a son named Orestes, just like my brother, both named for one of my uncles who passed away. Denice must have known him. I never did, except to know that my family loved him so much that children were named after him. The little Orestes who sits on my aunt's lap is wearing a red and gray track suit and is sucking his hand.

To me, cousins were people in faraway Australia or people in stories from Cuba. It was very special to me to be meeting these Cuban cousins. They try to tell me what my mother was like, how she held fast to her money (which she still does), and never spent an extra penny (which she still doesn't). They all talk about how hard she used to work. They are living in tough circumstances and they struggle with finding an appropriate way to express their jealousy. Even though my interpreter is my cousin, I find it awkward talking through someone else, so our conversation feels somewhat forced. I don't really know how to help them out, to know what's appropriate or would feel right. What do you give to a person who needs everything?

So I sit in my relatives' living room, a visible manifestation of what their lives could have been if their own mothers had gotten out like mine did. There is something in the way they talk that feels a bit like resentment. The stories they tell about my mother as a child have an edge to them. But how can I blame them? When I invite my cousin Maria Luz to come visit me at the Hotel Havana Libre, it causes an uproar at the hotel. Cubans are not allowed into the tourist hotels. They say it's a way to stop prostitution but she's obviously not a prostitute. I can't imagine how this must make her feel.

Years later, I am in Miami to meet Cubans who live here in the United States, a vibrant, very political community that has planted a tent pole in Miami and a few neighborhoods around the country. My mother came from Cuba over twenty years before the battle with Castro prompted our country to support Cuban emigration, so neither she nor I am part of the community that was united by the post-Castro politics of the United States. My mother didn't particularly care for Castro but she lived her American life in the politics of the here and now. She married an Australian and settled in an all-white town. Immigrating to the United States as a Cuban was not controversial back then. She obtained residency easily and sponsored my father's visa to stay after he finished school and got married. When my grandmother came, she was the first in our U.S. family to live in a Cuban community, in Union City, New Jersey.

She made me aware that there was this Cuban community out there representing people like me.

The true place of the Cuban community in the American mind was cemented with the arrival of 178,000 refugees between 1959 and 1962, most of whom settled in Miami. They accomplished so much it is hard not to want to be associated with them in some way. Their story is probably one of the most celebrated of all the Latino immigrant stories. They left because Communism threatened to rob them of their wealth, yet they had to leave everything material behind. All they brought with them was their intellectual capital. The Cubans believed they were only coming for a visit but they stayed on to become a phenomenally successful and powerful immigrant group, and a rich and exclusive one. Many of them had formed Cuba's upper crust, and in Miami they created a new elite that includes famous and influential performers and captains of industry, some of whom live in gated communities and on private islands.

Cubans are probably the most likely of all Latinos to say they are not Latino, but to identify with their country of origin, an attitude that has not endeared them to the many Latin Americans who live alongside them. They are more likely to be Republican than most Latinos, though Cuban support of the GOP eroded slightly in 2008. They are much more likely to associate with the politics of their island, just ninety miles away from Key Biscayne. When I first began reporting my documentary on Latinos, I felt only the smallest connection with the Cuban population in Miami that has become the face of Cuban immigration to the United States. My mother didn't leave Cuba over politics. She was poor and she wanted a chance to learn. The Cuban community we knew in New Jersey was not fixated on deposing Castro. There were even people who appreciated the accomplishments of the revolution and called for dialogue with the regime, people who felt the Miami Cubans were vitriolic and self-serving. But all the U.S. Cubans do share something in common that my family and I can relate to: We were handed an opportunity and we ran with it.

Modern-day Cubans have an enormous advantage over other Latinos. Successive U.S. governments have held Castro's regime in contempt and have implemented measures to help departing Cubans resettle and succeed. Other immigrants are severely punished for entering the United States illegally, while Cubans are immediately "paroled" and get work permits. In 1980, Castro allowed 125,000 Cubans to leave for the United States, including some criminals and mental patients, and they took advantage of American regulations. When Castro threatened to sanction another huge exodus in 1994, the United States shifted its policy to offer parole only to those who make it to dry land.

Even so, Cubans who make it to the United States have their work permits converted into legal permanent refugee status one year later without having to prove they meet the requirements of other asylum seekers. They also don't have to prove they can support themselves. They get job training, immediate economic assistance, welfare, health benefits, and they qualify for subsidized housing. Unlike other immigrants, they are not required to have U.S. relatives or other sponsors, nor do they spend years and thousands of dollars on immigration attorneys fighting to make their case. They are also spared the anxiety of not knowing whether they will be able to stay. Under the Clinton administration, the United States reduced the need for so many Cubans to make a treacherous journey to get here. He created a visa lottery that allows twenty thousand Cubans to legally immigrate each year. The welcome mat is out for Castro's victims.

As I was preparing to report on Miami for the *Latino in America* documentary, I had lunch with J. P. Souto. I wanted to debrief someone who is a child of a Cuban immigrant just like me but who lives in the thick of the community made famous by the Cubans. We met at Victor's Café, a high-end Cuban restaurant in midtown Manhattan. J.P. lives in Miami and he is the picture of that extraordinarily successful Cuban immigration. His grandfather, Jose A. "Pepe" Souto, came from a province of Cuba called Sancti Spiritus, where his family had been growing coffee since the 1820s.

The Souto family story line pretty much matches the Cuban-American story line, where my family's doesn't. When Fidel Castro overthrew the Batista regime, they left. Marxism meant nationalizing the coffee industry, so they were losing everything. When they realized they were never leaving Miami, Pepe began selling coffee door to door with his three sons. He had nothing but memories of a thriving business and the business smarts he brought here. By 1967, the boys were in college and their father had bought Rowland Coffee Roasters, the owner of Café Pilon, their main competitor in Cuba. By the year 2000, this family owned Tetley USA's espresso coffee business, and was selling Café Bustelo, Medaglia D'Oro, El Pico, Café Pilon, and Oquendo. They now have sales around $75 million and own the nation's leading brands of espresso. These newly minted Americans export millions of pounds of coffee to Latin America and they are not even a generation removed from the immigration experience.

When I walked into Victor's the chef was frantically preparing us tiny samples of Cuban Fusion food and it wasn't because I was there. Someone like J.P. is royalty in the Cuban community, and he looks it. J.P. is the picture of the Cuban man, dark silky hair and full red lips, an easy smile and great clothes. My first impression was that this was a man we wanted in our documentary, even if at that moment I had no idea what role he'd play. He was born in the United States but he is of Miami, with that barely detectable Cubano accent that says there is something Latin inside. He has impeccable manners and plenty to say. He is at ease calling himself a McCain Republican in a year Latinos in general went hard for Obama. His family business is a rarity in the United States in that they have three generations actively working together.

J.P. tells me the Cubans have been given enormous advantages over other immigrants but he also believes the Cubans made something with what they were given in a way that not every immigrant has. His business employs 250 people, many of them other Cubans whom his family has helped. J.P. runs their marketing operation and, as young as he is (in his early thirties), he already talks in the language of a community patriarch.

"We vote for McCain. We believe in strong families. We are a very particular group among Latinos. We don't even use that word. We say we are Hispanic or Cuban," said J.P., who looked tanned and buff in the middle of winter.

"All you hear is Spanish in Miami. If I was someone who didn't speak a word of Spanish, it would be like being in a foreign place. People assume you speak Spanish and that is the first language. I feel sorry for people who don't speak Spanish. The minority has become the majority in Miami."

At first blush, I have nothing in common with this really lovely guy. My mother was black and searching for opportunities when she left

Cuba. She didn't miss the poverty, the lack of health care, the erratic income source that was her father's gambling, or the obvious racism. She saw the United States as a "beacon for everyone, especially the poor." She was eager to take advantage of everything this country had to offer, and once she got here she never thought about going back. She expected a lot from herself. Her kids carried those same high expectations. We were reaching forward; the Soutos were trying to reestablish the past. They have a unit devoted to planning the fall of Castro, and J.P. cannot zero in on the date when his family gave up hope that their American journey was a temporary stop on their way back home.

While J.P.'s family may be wealthy they are not divorced from the dramatic experience that forms the psyche of so much of the Latino community. He told me a story that one day his family was dining at a yacht club in Miami and a whole Cuban family of rafters escaping the island washed ashore and hid in the brush. Their clothes were torn and their skin burned from the sun and they looked frightened and desperate. J.P.'s family ran over to help. They were deeply affected by the experience. It caused his parents to think about how they'd left everything to seek refuge in this unknown land. However different their reasons are for fleeing, like my family, they did flee.

On my first reporting trip to Miami I toured around with Gustavo Godoy, the publisher of the nation's oldest Spanish-language magazine insert, *Vista*. Gustavo is a Cuban force of nature, zooming around from one beachfront to the next, waving at the many people he knows and spitting out demographic information like a tour guide. Gustavo has a wispy gray beard and looks totally comfortable in a seersucker suit and snappy bow tie. He was born in Havana, where he studied with the Jesuits. Then his parents sent him to a military school in Indiana hoping he would learn English. They left Cuba for good in 1960 and joined the wave of Cubans settling Miami. Gustavo worked first in TV, then publishing, and became a sort of Mr. Miami. He can pick up the phone and get me on with people of the stature of Emilio Estefan at a moment's notice.

Gustavo and I walk the length of one of those tiny sand islands that host the footsteps of the bridges connecting downtown to South Beach. The view of a skyline cut from shiny high-rises speaks volumes about Miami. Set aside the usual urban woes of any U.S. city and

Miami is something to behold as a reflection of what immigration can do when it is embraced. Before the Cubans, Miami was this backwater Jim Crow town that was drawing increasing numbers of retirees but had little vibrancy to it.

"Miami was a very sleepy town, basically a tourist town," Gustavo said. "And there were a lot of people that had been retired from Illinois, from New York, from other parts of the nation, they would come and they would have a very pleasant, slow life." Now Miami hosts the Latin America divisions of 1,250 multinational corporations, according to the U.S. Chamber of Commerce. A survey of U.S. mayors found Miamians to have the third-greatest purchasing power in the country in 2008.

There have been subsequent waves of Cubans and other Latin Americans, often of less means but of equal energy. Together they have made Miami into a Latin American gateway, a place where half the population is Latino, more than half of those from Cuba. The majority of people in Miami consider Spanish their first language. More than half the businesses in Miami are owned by Latinos. Non-Cubans—Dominicans and Venezuelans and Colombians— are moving up in the economic hierarchy and their numbers could make them a political force, but Gustavo says immigrants from other countries are simply not moving up as the Cubans did, even though the Cubans have paved the way. He looks up at the sun melting over this skyline as he is talking and shakes his head.

"It's a very different promise for immigrants who are not from Cuba—totally different options, opportunities, and different law, frankly," I say to him.

"There were student loans for the children of the Cubans. At first, a very interesting thing, you would see doctors, engineers, architects, and lawyers and their wives working at hotels, doing beds, opening doors, or parking cars. And then a small Cuban-oriented industry started. Cuban crackers, Cuban bread, Cuban coffee, that's how it started. Little by little they were developing little businesses and some of them have become very huge and very productive. There is a difference. The fact that there's a positive, successful story of Cuban immigrants in South Florida has paved the way for non-Hispanics to see the benefits of having a wider, bigger Latino presence in this area."

"So you think that people look around here and say, 'This is a success story.'"

"This is Mecca, it's Mecca, the fact that the Cubans were here before and they were successful, [facing] the issue of language, the issue of work, the issue of where to live and where not to live, the issue of what schools to go to to take advantage of the bilingual education, to take advantage of one of the largest community colleges, which is run by Hispanics, mainly a Cuban. This place has been a source of education, and success in business."

But the opportunities for the newcomers, Gustavo tells me, have just not been there and it's made it difficult for them to re-create the success of those early Cubans. They created a template for how to take an immigrant group and make it successful. If it was followed for subsequent arrivals, he says, just imagine what this country could be.

"Is Miami a metaphor for 'so goes South Florida . . . so goes the rest of the nation?'" I ask him.

"I think the proof is in the pudding. You see the assimilation that we have had in South Florida. You see that there are good interchanges and communication between Hispanics, Cubans, and the non-Hispanic population in South Florida. Again when people get here, they get a new mind-set. There's a new mind-set."

"What's that mind-set? What is that message?"

"We are all in the same boat."

"Which is what boat?"

"Ah . . . we have to make it. We have to move forward. It's not just to say I want to be part of the American Dream. I have to work to be part of the American Dream."

❧

That evening I go meet Marlene Ferro. It's one of the half dozen Friday evenings Marlene has devoted to practicing for the celebration of her daughter Jenny's fifteenth birthday. The party is going to be a *Quinceañera*, an event that elevates the girl to princess status, and Marlene is planning to spend $20,000 on it. We thought *Quinceañeras* could be a theme for us since so many Latinos are celebrating them. The *Quince* is a Mexican tradition that was adapted from

French customs in the 1800s by the Francophile Mexican president Porfirio Díaz. The tradition spread to other Latin countries but has really flourished in the United States as much more than a simple Sweet Fifteen party. It's a family event, a celebration with religious undertones of what the family has accomplished, like saying before the world, "After all we've endured look how far we've come." Think of it as a Latin Bar or Bat Mitzvah.

In Miami the party might take place on a cruise ship, in a lavish banquet hall, at Disney, or in a private mansion. I found some that cost as much as $150,000, a sum that thumbs its nose at anyone who doubts that immigrants can rise above the way they came here.

"It's a big deal for a young Cuban girl," says Marlene. "It's when she becomes a woman. But it's about more than that. I spent years saving for this. It's made us grow closer. We go shopping together and pick things out. Jenny loves the spotlight. Her brothers are going to dance with her . . . this is about the whole family and celebrating how far we've come."

Marlene's parents came to the United States to "find freedom from Castro," she said, and they constructed a new life here very quickly. Her father was a baker. Marlene founded a home health agency and now she works shredding confidential documents. Her parents came with nothing; Marlene owns her home. She has three children in good schools and employs a cleaning lady from Honduras.

The scene that unfolds in Marlene's backyard nicely illustrates the story of what Cubans have been able to make of the benefits afforded them in this country. Thirty teenagers are practicing a synchronized salsa and chatting in perfect Spanish. It is Good Friday, and before they break for a dinner of baked salmon and black beans, the instructor asks them to raise their hands high in the air if they consider themselves to be Cuban. Every hand shoots up, waving as the girls erupt into laughter and the parents beam proudly on the sidelines. When she asks them who considers themselves American, just one or two hands rise. A girl asks: "Can we be both?" The teens double over in laughter.

The party is going to be held at a banqueting hall, where the manager told us we can see a window into the contrasts between how fabulously successful Cuban Americans are and how much Latinos from other countries are struggling. One of the servers there is Adreina Gonzalez, a soft-spoken Venezuelan woman who fled with her husband, Ivan, when she was seven months pregnant with her daughter. They came for much the same reason as the Souto family. President Hugo Chavez was socializing their country and they wanted the freedoms of democracy.

When people tell her to return to her country, Adreina tells them she would love to but she can't. She was a preschool teacher there at a nice school. Her husband had a business and they lived a stable, middle-class life. But voting records became public and when her bosses discovered she hadn't voted for Chavez, she was transferred to another school as punishment. One day someone killed someone's child right outside her classroom. Ivan and Adreina left because they were afraid.

The United States hasn't welcomed refugees like these with the same enthusiasm it showed for the Cubans who fled Castro. Ivan and Adreina are not eligible for any type of aid. They have spent a small fortune on immigration lawyers hoping to obtain residency. Adreina cannot teach without a certificate, so she waits tables and Ivan hands out fliers for a PR company. They feel humiliated by their life in the United States.

"Part of our immigration experience here has been to not be able to use the skills we were taught in school," says Ivan, who speaks more forcefully than his wife. "We are completely aware of how much better Miami is to live in than anywhere else in the United States because the Cubans have made so many possibilities for us here. We can speak Spanish, we haven't had to completely change our culture. But we do not have the opportunities they have. We came here because we didn't think we would survive back there. And we left our family and successful careers to work here and not get ahead and it does not feel like this country wants us or wants us to succeed. We have spent a fortune on immigration and we don't always get treated with respect. We work so hard and we don't feel like things are moving."

Adreina says she loves working the *Quinces* even though they make her jealous. "I live for my daughter," she says. "I dream that someday I might have a *Quinceañera* like the ones where I am a waitress. That would mean I came here for something. But right now I don't see that opportunity within reach."

Adreina and Ivan work two jobs. Adreina's second job is at a grocery store giving out samples of the espresso coffee sold by the Souto family. She declines to go on camera for our documentary because she feels like it would be too embarrassing.

Marlene Ferro lives in Westchester in Miami-Dade County, one of the most Cuban-American neighborhoods in the country. You can tell just by looking around. The thirty kids dancing in her backyard are 100 percent American, grandchildren of Cuban immigrants, yet they speak fluent Spanish, consider themselves to be Cuban, and live in a place where they can feel completely comfortable thinking that way. The teenagers are handsome, friendly, and well-mannered. They are family-oriented in a very different way than U.S. teens. The backyard party on a Friday night includes their parents, siblings, and even grandparents. There is clearly great respect for elders. This is cross-generational socializing that is uncommon in most of the United States. A lot of the kids identify themselves as cousins or "almost like cousins," and it's clear there's not a kid in the bunch whose parents Marlene does not know.

Marlene is fully aware that her success is a combination of hard work and luck.

"I don't know what we would have done without the help we got in this country. I don't really know what other people do without it," she says to me.

At the end of the interview I go to the kitchen and make *sofrito* with Marlene's mother. I have a good time and we chat about what it used to be like back in my grandmother's kitchen in Union City, New Jersey. The children's shadows crisscross dreamily against the garden walls while samba and son intermixes with salsa dancing in the warmth of a typical Miami Friday night. Spanish chatter spills into the neighborhood. A grandfather or two lights up a cigar and eases back into his lawn chair to watch the youngsters play. Everyone here is perfectly comfortable expressing their Cuban culture in this piece of the United States. That is the Miami the Cubans have built.

On the same trip, I interview Helman Lara in an empty warehouse he had once built into a thriving business. His story brings another contrast to the successful Latinized Miami. He has come to Miami from Bogotá, Colombia, on a special visa for people who want to do business. Helman was supervising goods being shipped back and forth between the United States and Latin America and making a handsome profit. He had even created jobs for about a dozen Americans directly and brought business to truckers and delivery people and the warehouse where he kept goods. Helman has a PowerPoint presentation on his laptop showing all the work he was doing just a year ago.

But on a trip back to Bogotá, where his wife and children still live, his visa was held up for four months, time that cost Helman critical business. He missed meetings and couldn't supervise his staff. The economy in Florida is bad enough that four months of delays on a business deal are enough to sink a business.

Helman Lara is so frustrated he has a nervous tic when he talks. The volume of his voice rises as he frantically recounts every conversation with immigration authorities. "I had so much. I came back and forth and I was so proud of what I did. But I feel like I have no American Dream now, it's nothing, it's a waste. I feel like I have been treated like a Mexican who crossed the border illegally rather than a person who came to create trade," he says.

Helman's eyes fill with tears when he talks about his experiences with his immigration application. He is a square-shouldered guy who looks comfortable in suits. His brown hair is neatly combed and cut neatly above his ears, which sit flat against his wide face and pretty Latin features—long eyelashes, full red lips. He is proud and handsome and successful. It is very hard for him to fail at anything, especially business. While he was trying to keep his business going, he missed so many key dates in his daughters' lives. He feels like it's all been for nothing and he has decided he's going home for good. Some would say that's okay, as economic hard times mean fewer jobs for Americans as it is. But Miami is struggling to find educated, fluent Spanish speakers to work in the thousands of companies that do trade with Latin America and, several generations into it, the Cubans are no longer enough. Miami actually needs more Latinos.

Tammy Fox-Isicoff is a lawyer who represents Latinos in every conceivable circumstance in Miami. She told me that she could fill her office with legal immigrants who are taking their skills elsewhere. They believe they can earn more money back home. This is a new and shocking phenomenon that has yet to be reported. The economy going sour has not just meant a decline in the number of poor people crossing the border; it has meant a decline in the number of people with the necessary skills and innovative ideas who come here legally and want to stay. There are Ph.D.'s who rob their own countries of their talents and innovators who open businesses here with ideas off the streets of Bogotá and Buenos Aires. After all the sacrifices and separations they have endured it's unfathomable that they'd just turn around and go back one day when they have legal permission to stay.

Fox-Isicoff and several other immigration attorneys told me that they sense a change in the attitude of immigrants.

"They feel like they are not wanted, and I'm not talking about some guy who crossed the border. These are people who obtained visas, people with green cards, who have permission to stay," said Fox-Isicoff. "They are throwing up their hands and saying, 'I'm not wanted here. I'm not happy. I miss my family. I miss my culture. I am not sending money back and I could maybe do better at home.'"

She told me that at a conference of immigration lawyers in Miami the week I was there, this story was told over and over again by lawyers who obviously have a stake in not seeing their clients return. The people who come to this country, like my mom, have a plan in their heads that caused them to leave to go build a life elsewhere. These plans require that they make a place here for their families, not just make money. It's about making a life, not just making a living. So when they cannot make a life, they leave.

The statistics on returning Latinos who forsake a U.S. visa to return to their home countries are hard to come by. It's clear that a crackdown on illegal immigration and a bad economy are taking a toll on the flow of illegal immigrants. Mexican banks report that people are sending less money back home. (In June 2009, the AP said that remittances back to Mexico in April 2009 totaling $1.7 billion were 18 percent less than in April 2008, the biggest fall on record.) Border Patrol is making fewer arrests with a lot more officers. But it's very hard to quantify the number of legal immigrants who have chosen to reverse their decision to come participate in the American Dream.

At his lawyer's office Helman Lara reviews a mountain of paperwork that has cost him tens of thousands of dollars to prepare. Helman is a very formal guy with a substantial ego that has obviously been reduced in stature by this whole process. He jokes with his lawyer, Richard Lind, that he must have funded him a new swimming pool by now. Richard explains that a post-9/11 mentality has influenced how U.S. immigration agents deal with folks south of the border.

"This is the one form of immigration they have an affect on and no one wants to be the one who let in the wrong person so they just say 'no' to everything," he says.

I had asked Helman if I could interview him at his home but he finds it too embarrassing. His drop in business has forced him to sleep on his grandmother's couch in her retirement community.

"I do not want to go back," he tells me. "I want to do business here. I never asked to stay permanently. I just want a respectful process when I come and go, not being pulled off into rooms to be questioned about my intentions or asked if I have sufficient ties to my country when I have a whole family living there. I can't afford to have months of delays every time I go in and out. I'm exhausted by this and I feel like my dream has gone nowhere."

On my next trip to Miami I take a step into the past. I drive out into the far reaches of West Kendall, where there is still a bit of wilderness. The day I visit Camp Matacumbe, I am dressed in black and the sun pounds Miami like one of those puffy mallets you use to hit the drums in a marching band. I am cooking in the heat.

I have come to meet Senator Mel Martinez, the first Cuban-American U.S. senator ever and one of just three Latinos currently in the Senate. When he steps out of the car the senator is wearing a snappy serge blue polo and looks fresh and cool. He is tall and good-looking and has those charming Latin manners that make you want to like him. Somehow being around Senator Martinez makes the heat lift and we both begin marching around the place exchanging stories.

The twenty-two acres around us are being used by the city as a public day camp but it looks lonely today because there are no children. Big parts of it have been designated as a nature preserve and birds of every color seek refuge beneath the canopy of South Florida slash pines. Raccoons, foxes, and possums poke around at dusk. The area is imperiled, which is a concern because it is a stopping place for migratory birds that have nowhere else to go. It is a metaphor on so many levels for what this place is all about.

Melquiades Martinez was fifteen when he flew from Cuba in a DC6 and landed at the Miami airport. He was taken with a group of other Cuban children down a hallway labeled "Children Coming Alone Come Here." After giving up the most basic information about his family, he was driven to Camp Matacumbe. It was dark and the forest was quite thick. It looked nothing like Sagua la Grande, where he had grown up playing baseball with his brother, Ralph, and fishing at the beach with his father, who was the local vet. There were dark cabins nestled among the trees and it was very quiet. The children were taken to the largest structure, a dining hall that had cots with army blankets lining the walls. He remembers all the details vividly. There was linoleum on the floor, which he had never seen, and they got to drink cold milk out of cartons, which was also new to him. He got to eat these wonderful cookies made of oatmeal. Then they all slept together on the floor.

"This is it," he tells me, staring down at the linoleum, which has survived the years. "This is where I began my life in America."

Mel's happy boyhood had been interrupted in 1958 with the sound of gunfire from the incoming forces of Fidel Castro's revolutionary troops. He has retold his story in a book titled *Sense of Belonging* in riveting detail. His Catholic school, Sagrado Corazón de Jesús, was shut down and the priests were expelled. His new school books celebrated Communism. Mel was defiant and helped smuggle communiqués against Castro. Boys not much older were being sent to prison and a sixteen-year-old in his town was executed by a firing squad for smuggling a rifle.

In 1961, Mel's parents told him he had to flee without them. His new baby sister, Margarita, had just celebrated her first birthday. He was also leaving behind his brother, his mother, and his father, who squeezed his arm and told him they'd be reunited in three months. He was sending his oldest son on his first trip alone in his entire life.

Camp Matacumbe belonged to the Catholic Welfare Bureau in Miami. It was a summer camp with a pool and a basketball court. Its history as a place for refugees began with Father Bryan O. Walsh, an Irish priest. In 1960, a Cuban man had brought him a fifteen-year-old boy named Pedro (Peter) who had been sent to Miami from

Havana and needed help. Cuban parents, like Mel Martinez's, were panicking because they feared their children would be victimized by Fidel Castro's Communist revolution. (Some historians argue that the CIA was also spreading warnings about what could happen to children if the revolution was allowed to endure.) Parents who were not aligned with Castro wanted to send their children to nearby Miami until things quieted down. Father Walsh convinced the U.S. Department of State to give him the power to waive visa requirements for these children so they could board commercial flights to Miami.

To the U.S. government, Communism was a dark specter that had invaded a romantic island befriended by the United States. Something had to be done to save these children. The United States was so eager to help they even gave Walsh money to care for the children once they got here. Walsh connected with the headmaster of an American school in Havana called Ruston Academy. They launched a rescue operation together called "Pedro Pan" (Peter Pan) that flew in fourteen thousand unaccompanied children in twenty months. Mel was one of the Peter Pans.

As the children, mostly boys, arrived in ever-growing waves, Camp Matacumbe was dubbed "Boystown." When Mel arrived at Boystown in February it was colder than he was used to and he immediately thought he'd made a mistake.

"I look back on it now and I realize how very homesick I was," he told me. "It was the saddest, most depressing time of my life. I was very lucky that this journey was marked by the generosity of so many people, but I was young and away from my family and it was frightening."

Mel has a son named Andrew who is fifteen now, the same age Mel was when he arrived.

"Can you imagine sending Andrew off to another country where you know no one and he won't know the language, not knowing whether you will see him again?" I ask.

"He's just a little boy," he says with emotion. "I just can't imagine it. I was so worried about my situation then, about what could happen to me and where I would end up. I wondered how I would get to my parents. I was really depressed. I thought for those first few days that I really wanted to go back."

Boystown still has the dreary little yellow buildings where the

Pedro Pan children stayed. They are boarded up now and several have been invaded by bees. Miami-Dade County bought the land for $2.4 million with grants and money raised by the Pedro Pan alums, who hope to erect a memorial or museum there.

Many of the children were reunited quickly with parents or other relatives, who swept into Miami right behind them. But a large number stayed at Boystown or were dispatched to other camps, schools, dormitories, and private homes all over the country. Mel ended up spending time with two foster families in Orlando, the Youngs and later the Berkmeyers. They treated him like their nephew, even better sometimes. He went to a Catholic school that was even better than the school where his foster brothers went. "They were very generous and I was well taken care of but it was awkward," said Mel. He barely spoke English at the time but was staying with families who spoke no Spanish.

"There were these cultural things. They'd take their kids to the store in shorts, which didn't feel right to me. I didn't understand their rituals. The boys were not aggressive and romantic with the girls like Cuban boys were."

In October of 1962, the Cuban Missile Crisis stopped the airlifts off the island, leaving separated families at the mercy of the U.S.-Cuba relationship. Modern Latino Miami was born even as thousands of children were left stranded waiting for months and even years to see their parents again. Some stayed with foster families or at Catholic facilities in a hundred cities around the nation. They became the largest group of refugee children in the Western Hemisphere.

"It was around my birthday," Mel recalls. "I knew we were really separated then with me here and them there and the missiles in the middle. My family was totally caught up in a Cold War drama."

After spending a full hour in the heat of Boystown, the senator and I retreat to the Biltmore Hotel so I can interview him on camera about the years that followed. I think we're both relieved to leave the site of such dark childhood memories for a grand setting more reflective of his present. The Biltmore is a National Historic Landmark and we settle into a suite for our interview. Mel, ever the Latin man, orders everyone lunch and jokes about having a "Dennis the Menace propensity" in the back of his head that our cameras will have to avoid. His journey from isolated teenager to U.S. senator was not an easy one, but he repeatedly tells us that it happened because of the generosity of this country—the people, the church, the government who gave him refuge.

Senator Martinez remembers what it was like to be reunited with his family. He was older and taller and they stepped off a plane in Orlando with nothing to their name and no place to go. The Berkmeyers decided to take them in as well. He remembers sitting in the back of their car between his mom and dad holding their hands and barely being able to contain his emotions. He just wanted to hold them. But as soon as they were settled, his role in the family went from child to translator and cultural ambassador.

"We came here already educated, professionals, and we worked very hard. We were a lot like the Jewish Diaspora," he said. "We had a solid background and ended up with no place to go back to. We had to make it here."

Mel is just one of the successful Pedro Pans. I interviewed others, like the auxiliary bishop of Miami, Felipe Estévez, and the singers Willy Chirino and Lissette Alvarez. The group includes numerous business leaders and other politicians. It is a very successful group.

"It is really remarkable," Mel Martinez says.

"Is it the most successful immigration in U.S. history?" I ask.

"Probably."

"How so?"

"In one generation to think I could have become a lawyer, much less U.S. senator. . . ." He pauses, as if overwhelmed by that fact.

"What about this place let that happen?"

"This country provided the best opportunity for success."

But that opportunity has long since faded. Boystown no longer operates at Camp Matacumbe, but it has not gone away. The Catholic Welfare Bureau, since renamed Catholic Charities, still cares for refugee children with the same eagerness it showed to boys like fifteen-year-old Mel Martinez. But the U.S. government now has other plans for the unaccompanied minors who come here.

When I arrive at the new Boystown, in the Miami community of Cutler Bay, my first impression is that it looks like a more modern summer camp than the old one. The building is a cheery yellow surrounded by clipped grass soccer fields and short healthy palm trees. The front doors open onto a cafeteria with the kind of round tables and chairs I'm used to seeing at the motels where I sometimes stay when I'm on the road for CNN. But looming over the room like a somber reminder of why children are here is an eraser board listing the daily schedule. "1 pm—IMMIGRATION COURT," reads the top entry.

There is capacity for sixty kids here but today there are thirty-one in various stages of being adjudicated for having illegally entered the United States—alone. The lawyer for many of them is Michelle Abarca, an attractive Nicaraguan woman, who came to the United States when she was twenty-four and went to Northwestern Law School. Michelle has these rounded cheeks that make her look like she is smiling even when she is not. She is dressed in a summery suit that is totally appropriate to her station as a lawyer with a nod to the Miami humidity. But she doesn't look formal at all. She is an attorney who represents kids. Michelle moved to Miami to be closer to her family and the familiar warm weather. She planned to do some kind of immigration law and she discovered this population of lonely and depressed children with a need for legal representation. She stepped forward as one of many pro bono attorneys at the Florida Immigrant Advocacy Center who take their cases.

Michelle reviews some of the child clients who are living here at Boystown waiting for a judge to tell them what comes next. There is a ten-year-old boy from Honduras who crossed the Mexican desert with a smuggler who ditched him midway. He walked three days to reach the United States in search of a mother he'd only seen in photos since he was six. Then he was grabbed by Border Patrol. There is the teenager who crossed the desert on one leg hoping to earn enough money in the United States to get a good prosthetic. He was captured clutching the old one because it had become too painful to use. There are kids who are not old enough to be in school yet, smuggled on planes and trains and boats by total strangers, even a four-year-old who crossed the desert with his father, only to be separated from him and sent to detention. In many cases, there is no one in this country who wants them and no one in their home country who wants them back.

The children live at the camp in near anonymity; some of the seventy-two hundred children captured by Border Patrol or customs agents are farmed out to one of forty-one detention centers in ten states. Up until a few years ago, the program was supervised by U.S.

Immigration and Customs Enforcement (ICE), but the kids ended up getting treated too much like adult prisoners. So the program was handed to the Department of Health and Human Services, where people are used to caring for children. They technically live in the custody of their Office of Refugee Resettlement, which views the kids as child welfare cases and cares for them like the children they are. They subcontract to agencies like Boystown in Miami.

Permission to visit the camp with cameras is rarely ever granted and getting it was a process that took us many months. The children's lawyers asked that we not use their names and the Department of Health and Human Services limited how we could use their images. Ultimately we had to deal with lawyers for the children's parents to be able to show them on TV. Everyone was trying to protect someone or something. But we insisted on doing a story about the children there anyway because this place is very special. The story of how these refugee children have been viewed over the years is in many ways the story of our country's uneasy relationship with all the refugees from Latin America who come searching for a better tomorrow. It tells us a lot about what can happen when the United States embraces them and what can happen if we don't. Since they are children, it is a measure of how we act when the people asking for our help have nothing on their minds but hope.

The Boystown at Camp Matacumbe continued to operate as a refuge for unaccompanied minors until nearly three years ago, when it became so run-down that Catholic Charities found another site. The new Boystown is in a residential neighborhood and has adopted the second name Children's Village, even though they still have more boys than girls. With that move, and the transition to being a part of the Department of Health and Human Services, it looks more like a child care facility than a detention center.

The director of Boystown is a woman named Karen Husted who acts like a cross between an aunt whom your mother has entrusted with your care and a truant officer at your school. She has brownish hair with a curl to it and dresses a bit more formally than the staff, which is hovering around the place in jeans and T-shirts. But she has on the shoes of someone who is not comfortable wasting time behind a desk when there is work to be done. Her milky-colored skin is a sharp contrast to the dark leathery look of the children who march back and forth between the open-air buildings around us.

When I arrive, she runs out ready to give me a tour of a place of which she's obviously quite proud. The facility has gates made of thick horizontal metal bars out front and between all the different sections inside. But it doesn't feel at all like a prison. Nothing is locked. Instead, they have alarms in a few places and plenty of staff looking after everyone. Karen says the children don't try to leave since they have no place to go.

In the main cafeteria Karen has everyone preparing for a graduation. A boy who was released to foster care has graduated from high school and she's arranged to give him a party. She takes me to see the boys' dorms, where light-cream-colored walls are decorated with drawings and sturdy wooden beds are covered with colorful bedspreads. Everything here is donated and it's nice and new, and toys and stuffed animals spruce up the nearly bare rooms. The children are between classes and playtime so they're sitting in a common room doing some schoolwork. They are watched from a glass office on one end and staff members walk around supervising them. They are oddly quiet for kids their age.

The boy with the deformed leg is sitting in a wheelchair in hospital pajamas. He wheels over quickly and grabs Karen's hand. *"Que dios te bendiga,"* he tells her enthusiastically. "May God bless you." "Thank you," he adds. His smile is enormous. *"Te quiero,"* he says. "I love you." "I love you, too," Karen says to him. Karen only met this boy a short time ago. Karen began her work at Boystown/Children's Village two and a half years ago, just as it was being moved to this site. She had been a social worker since 1982, when she met some of the unaccompanied minors.

"Their stories, the resilience, their willingness to learn. I can't even describe it," Karen said.

"Is it hard for the kids to make the difference between 'you're detained' and 'but you're not in jail'?" I ask her.

"I think initially it is difficult for them, because when they first get here they're very nervous. They don't know if they can trust, they don't know what to trust, where they're going. So I think it is difficult when they first arrive. We try to do things that are childlike with them, taking them on outings, you know, to sports teams here, to many games, to the aquarium, to see movies. They're going to the zoo on Thursday. So we try to do as many 'normal' kid activities as we can with them."

"Is this a hard job for you? Is it emotionally difficult?"

"Um. Yes, yes . . ."

"Why the pause? That was a long pause."

"I know, I know. I wasn't sure how to answer that properly. So yes, it is difficult."

"Why?"

"The children are wonderful," she says, her emotions welling up.

"You fall in love with them?"

"You do, you have to. You would, too, you will before you leave here. I guarantee it."

"And you don't want to see them go back?"

"No . . . No."

"Does it sometimes seem unfair?"

"No, it always seems unfair."

"Always?"

"Always. Because they struggle so hard to get here but they don't consider poverty enough [reason] for somebody to stay here. And a lot of the children are driven by poverty."

"How poor are they?"

"You have a fifteen-year-old who feels they have to support their family back home. They feel the weight of their entire family on their shoulders. That's what these children go through. They come here to work. And you know, when they're here, they don't want to be here, they want to be working, because they feel that they have to support the family. That's a lot on a fifteen-year-old. And that's what many of them face. They feel that they're the only one who can support their family back home."

Most of the children come from Central America and stay an average of fifty-one days, according to the Office of Refugee Resettlement. They are usually looking for parents who came to the United States illegally to find work. Others are escaping poverty and abuse or, young as they are, looking to work to help their families back home. The goal of the centers is to care for them while the courts decide whether to deport them or release them to suitable adult guardians, foster parents, or relatives while they wait for judges to rule on petitions to stay in the United States. Meanwhile, they get some schooling and are fed and clothed and given whatever perks Catholic Charities can extract from its donors. That includes computers and Ping-Pong, Nintendo and Atari, books, TV, and toys for some of the little ones. They have gotten tickets to see the Dolphins, the Panthers, the Marlins, and the Miami Heat. The Pedro Pan alums are paying for them to go to the Miami Zoo.

Karen says they provide Spanish-speaking staff around the clock. A banner in the back of one of the playrooms is labeled *"Sueños de los Immigrantes,"* or "Dreams of the Immigrants," and here children have written up their wishes. The most repeated of these is simply to stay.

Catholic Charities celebrated its fiftieth year in Miami in 2008 and Karen believes its work continues because for people like her it is an expression of their faith. The boy in the wheelchair is an example of that. Boystown is a detention center where he is to be cared for until an immigration judge decides his fate. But the boy had come to the United States dreaming of earning enough money to get his leg fixed. So Karen tapped her network of contacts and convinced the Shriners to pay for his surgery. Doctors amputated his deformed leg and he is being fitted for a proper prosthetic. When he clutches her hand and gives thanks, Karen feels like Catholic Charities has fulfilled its mission of doing the best it can in the time they have these kids.

"What kind of shape are they in when they arrive?" I ask her.

"Difficult."

"They're traumatized?"

"Yes, traumatized."

"Do they sleep?"

"It's difficult."

Karen points out that they are caring for children as young as four and that all the children have experienced traumatic events, like being dragged away from their parents, seeing family members perish in the desert or waters of the Rio Grande. There is a group of Haitian children rescued from a boat that capsized off the coast of Miami. They saw people die. There are those who travel great distances alone, clutching photos or phone numbers of mothers they haven't seen for years, only to be caught before they reach them.

There are several who managed to arrive here safely, only to be captured months or even years down the line in immigration raids. Then they are separated from their parents once again. Children as young as fifteen sometimes come in handcuffs. Karen is especially upset by seeing that.

"What do people assume about these kids?" I ask Karen.

"That they're dangerous."

"And?"

"Oh, no. You just look at them and you don't want to see their dreams shattered."

"Do most get to stay or do most go back?"

"Most go back."

"Is that hard?"

"Yeah."

We walk outside to talk, very much aware that many of these kids have learned enough English to understand what we're saying. The sun is burning out and the green grass fields are almost glowing. There is a basketball court and a place where the kids can play baseball, but Karen says what really makes them happy is to play soccer, which they do even in the heat. She tries to help them focus on improving their English since it is the one skill she can provide that could help them if they do get to stay. I tell her it's a "really nice place" and she looks proud but a bit sad. "It's still detention," she says, and mentions again how troubled she is when she sees the handcuffs.

I ask to see the classrooms and we exchange the heat of the grassy field for a cool room decorated with construction paper drawings, posters, and maps. Some of the kids get more school here than they ever got back home. There are three county schoolteachers, including John Hung, whose Spanish accent is almost as thick as the students', barking English drills at nine very enthusiastic pupils.

"They are very hardworking. They are anxious to learn English," he says. "It's sad because when you have them prepared they need to leave. This may be the first and last time they see a classroom."

I ask a girl if she would like to stay in the country and she nods her head firmly. "Is that why you are trying to learn good English?" I ask.

"Yes, ma'am," she replies firmly.

When classes end I go back to the playroom to spend some time with the children. A four-year-old boy sits on the floor and draws me pictures.

"I'm waiting here for my father," he explains. He is Cuban, which makes all the difference in the world. He will get to stay and receive all the assistance Cubans are entitled to in this country. The day before, a Honduran boy just a few months older had left for an uncertain future to stay with relatives in Los Angeles. Their beds were in the same room, with safety gates to keep them from falling out and baby toys scattered on the bedspread. Now one bed is empty and the Cuban boy is by himself. He is dark-skinned and has close-cropped hair that makes his ears stick out. He's wearing a striped brown shirt and checkered pants and red Crocs patterned in the form of Lightning McQueen from the Disney movie *Cars*. We balance pens on each other's heads and giggle when they fall over.

I enjoy playing with him because he's a funny little guy and reminds me of my twin four-year-old boys, whom I always miss on these reporting trips. It's very hard to process the idea that someone the age of Jackson and Charlie has been separated from his family and is hanging out playing at a shelter in another country. Michelle is his lawyer and she's watching as I put crayons on my head and pretend I can't find them.

"Can you imagine I have to sit down and discuss his legal situation with him?" she asks. Michelle is accompanied by two of her colleagues today, a paralegal named Julie Irvin, who is there to do a presentation to new children on their legal rights and Lisette Losada, another lawyer supervising her colleagues. Jill Volovar, a representative of the Office of Refugee Resettlement, is there to watch us, in addition to Karen and two employees of the shelter. I have my coauthor and two photographers. There are ten people watching me balance pencils on this four-year-old's head and he is erupting into peals of laughter.

Everyone is worried about something different: Michelle about representing the boy in court and working in his best interests even though he can provide her with next to no information. Her colleagues are concerned because making presentations on legal rights to children is almost absurd, and they're not quite sure what to do with this boy. Karen is worried we'll upset a small child and the employees are distressed because the five-year-old who had been sharing his room has left, so they know he will soon begin to feel lonely. My own colleagues are trying to sort out how to tell this boy's story and realize that as dramatic as it is to see such a small boy in custody, we need to interview someone who can answer questions and represents the average child here, someone who is several years older. Without even saying it, I think we all just decide that the sight of a preschooler in detention is just too much to handle for now and we move on.

Michelle introduces us to a boy they believe to be eleven, although he insists he is ten. No one has ever celebrated his birthday enough for him to know the exact date. He thinks it happens when it begins to get warmer so it is around this time. The boy's grandmother brought him from Honduras to Mexico, but she was captured and he continued his trip alone. He has not seen his mother since he was six and is desperate to be reunited with her. The boy imagines she must still look a bit like the photos she sent him a few years ago. He was so determined to get to her that he traveled for three days in the desert until he was captured by Border Patrol. They let him call his mother in L.A. and she told him not to worry because she would fix his legal situation and they'd be together.

His story of detention is one told by many of the kids we'll meet that day. Before coming to the shelter, the children remember being put in holding pens and isolated so they did not come into contact with adults. They all describe it as a jail cell and talk about the cold and the loneliness. It's obvious this is one of the most traumatic things they've experienced along the way.

"I was crying because I was by myself. They gave me juice and crackers. It was dark and I was so cold. I got very sad. I was in there so long," he said.

"What's been hardest?"

"Everything has been so hard for me."

He has clearly been crying today so I ask him why. He had made a friend at the shelter and they were trying to stick together. She was a nine-year-old girl from his country. But when he went to class today she was gone and they told him she was being deported. He was so sad he couldn't stop crying. I ask him if crossing the desert was hard and he suddenly toughens up and looks a lot older than his years.

"It was nothing," he says stiffly. "Fine. I just wanted to get to my mother." His personality shifts are jarring. He looks like a boy one moment and a young man the next. Yet he is not even a teenager, so the man part is disturbing. He is tough when he talks about his walk through one of the hottest deserts on Earth, but a baby when he talks about the departure of a girl he met weeks ago. Like all the boys, his skin is darkened and leathery from too much exposure to the elements. His round dark eyes look like they spent a lot of time being rubbed and he speaks in a very low voice, almost as if he'd prefer to be saying nothing at all.

Michelle has a girl she wants us to meet because she thinks she might be the right child for our documentary. She is fifteen and came from Central America at thirteen. She asks us not to use her real first name or identify her country precisely. These children's legal cases are very complicated and they do not want to jeopardize their chances in court. We later obtain permission from her mother to use her image, which I can immediately tell is going to be very powerful. We decide to call her Marta.

Like many children here, Marta was captured after having successfully crossed the border and reunited with her mother. She looks embarrassed and suspicious of everyone at the same time. She boldly walks over and sits down next to me, sensing that she has been brought in so we can talk. I strain to get a good look at her since she keeps looking down or away or hides a bit of her face behind her hair. When I finally get a full glimpse I realize she is very pretty. Marta has big round dark brown eyes and long lashes. She is a slight girl with dark hair cut unevenly above her shoulders. She stares out of the corners of her eyes at Michelle. It is clear Michelle is the only person she trusts even a little. Michelle is smiling at us, so she senses it is okay to talk.

Marta is clutching a happy-looking gray stuffed hippo she has borrowed to give her something to hold. Her eyes are so sad it's hard to look at them sometimes. She keeps focusing them downward at the hippo, and I take those moments to look away from what I'm seeing. She is so vulnerable it's painful. At first she tells her story in whispers. When she was six years old her mother left her and two younger siblings and went north to look for work. She ended up in the South at a chicken processing plant, undocumented and working insane hours, but she was able to send home money and occasional photos.

Marta desperately missed her mother and felt disoriented. Her father died and she was left in the care of her grandmother, a woman she says is not very old but is so worn out she appears ancient. She said her grandmother's house is big but in very bad condition. When it rains, water pours into the house, destroying everything. There was not enough food to eat. There was not enough of anything. She is trying hard to speak to me in English and what she's saying sounds almost more dramatic from the effort.

Her mother slowly became a voice on the phone, someone to cry to in moments of sadness and desperation. She gives the hippo a squeeze as if to steel herself for what she's going to say next. Her grandmother developed kidney cancer and she saw herself ending up alone with two younger siblings and no one to take care of them.

"I told my mother, 'Please. I want to come be with you,'" she says half in Spanish and half in English. "I had no idea what would happen to me on the trip. I was so nervous. But I needed my mother. I was so afraid."

So when Marta was thirteen, her grandmother took her to the Mexican border and handed her off to a total stranger who was to take her to the United States. But that woman left her in Mexico and refused to go on. So her mother sent more money to a second smuggler, who took her to the border. That's when, she says, she became a *mojada*, or wetback. The new stranger told her they needed to cross a river to get to a place called Fort McAllen. Marta was terrified. She did not know how to swim. So the woman took the tube from inside a tire, blew it up around her waist, and launched her into the Rio Grande.

"I felt like I would not get past the river but I did," she says with great relief. On the other side, they boarded a bus and she was given paperwork belonging to the woman's nine-year-old girl, "like a normal person traveling with their mother." But when they got to the Texas border, Border Patrol came on board to inspect the travelers. The woman told her to pretend to be asleep, but the agents shook her awake and asked questions. She answered with the details of a set of paperwork she'd been given by the previous smuggler.

She describes the next part with the same scared tone of voice as the ten-year-old did.

"They took me to a room with adults and it was really cold. I was scared. It was dark and I was crying. There was no place to sleep," she says. She also remembers getting juice and crackers and worrying that she would stay in the jail forever.

Marta was released to a detention center, a place she recalls as not being as nice as where she is now but much safer than the jail. She got a pro bono lawyer and went to court. She was at the center for three months before being released to a couple connected to her mother because she is godparent to the couple's child. She was given a court date when the judge was to review her immigration case and told that if she did not show up it would cause her to be deported without a hearing. She remembers clearly the instructions of the judge. He told her to stay out of trouble, to go to school, and to not go see her mother. The first thing she did was to go see her mother.

Marta lapses into Spanish to describe the reunion because the words are rushing out too fast to translate. But it's not from the excitement. The reunion seems to have made her feel more shock than anything else.

"When I first saw her she ran up and hugged me. I had not seen her since I was five or six except in photos," she says, and then inhales very deeply. She pauses for a moment while the rush of disappointment sends tears settling in the bottom of her eyelids.

"I didn't remember her. I didn't remember. She was thinner back then. She had gained weight. Her voice sounded different than on the phone. I hugged her too but she didn't feel like I thought she would feel."

Her eyes are wide as she talks about the reunion. She is out of breath and keeps wringing the arms of the gray hippo. Her face turns from side to side, as if she is talking to me, my coauthor, her lawyer, everyone in the room, about something she believes we should all find equally shocking. Her tone is more intense than it was describing her dying grandmother or her dead father. It's more intense than the story of crossing the desert or floating across a river in an inner tube. This moment is more burned into her mind than her capture on the bus or the nights in the jail cell. Her own mother, whose absence haunted her for seven years, is someone she does not know at all.

Marta's mother had met a new man since leaving her home country and they had a new daughter, a girl just a few months younger than Marta had been when she was left behind. Marta saw the boyfriend as an opportunity to replace the father she had lost and she was excited about having a sister since she missed her siblings back home. They lived in a rented house and had a whole network of friends and relatives she did not know. She threw herself into getting to know her mother and learning English. Her school in the South was a shabby place, she said, but she loved every moment she spent there. She had very little education in Central America and she loved being able to go to school. She loved math and English and health. She even adored her homework. She loved the feeling of sitting down with a workbook at night trying to figure out answers.

Marta made new friends and they'd study together like normal girls and go to the mall to dream about things they'd buy someday. Her mother would spoil her with little gifts to keep her from being jealous of her little sister.

"I can't treat you like you're little but I still love you," she'd say. Marta thought her mother treated her better because she felt so guilty they'd been separated for such a long time. As the weeks and months passed, she started to care for this new lady she had met. She warmed up to her half sister and tried to help around the house. Her mother worked six days a week and she'd try to fill in for her when she was away. But the boyfriend was jealous of the attention Marta's mother gave her and indignant there was this new child on the scene. The new household was not a happy one. Her mother and the boyfriend fought all the time and she was left to try to keep her and her new sister out of the way. Things got broken and screaming woke her up at night. They both worked odd hours and she'd never know when someone was going to arrive home and the fighting would start once again.

The tension came to a head over her *Quinceañera*. To someone as poor as Marta's mother, this couldn't be a banquet hall affair but she wanted a party for the girl whose life she'd half skipped. The boyfriend went into a rage.

"Paying for you to cross the border was your *Quinceañera*," he fumed. Marta said after that "he crossed a line" and began doing things to her that fathers shouldn't do. Her rapid-fire storytelling ends in silence when she arrives at this fact. Her big round eyes fill with tears. She pulls the hippo up to her face. There is not much more you can ask of a girl who has just told you this story. Her sponsors, the godparents, reported to immigration that they could no longer care for her. She was supposed to be staying with them and they had let her stay with her mother. Whatever was happening in that home was inappropriate enough that they no longer wanted a part of it. Marta's mother was desperate. She found a couple willing to adopt Marta and sent her to live with them. In court, the judge insisted Marta provide information about her mother so they could call her in to sign some paperwork. The request sent Marta into a panic. Her mother is undocumented and she was afraid they'd turn her in. So Marta was detained and she was ordered to be deported. That is how she ended up at Boystown.

When I leave Boystown after meeting Marta, I feel like I've left home knowing the stove is on and no one's home to do anything about it. She is a child and she is so alone. The staff person who sees her back to her room puts a kind hand on her back and they walk off into the hot afternoon toward dinner and bed, even though the sun is still high in the sky. Michelle is very somber as she says good-bye to her and promises they'll speak the next day. She doesn't really have much new to tell her but she has plenty of more things to ask her. Michelle needs to prepare a case for her, just like she does for the other children. She is supposed to be acting in her best interests and that means finding some way for her to stay here, even if that has to happen without her mother.

I meet another former resident of Boystown, Willy Chirino, and his wife, Lissette Alvarez, who are both Pedro Pans. The couple are well-known Latin singers who own a house in one of those swank Miami neighborhoods that Cuban Americans have filled with stylized homes. On his album covers, Willy looks tanned and buff, with that shadow of a goatee so many Latin performers have. In person he looks more like his age, sixty-two, but is still someone who clearly takes care of himself. He has fine hair on his forearms and longish sideburns that give him a bit of a cowboy aspect. Willy was born in Consolación del Sur, a small town in Pinar de Río, Cuba, where tobacco blankets the green fields. He was the son of the town's state attorney and a pharmacist. Willy always loved music and remembers vividly meeting the famous performer Benny Moré when he was nine and deciding he wanted to be like him. But at thirteen his parents sent him to the United States on the Pedro Pan airlifts hoping he would escape the limits of Communism. They told him he'd likely be back in time for his cousin's *Quinceañera*, which was coming up in a few months. That was forty-eight years ago.

Willy remembers the loneliness and fear of his first days in that forest camp the same way Senator Martinez does. He also remembers the linoleum floor and the cold carton of milk. But he mostly remembers the excitement. He was moved with a group of boys to St. Raphael's Hall, a home the church established for Cuban boys where they were watched by four couples. The Pedro Pans describe it as the nicest of the shelters.

"I remember we had some great food and a good education, they took us to Sears to buy clothes and every Friday we got a dollar fifty, which was a lot of money back then," he says. He would watch television and mimic the drummers. By the time he was reunited with his parents, he was much taller and the priests had bought him a set of drums. He got a gig playing at a Catholic hall. He moved into a bungalow with his parents and two sisters and everyone began to work. He was fifteen.

Willy's first years as a performer were heady but stressful. He worked at the Bamboo Club on Alton Road for $11 a night, which was more than anyone in his family was making. He needed to be at school from seven in the morning to three in the afternoon. Then he'd come home to eat, take a nap, have dinner and shower and go to his nightly gig. He would not wrap up until three thirty in the morning.

By the time he was seventeen, Willy had performed with major Latino musicians like La Lupe, Tito Puente, and Ray Barretto. On one of his trips to New York he had a chance meeting with Lissette Alvarez. "She was like the Britney Spears of her time," he remembers. Years later they would meet again and marry.

Lissette's parents, Olga Choren and Tony Alvarez, were singers known as *Olga y Tony*. Lissette grew up touring (she was born in Lima when her parents were on the road). Olga and Tony recorded a song with Lissette when she was five. Lissette has catlike eyes and that bleached blond hair preferred by Latin performers of a certain era, only hers is tinted in a modern color that makes a striking contrast with her dark clothes. She is curvy and tiny and wearing impressively high heels. She has been performing so long that there is no part of her personality that suggests she ever belonged anywhere but onstage. She has often sung in English and even done translations of

American pop hits. Latinos of her parents' era idolize her to the point that Lisette Losada, one of the lawyers we met back in Boystown, was named after her. Her parents' fame drew attention to them in Cuba. They knew that as famous people their life after the revolution would be limited and they sent Lissette and her five-year-old sister away through Operation Pedro Pan.

Lissette has trouble telling her own Pedro Pan story because it is so traumatic. She left Havana at fourteen promising to care for her little sister.

"When they said good-bye to us, they were very quiet and tense. They told us they would see us in three months. I told them this would never be over. They had kicked the nuns out of my school," she said. "I was very lonely when I got here. I had to fight off the melancholy of the era."

Lissette ended up at a Catholic home in Dubuque, Iowa, where she was separated from her little sister. She remembers how terrifying that was and how she would sneak off to try to see her. Then they were at a foster home, where things were going well until one day, when she was at school and was called to the main office and handed her luggage. The family didn't want her anymore. She would be separated from her sister for three years, staying at another foster home that she remembers as a terrible place. When they were all reunited in Miami, it was a tough mixture of pain, resentment, joy, and melancholy. She and Willy have six children, three from Willy's first marriage, kids they keep very close to home even as they are grown men and women.

Willy has never been back to Boystown but Lissette has. It was disturbing for her to go back there. They live another life now and that life has been good to them. When I met with Willy he was preparing to play a concert in Miami's American Airlines Arena, an arena he's dreamed of playing since it opened ten years ago. They are both hard-line conservative anti-Castro activists. Willy held a press conference daring Raúl Castro to broadcast his concert in Cuba. They have grown very comfortable in their new U.S. home but have not abandoned their desire to see Cuba returned to the way it once was.

Willy and Lissette's house in Miami is a grand affair. There are cubbies and spaces etched in the woods and stone walls to accommodate fine pieces of art. A Grammy award sits on the mantel of the fireplace.

There is a room just for playing pool, several sitting areas and living rooms, and bars. Wood planters of tropical flowers weave around the many staircases that lead to other floors with even more rooms. To someone living in Manhattan, the kitchen is a dream.

Willy and Lissette are warm and enthusiastic about our interview. That Cuban connection can't be beaten. I am as thrilled to meet them as they are to meet me. We belong to some Cuban club of people whose hard work has paid off just enough to justify our outsized Cuban egos. Their various children are just a few years younger than me and they've had equal success. One of their daughters plays guitar for Shakira.

None of this wipes away the realities of the past. I tell them about the children I met at Boystown and they get very serious.

"A lot of them are likely going to be sent back. Is that fair?" I ask Willy.

"It is not. It is not. I mean, how could it possibly be fair? But life is not fair. We all know it. This is a tough decision for everybody involved. But fair, no, of course not."

"Do you think the treatment of refugee children should change?"

"Children are children and they should be treated fairly and they should have every opportunity. . . . I do have a foundation that helps in the process. . . . All of us, who have been successful in this country, for so many years, who have achieved the American Dream, have to help in the process. Separated families are our big tragedy if you talk to any Cuban family. The biggest pain comes from the separation, parents over there, children over here, vice versa. That happens to Mexican families, to Honduran families, to Salvadorian families, and that's very painful.

"Is it fair for Cubans to have certain privileges? Probably not. Are we thankful that the laws are this way, and for us it's different, because our trajectory is different, because of what Cuba has had to endure for so many years, that dictatorship? Yes. But are we doing enough about it? I don't think so. To make it fair."

Earlier, I had asked Senator Martinez the same question. He is a member of Congress about to immerse himself in the controversial issue of immigration reform, so his answer is extremely consequential. Will it make a difference to this country if these new refugee children are not given the same opportunities he was given?

The senator is acutely aware that, in this country, the opportunities he was given require congressmen like him to fund real programs. So he won't go that far. Instead he points to his support of the DREAM Act, which would enable undocumented children who excel in school to go to college and have a path to citizenship.

"It's not even about who pays, it's about not putting an impediment in the way. The way I paid for my schooling if anyone put a pebble in my way, I would have stumbled."

But he has to pause before answering whether there is a difference between the DREAM Act children and Marta.

"There is really no difference," Martinez finally says. "I don't know. You're really driving at a really great unfairness that our system has, which is that some of these children are getting lost in a system that is destroying their lives. And it's only because we are saying, 'Oh, but that's the law, we've got to enforce the law.' I don't know. I'm too much of a lawyer to tell you that the law doesn't matter though. The law does matter, but it isn't always fair. I feel for them. I could be a great advocate for them . . . because you can't help but look in their eyes and see that same hopefulness that I had. . . . The fact is that the same hopefulness is in that young child's eyes, who just wants to be gone from that place. She just wants a chance to go over to McDonald's and get a job. And start her life here, maybe go to school, fulfill her dreams, and I mean, I can't give you an answer for that one. I mean it's tough."

It is hard for Lissette to talk about this issue. She has achieved fame but never escaped the trauma of those three years, so she has trouble getting the words out. She was about Marta's age when she came to Miami with her little sister.

"Yes, you are going through so many changes, hormonal changes, and becoming a woman, and you're still a child in a way, and being away from your family that is supposed to give you guidance and . . ." Her voice trails off.

I tell Lissette about Marta's situation.

"I was in Boystown about five or six years ago. I went to see the kids there," she tells me.

"What was your experience like? What did you think?"

"You know the kids live day to day, let me tell you. And they, like, always have this hope that they're going to get out of there and that this is an adventure. And it was very nice, at the time that I went there, they had little apartments with their TVs, and they were fine. I mean, of course you don't know what goes on inside. You know, you just see them there and they were being taken care of but it's very tough. You know it brings back all the memories."

"Do you remember those days as a Pedro Pan very clearly? I mean, you teared up the minute we started talking about it. I'm sorry, I didn't mean to bring up what was obviously painful. Do you remember it like it was yesterday?"

"Yes, I do. Well, sometimes. It's strange, you know. Sometimes it seems like it was a million years ago. And you see how it makes me cry still, so it comes back really easily."

"Can you believe how much success you've had, at those most terrible moments when . . . ?"

"The melancholy and the shyness, of course, and I come from a family that were very famous people when I was a little girl. I was born on the road. So I grew up with sort of this abandonment kind of a situation, and then leaving Cuba and all that, the trauma, it was incredible. You grow from that and you write songs. That's what alleviates it. You know, to be able to sing and write songs, and express yourself that way."

Lissette gets up and grabs the hands of one of her daughters and motions for the family to come gather around the piano. Another daughter picks up a guitar and Willy sits down at the piano. As they settle down to play some music, Lissette throws out just one more thought as she shakes her head and blinks back her tears.

"We have to pray that they can be reunited with family wherever. My sister was five. She did not understand why she was there."

They begin to sing songs, American pop, old Cuban ballads. Lissette uses the music to break her sadness. She sings *"Doña Soledad"* to me and I get a serious kick out of it. They have songs about immigration and triumph and just having fun in Miami. This family has come so far.

The days at Boystown pass very slowly for Marta. The staff wakes her up at seven a.m. if she's not already lying in bed awake, as she often is. There is some school but not that much. The second time I see her she has just returned from the Miami Zoo, which Marta referred to as a day of "seeing animals in cages." She is in pajamas some days by four p.m., after her second shower to wash off the sweat from running around all day in the heat. She has not made many friends here because she knows they will leave without notice. Marta jokes with two girls who have been in the United States since they were toddlers and are now fifteen. They don't even speak Spanish but they may be deported back to Honduras. Their home was raided and their parents taken away. Their father was deported and their mother is detained. Like everyone else, they're waiting to see what will happen to them next. My staff brings them ice cream and they take the bars quietly and eat them alone. You've never seen children so unexcited about ice cream.

Michelle is working up to telling Marta some tough news. She pulls us into a classroom to give us details. Michelle believes the only chance Marta has of staying in this country is for her to file for a special visa reserved for children who have been abused, abandoned, or neglected.

There is little doubt that Marta fits into this category. She lived in abject poverty back in Central America, and with her father dead and her grandmother dying, she has no place to return to. Her mother abandoned her and, despite her efforts over the years, she hasn't been able to adequately care for Marta since then, even exposing her to the abuses of her boyfriend. She even had to ask Marta to leave her home for her own safety.

What this means is that Michelle will advise Marta that she should go into court and make allegations of abuse, abandonment, and neglect against the mother she dreamed half her life of rejoining. There could be repercussions in the household for the younger child, the boyfriend, even the mother. Marta's mother has no idea how abusive the boyfriend was and this means she will likely find out. If she wins, the law does leave open the possibility that Marta could be reunited with her mother down the road. But the judge could stipulate that she'd have to abandon her boyfriend, move, or even turn herself in.

"It's very hard because I have to make sure that this is what she wants," Michelle explains. "She is making a decision to do something that will have an enormous impact on her family, but I'm her lawyer and I want what's best for her. It's tough to expect a child her age to know the right thing to do. We're the child's attorney and we want to be their guardian but we can't be. If the child says they want to go back to an abusive situation or poverty in their country, I represent them and I have to do what they want. These children are being treated like they are adults and expected to know what's best for them. Marta has a very compelling case and is a very vulnerable child, but she is just a child."

Michelle says she is hoping the couple who wanted to adopt her are still in the picture, although for now the federal immigration charges ignore the fact that there was a pending state adoption case.

"She will be a great asset to this country if she is allowed to stay. She needs to walk into court and tell a judge what has happened to her. That she came here as a thirteen-year-old alone to see her mother and now has no one, that she is learning English and is a good kid and wants and needs to stay here."

Michelle is not certain what Marta will decide. While we are talking, Marta has changed into a white T-shirt and flannel blue pajama bottoms with drawings of little girls on them. She ties her hair back and it makes her look a touch older, more like the young teenager she is than the girl she looks like. Her stomach has been troubling her since she arrived and the doctors told her she is nervous. She was finally diagnosed with gastritis and is eating bland foods. She is allowed to receive phone calls so she keeps up with the kids back home. She recently learned her mother lost her job at the poultry plant and she is anxious because she wishes she could help her out. She is obviously very loyal to her mother.

"I miss my school," she says. "They have a dance this Friday. I know I'm falling behind here. I was just learning algebra. I had almost caught up to the other kids."

Even when she is just chatting, Marta looks as if she is about to cry. She remarks that she really loves algebra and has a friend back home who studies with her. She was hoping they would stay in school together and someday graduate on time. Her English sounds better every time she speaks. She listens intently to the TV set in the playroom and mouths the words.

There are some younger girls there today, a five- and a six-year-old, so the bigger girls are helping them with their hair. Marta is frustrated that her hair has not been cut in some time. She didn't really want to go on the zoo trip so she's in a bad mood.

"Estoy desesperada," she whispers. "I'm desperate."

"I want to get out of here. I want to go home. This is driving me crazy," she says and walks back and forth across the floor, as if walking quickly would get her someplace even though she has no place to go.

The little girls have pulled out some big bold markers so they can draw. The older girls have grabbed the black one and are drawing things on each other's shirts, signing and dating them so they will remember each other in case one of them goes away. Marta isn't that interested. She wrote on the top shoulder of her shirt, just high enough so she can almost see it if she dips her head and looks behind herself.

She puts on a shirt belonging to one of the other girls. She glances over her right shoulder and pulls it up to see what's written on the back.

"I want my mom" are the only words she can see. She smiles and decides this is the shirt she will wear for us to take a final picture.

3

have a magical day

THE DAY I fly to Orlando to meet Carlos Robles the temperature is as high as it is in his hometown of Fajardo, Puerto Rico. The same humidity, too. Occasional puffs of cool air cut through the midday heat, which hits eighty degrees by noon and hangs there until the sun sets. The weather helps explain why so many Puerto Ricans relocate to Orlando in search of opportunities.

"The truth is I wanted a new job and couldn't see myself moving too far north. I can't stand it when it gets below sixty," says Carlos.

He has been in Orlando for two years and so far only the most extreme winter chills (extreme, that is, by Orlando standards) have rattled him. Puerto Ricans are the only U.S. citizens born on a piece of U.S. soil where Latin culture and the Spanish language are dominant. They are not immigrants or the children of immigrants like all the other Latinos. Since 1917 they are U.S. citizens and, despite their island's colonial friction with the United States, they are basically Americans born and bred. Taking a trip to Puerto Rico, lovely as that might be for me, isn't going to tell me much about Latinos in the larger American experience because the island in many ways operates like its own Latino country. So, instead, I've come to Orlando, Florida, a favored destination for islanders looking to come to the mainland.

I meet Carlos in the sun-splashed garden of the Valencia Community College Center for Global Languages where Carlos is taking a class. Students from all over the world study here to improve their pronunciation and understanding of the English language. They used to call the classes Accent Reduction but no one enrolled. So they renamed them English Conversation class and now they're full.

PREVIOUS PAGE, TOP: Vanessa Rosas.

PREVIOUS PAGE, BOTTOM: Carlos Robles.

Carlos is a fair-skinned, chunky guy with short dark hair and a squared-off goatee. He is sweating and antsy and shakes my hand like he's just walked into a do-or-die job interview. When he says, "Eh-lo," I think of my grandmother with her two words of English. I tell Carlos that I know Spanish but that if I were to talk to him in Spanish he'd be doing this story about me. He starts smiling little by little. I recall how my mother used to say "hog-dog" all the time for hot dog and get a snicker of recognition out of him.

Carlos's features could make him from anywhere Latin, except that his Spanish is very Puerto Rican. When he speaks Spanish he replaces his *r*s with *l*s and he talks like he's about to start singing. It's a happy form of speech, very homey, almost like teasing. But in English he sounds like he's spitting out phrases. He is hesitant, throwing out each word almost like he's asking the question, "Is this the right word, am I pronouncing it right?" So this guy who was born on American territory, educated in American schools, is about to begin barking out language drills in a classroom so he can communicate with his fellow Americans here in Orlando. He laughs at his whole situation.

I meet another Puerto Rican student in the garden. Santos Martinez is tall, black, bald, and looks like the basketball coach he is. He coaches in English but feels like he's not communicating with the parents. "I can't do that if the fathers keep looking at me like, 'What did he just say?'" says Santos. He rattles off his personal résumé to explain why he's here. "I'm part-time [at] JetBlue, no wife, no kids. In my culture that's a loser." His language limitations have kept him from rising professionally or meeting the American wife he's looking for. Santos, Carlos, and I trade words before class begins. Carlos can't say the *th*s properly. Instead of "thought," he says "tawt." I ask them what's the most difficult word to pronounce in English and Santos says, "Crocodile." I ask him how you pronounce it in Spanish and suddenly we're all standing there sputtering: "Co-co. Ca-ca-ca." We all begin to laugh.

Carlos's journey to Orlando began in his hometown of Fajardo, known as *La Metrópolis del Sol Naciente*, the Metropolis of the Rising Sun. It's a small town on the east end of Puerto Rico where recreational boats float in the Atlantic Ocean and big ferries take off for the islands of Vieques and Culebra. Nothing in Fajardo seems to move quickly, not even the cooling breeze that comes off the ocean. Like Orlando, it's a place many people associate with a good vacation.

Carlos worked as a police officer in nearby Carolina, where an international airport sits beside a string of resort hotels, lazy beaches, and a very large shopping mall. His territory included the towns of Loiza and Canóvanas, which have housing complexes with substantial drug problems. Carlos felt he was on a road to nowhere good. The pay was low; his family was threatened by the drug dealers; his mother was always praying for his safety. Homes on the island are very expensive so he felt he'd never be enough to buy something nice. He had to get out. But it made him sad to walk away from the tranquility and tropical weather he loved.

Years earlier, his aunt and uncle had moved their family to Orlando after his uncle was transferred there by the navy. There were a lot of Puerto Ricans in Orlando and the family found the weather and atmosphere familiar. Carlos and his family visited so often that his grandmother purchased three small apartments to use as vacation homes for all her kids and grandkids. When Carlos decided to quit his job to search for new opportunities, his grandmother offered him a free apartment in Orlando so he could join his aunt, uncle, and two cousins. He was gone in weeks.

This is a familiar story for many Puerto Ricans who relocate to Orlando. The island has 15 percent unemployment and there isn't enough affordable housing, while there are more opportunities for jobs and homes on the mainland. Jorge Duany, a professor at the University of Puerto Rico, researched the phenomenon of Puerto Ricans moving to Orlando. He discovered official efforts to encourage Puerto Ricans to move to Orlando dating as far back as the 1950s, when central Florida needed more farmworkers and the island's government began a program to encourage migration. That was followed by another contract labor program in the 1970s.

Puerto Ricans are U.S. citizens and the island had a lot of trained agricultural workers. Since the island had lower salaries, the Puerto Ricans were a cheap, hardworking domestic labor force. The workers made more money on the mainland, bought homes and stayed. Friends and relatives followed. In 1971, Disney opened and real estate speculation drew even more Puerto Ricans. Disney also liked Puerto Rican workers. They sent representatives to the island to visit schools and job fairs. They even offered cash relocation bonuses at one point.

Orlando in general was exploding with people. The local chamber of commerce estimates one thousand a week were coming at one point. Research by the Pew Hispanic Center in 2002 determined Orlando's Latino population had 300 percent growth since 1980. The U.S. census said the place was adding 347 people a day in 2001, and there's no denying that Puerto Ricans were a big part of that growth. They represent 56 percent of the Orlando Latino population, and that doesn't even count the many Puerto Ricans who travel back and forth.

As the population of Orlando became more Latino, other companies looked to diversify their workforce and offer bilingual services. Puerto Rican employees filled both those goals without having any immigration issues. NASA, just forty miles away, sent recruiters to hunt for talented engineers at the University of Puerto Rico in Mayagüez. Florida Hospital in Orlando signed an affiliation agreement with the University of Puerto Rico in 2005. Between 2000 and 2006, according to census figures, 200,000 of Puerto Rico's 4 million people moved to Florida. After the farmworkers came blue-collar laborers and then professionals. They didn't just come from the island but also from big mainland cities like New York and Chicago, traditional destinations for Puerto Ricans. Almost half the Puerto Ricans in Orlando come from other cities on the mainland, Duany found in his research. He also discovered that the newcomers are mostly white, well educated, and have more than double the median family income of their counterparts back on the island. The move is paying off.

When Carlos came to Orlando in 2007, he was hoping to become another Orlando-Rican success story. Very quickly he had a job as a manager at Kay-Bee Toys. There were four managers and he was the only one who spoke Spanish, an asset. He was earning good money. He met Puerto Ricans from New York who were looking to move to Orlando because they found their city so cold and fast-paced. Carlos is funny and friendly and gives off the air of a guy who likes to be liked. He tried hard to fit in with the other managers. But they weren't very friendly. Every time he opened his mouth, they would look at him like he was an idiot. "I cried in my bed because I can't have a conversation with the people. It was really bad," he said.

Like all Puerto Ricans, Carlos was taught English in school and expected to speak it fluently. Yet once he left school, there just weren't opportunities to have real conversations in English. His vocabulary and accent suffered. The Puerto Ricans from New York all spoke English and people expected him to speak it, too. But the white people in Orlando would just smile politely and walk away in the middle of a conversation. "I'd look at them and think, 'That guy has no idea what I just said to him,'" Carlos remembers. The other managers at Kay-Bee Toys wouldn't even smile. They would just bark orders at him as if he was their subordinate, pushing him toward grunt jobs and making jokes behind his back. His supervisor called him a Mexican. Carlos thought it was funny because he was considering joining the Border Patrol at the time and the ads all asked for fluent Spanish speakers.

He tried to let their remarks roll off him but it slowly began to get to him. He'd never felt this way back on the island, where he was a swaggering American police officer bossing around a whole group of motorcycle cops patrolling for drug dealers.

"Oh, my God. It was humiliating. I wanted to punch them sometimes," he said. "I just kept telling myself I'd start to speak better and one day I'd be this professional guy they'd look up to."

There are nearly eight hundred students taking the English speech classes at Valencia and it is repeated five times a year. It is a little odd to see Americans taking classes to reduce their accents alongside people coming from foreign countries, but Puerto Ricans are a twist in the discussion of Latinos in U.S. culture.

After Kay-Bee Toys shut down, Carlos decided he wanted to wrap his arms around the language and enrolled in pronunciation class. He is taking a second round, twice a week from 6:00 to 8:30 p.m.

"I'm taking the class because I saw that I can be more professional and I think that I can have a better life and I need to talk English. I'm in the United States, so I need to talk," he said.

"Well, Puerto Rico's part of the United States," I point out.

"Yeah, but we always talk in Spanish. We never talk in English over there."

Carlos looks like he used to have the imposing build of a cop. He wears the reflecting sunglasses you'd expect to see on a police officer who works in warm weather. Inside his classroom, words are written in red that make Carlos's head hurt: kitchen, corner, and victory. Cabinet. Thought.

"The Latinos hate the words with the *th* and the *v*," says Marisa Dawson, the teacher. "The Asians have great grammar but they've never had to speak, so their pronunciation is terrible. The Puerto Ricans should know more than the South Americans but they don't. They all learn it in school but it's kind of like learning high school French. If you never use it, you lose it, and when they come here I think they're surprised how much they need it. The South Americans are prepared because they know they won't get anywhere if they can't speak English."

Carlos is sitting between a Colombian guy and a Venezuelan. Neither of them really wants to be in the United States but they were forced to leave their countries. Miguel Ortega was a surgeon back in Colombia and now he's "the cable guy." He tried being a medical assistant when he first got to Orlando but it paid $8 an hour. It is too dangerous in Colombia or he would go back. The paramilitaries killed people where he worked. He is determined to be a doctor again so he is studying to pass the required recertification tests. He has passed the first few but the last one requires English conversation, so he needs this class to work.

Luis Sirit was in the Venezuelan navy as a commander. He also wishes he could go home but he says he is on the wrong side of politics there and that can be deadly.

"I could do just fine in Orlando without learning any English, that's how Latino it is here," he says. "But I'm cleaning swimming pools. I didn't study to clean swimming pools."

Both of the men voice a short list of laments about living in the United States: the food is not fresh, the parties never seem to include music or dancing, the people aren't as close to their families. Luis says he keeps inviting people over to show them how much fun Latinos can be and he says they really enjoy his culture. He especially likes the Puerto Ricans, like Carlos, because they are Americans with a Latino personality.

Luis and Miguel don't find it odd that there is an American in their class. "Spain had Puerto Rico before the United States," says Luis. "He's Spanish like the rest of us. Plus the Americans can't tell the difference. They think we're all Mexicans. So we have to stick together. Once we're all here, we're all Latinos and we have more in common than we do different."

Carlos pokes the two of them in the arms and flashes his broad smile. He has the same goals they do even though he's not from a foreign country. He doesn't want to be reduced to working in a toy store again. He is scheduled to take the Florida sheriff's exam for the second time. Back in Puerto Rico he passed the police test with a score in the high nineties. Here he got a seventy-three on the sheriff's test when he needed an eighty.

"There was this word all over the test, 'accurate,' and I thought I knew what that word meant but I didn't and it was a problem. Everywhere I looked it said accurate and accurate and accurate and every time I thought I knew. When I was done I went home and looked it up and said, 'Oh, no.' I had messed up so many questions," he remembers. He thought he'd do better since he was educated in Puerto Rico, but the words tripped him up. His computer is always on a translation Web site now.

Gabriela Lemus, a policy director for the League of United Latin American Citizens (LULAC), studied the growth of Latinos in Orlando in 2003. She found that the school system there had reached a "critical mass" because of the large number of Latinos who don't speak English. As the Puerto Rican community grew in the nineties the number of students nearly doubled, and they didn't have the resources to keep up. Now, nearly one-third of the Latino population in Orlando is under twenty and parents are not in agreement as to whether they want their children immersed in English or taught to be bilingual.

LULAC thinks part of the problem is that Puerto Ricans don't have the political clout to get the resources they need. Island Puerto Ricans vote in much higher numbers than those on the mainland. Turnouts are so low in central Florida that the island government runs voter registration drives in Orlando. Another problem is that the broader Latino community is not united.

"Orlando has not really experienced any major crisis affecting Latinos. Orlando Hispanics have yet to witness a backlash that would cause them to depend on one another for support," says the LULAC paper titled "Orlando, Fl: A Study in Hypergrowth."

". . . Discrimination is exhibited more subtly and is primarily based on accents and language."

We caught up with Carlos again when he had gone to his fiancée's apartment to study. He sits at her kitchen table with a stack of dictionaries, this big cop thumbing through these delicate language picture books full of words he can't say. His life has become all about learning English and passing that exam so he can put together a life for his fiancée.

Carlos met Keila Pagan, a newly arrived Puerto Rican, at a bar in Orlando. He was out with a friend who was drinking away his marital problems and the two of them got very drunk. He said he came on too strong but managed to extract a cell phone number from Keila so he could apologize the next day. Seven months after the bar encounter, she is expecting a baby, he is calling her his fiancée, and the language classes feel a lot more pressing. She doesn't speak much English. He thinks they'll need it to take care of their new family in Orlando and she is due in seven months. The pressure is on.

The walls of Keila's apartment are bare except for her bachelor's degree from the University of Puerto Rico in elementary education and her teaching certificate. The books are all English-Spanish dictionaries except for the one about taking care of your new baby. In between homework assignments, Carlos pulls food Keila has frozen for him out of the refrigerator and runs hot water over the plastic container. He's been eating a lot better since she came on the scene. She has left him steaks with Puerto Rican seasonings and yellow rice with instructions on defrosting and cooking and reminders to leave enough for her to have dinner when she gets home from work. He runs off to the gym every so often to make up for the fact that he's gaining weight. There's no point in passing the sheriff's test if he fails the physical. Then he races back to study some more. Carlos misses Keila. She sends him texts on his cell phone telling him she loves him. "I love you more," he responds. He usually picks her up and drops her off at home before going to his language class.

Keila is twenty-five and comes from a very small town called Cidra. She graduated from college just two years ago and left the island because she couldn't find a teaching job. She is licensed to teach K-to-3 kids but she was making $5.25 an hour at a Subway. Her best friend had a great job at an engineering firm in Orlando and had just married one of her Puerto Rican coworkers. They offered her a place to stay so she moved in with them. Then Keila got a job at Wendy's earning $7.25 an hour. There were not many Puerto Ricans where her friend lived and she felt out of place. So she got her own apartment closer to Orlando where she didn't really need to use her English. She could hop on these bright purple buses stamped LYNX by the Orlando transportation system and be among other Latinos in a few minutes.

Once Keila solved the problem of where she lived, work became a stumbling block. She says she was shocked at how racist people are. At least one person every day asked her if she was Mexican derisively. When she told them she is Puerto Rican they'd smile awkwardly like she had some nerve making a distinction. There were a lot of black customers and she expected them to be nicer since she knows many black Puerto Ricans. But they seemed to have the same low opinion of Latinos, she said. There were no Latinos when she started working. But every time there was an opening, one would get hired. She thought maybe the whites and blacks resented the Latinos for getting the jobs. But as the months went by, she rarely saw blacks or whites applying for the jobs. She understood everyone's English perfectly, but when it came time to talk back she would just freeze. It was hard for this teacher to admit she had a lot to learn about language. "I get all the concepts and words but it's so humiliating to talk it," she said.

Carlos picks Keila up at the Wendy's most evenings before leaving for his class. She begins taking off her uniform as soon as she hits the sunlight. When they walk into her apartment, she opens all the blinds and the room brightens. "I know everyone says this but I came for the weather," she says, laughing. "I grew up in sunshine. I need sunshine." Carlos mentions that he would have moved in with her instantly. Carlos's brother and his wife moved to Orlando after his brother got a job as a chef at a Disney restaurant. His sister-in-law was pregnant and by then so was Keila. They were both beginning to feel like Orlando was a new hometown. When they are home together it all feels right.

Keila says she would go back to Puerto Rico if it wasn't for Carlos and the baby. "The Americans make so little effort it makes me angry and I don't like being angry," she said. "I know it bothers them that I don't speak great English, but I grew up in America speaking Spanish so I don't understand what they're so angry about. At least I'm making an effort. They could also try. When they come to San Juan on vacation, they speak English and expect you to speak it back. I don't go to Orlando and expect them to speak Spanish back. I try to speak English. Then they get all indignant that I'm not fluent. They treat us like we're from some other country, like foreigners. I can't even imagine what it must feel like to be a real foreigner.

"People seem to resent us for getting jobs in our own country. What am I supposed to say to that? I didn't come here to fight with anyone. I'm moving from one place to another in my own country," she said.

Keila says people are offended by her pride in her Puerto Rican roots. She got her driver's license and put down her two first names and two last names because that's the way Latinos use their names. She says she wants her child to be fluent in Spanish. She has tried to make friends in the United States but isn't comfortable with the culture.

In Spanish Keila is an entirely different person than she is in English. She is bright and well-spoken and pronounces her words with the caution of a language teacher. She had hoped to teach Spanish in Orlando but doesn't want to apply for jobs while she is pregnant. She thinks Anglos and even other immigrants can learn nice things from Latinos and should. She is very much against assimilation. "Assimilate into what?" she asks me. She thinks that Anglos are always rushing around and have the type of parties that start and end at a certain time. She complains that everyone stands around talking about themselves or where they work. No way. It's much better that they learn to have parties where you don't have to ask if you can bring your family and where people never even know what your job is. She would rather be at parties where you can "dance, cook, make good jokes and have enough fun to drag the party out until the sun rises."

Keila is going to take the same language class that Carlos is enrolled in because she wants to speak better English.

"I know I'll be teaching here eventually and that if I were in Puerto Rico my name would be on a waiting list forever," she said. "That's what's great about the mainland. You can be whatever you want. But it could be so much better here if they'd stop resisting integrating us. They're so afraid we're going to change them that it hasn't occurred to them that we just might change them for the better!"

Keila is due for her second appointment with an ob-gyn since she confirmed her pregnancy. The first exam didn't go well. She and Carlos thought they were going to get a sonogram but they misunderstood what the doctor said. He spoke only English. Carlos spent the first exam frustrated and didn't ask the doctor any questions and Keila said it left her wanting to go back to Puerto Rico. LULAC's study found vast discrepancies in health care between Latinos and Anglos in Orlando, even as the community actively recruits Puerto Rican medical service providers. "Barriers in language and communication barriers have resulted in the misdiagnosis of many patients," says the report.

For their second appointment, Carlos drives Keila early in the morning to the Seminole County Health Department, where a new clinic offers health care to expecting mothers. Mike Napier, the administrator there, used to be married to a Colombian woman and is very sensitive to the needs of Latinos. A few years back, he noticed a sudden rise in infant mortality in his county and became concerned. The number of Spanish speakers having babies was on the rise and he was afraid they weren't getting enough information on prenatal care. So he got funding to bring in private physicians who specialize in obstetrics and made sure that several of them were bilingual. One of them was Dr. Juan Ravelo, one of those tall, handsome Cuban doctors who affirm the positive Latino stereotype that gets pinned to Cubans.

Dr. Ravelo greets Keila and Carlos in Spanish and clears up some misinformation from their last appointment. She is eleven weeks pregnant, not far enough along for a sonogram. She has a rash on her arms that is related to the pregnancy but can be treated with cream. She and Carlos are all smiles when he says he will be seeing them going forward. A Puerto Rican nurse goes over prenatal care with Keila. Then Dr. Ravelo asks her to lie down and brings out a heart monitor. A few slurpy sounds later and a clear, fluttery fetal heartbeat pounds through the monitor. Carlos's eyes fill instantly with tears and he squeezes Keila's arm. *"Te quiero. Te quiero,"* he tells her and kisses both sides of her face and then the top of her head.

"I really need to learn English," he says between big smiles. "I'm having a baby here. I'm going to raise a baby here. I need to know how to say more than the baby in English!"

"Me, too," Keila adds softly.

That evening, Carlos's family gathers at the small apartment given to him by his grandmother. His brother's wife had her baby just a month ago so Carlos's parents flew in to surprise their sons and meet Charlene Gabriela Robles. Seven adults surround this tiny little girl with fuchsia pajamas talking baby talk in Spanish. This is a family that is deeply connected to their children. Carlos's father, Carlos Robles Figueroa, named his sons Carlos Osvaldo and Carlos Alberto.

To have both his sons move to Orlando has been a mixed blessing for Carlos's father. He and his wife have traveled all over the world, enjoying their retirement from being full-time parents. They are glad to see their sons working hard, pairing up with nice Puerto Rican girls, and giving them grandchildren. But the apartment complex where the grandmother Lydia bought her units has converted from a place for retirees to a rough complex filled with gang activity. Carlos woke up one night to find two dozen teenagers attacking each other with shovels. Some of his neighbors own pit bulls for security. Everyone is worried about crime. Carlos's father also worries about what living in Orlando will do to his sons' self-esteem. He is a professor of Puerto Rican and U.S. history at the Inter American University of Puerto Rico. Puerto Ricans are fiercely patriotic and it irritates them when people treat them like anything less than Americans.

"We have been U.S. citizens since 1917. We have fought in every U.S. army since World War One even though we cannot vote for the U.S. president or Congress. We are fighting right now in Afghanistan and Iraq," says the professor, whose English is stronger than that of his two sons.

"The relationship of the United States to Puerto Rico has been one of mutual love and mutual need. It's deeply insulting that so many people here don't even know where Puerto Rico is and keep thinking we're a part of Mexico, which couldn't be a more different place. It amazes me how critical they are of us for not speaking better English when we were educated in American schools. They should be mad at the schools. It doesn't even occur to them that maybe kids on the mainland should be taught to be fluent in Spanish too since so much of their country has Spanish speakers now. I know my sons will learn to speak better and move forward. But I have no interest in them losing their Spanish or their culture because both things are part of what it means to be American to us."

His sons and daughters-in-law nod respectfully as he speaks, then turn fourteen eyes to the seven pounds of baby girl at the center of their discussion. *"Que mucho se espera de ti, niña bonita,"* says her father. How much we expect from you, pretty girl.

The language issue has been more than just an obstacle to some Puerto Ricans who have moved here. Roberto Cruz of the Legal Advocacy Center of Central Florida tells of a case where dozens of Puerto Ricans were targeted by a shady lending scheme because of their weak English skills. A company called 4 Solutions promised to refinance homes of owners who were having trouble making payments. In some cases, they'd even take over the mortgage for a few years. Borrowers were promised that their payments would ultimately fall. They signed refinance papers but realized later that they'd actually agreed to sell their homes to investors who believed 4 Solutions would pay the mortgage. When the company didn't pay, the homes fell into foreclosure. The original owners couldn't buy them back because the mortgages had grown.

"Language was definitely an issue here. These people were told they were refinancing but the paperwork said they were signing away their equity," said Cruz, another Puerto Rican who relocated to Orlando.

"You would think Puerto Ricans would know better English but it's a myth. A lot of Puerto Ricans, especially ones who are poor and have less education, don't speak and read the language strongly enough."

One of Roberto Cruz's clients is Paula Rivera from Bayamon, who moved to Orlando in 2000 to care for her sister, who was suffering from Alzheimer's. In Orlando she felt like she could improve her quality of life. She earned $10,000 from the sale of her house on the island and signed a rent-to-buy lease in Orlando. She heard an ad on Spanish radio about "great rates" and how you could save money. She was promised her monthly payment would fall from $965 to $600. She didn't figure it out until she got a call from a guy named Vincent Vasquez who claimed to be the new owner. Now she is living there with her sister and a grandson and is counting on God and Roberto to keep her from losing her home.

"The problem here was everything was in English and I speak so little English," she said. "They spoke Spanish and I thought I could trust them."

For others, the gamble of moving to Orlando has paid off handsomely. Haydee Serrano speaks very little English but she was making a living in Boston when she embarked on a vacation to Disney with her two sons and her four-year-old daughter. She had left Puerto Rico years ago searching for opportunities. "It was so cold in Boston," she said. "I didn't get the culture. I had a great job but I was really very unhappy. My kids and I didn't like it there." She was only in Orlando two days before she knew this was the place to be. The suburbs reminded her of the sprawl near San Juan just off the highway. A few weeks later, she had moved her children to Florida with no job, no money, and no prospects. She spent her first months living in a seedy hotel cleaning toilets at a chain restaurant. But five years later she owned a home and belonged in a community.

Haydee's daughter celebrated her fifteenth birthday, her *Quinceañera*, at Disney. The theme park is marketing the parties to Latinas in expensive packages that can run tens of thousands of dollars. There are carriages and Disney figures and fireworks, as magical as Disney itself. Mirroring what we found when we looked at these ceremonies in Miami, to Haydee, it was as much a celebration of her family's success as it was her daughter's birthday. Even the staff cried to see how proud the stout woman with the thick accent looked escorting her princess at the place of magical dreams. Haydee's son just moved into her house so she races home to cook him rice and beans each night. She says she has been touched by good fortune. She recently got her hours cut back at the job she has as a medical assistant but she took on foster children anyway. She feels like it's her way of returning the help she got when she first moved here.

The trouble some Puerto Ricans have communicating is only a hurdle for some Puerto Ricans in Orlando. In fact, in the 2000 census, 63 percent of all Puerto Ricans in central Florida claimed they could speak English very well. But it's not the only hurdle they face. Vionette Pietri moved to Orlando in 2003 to preserve family ties. Her nephew is her closest relative and he lived in Orlando.

"Family is everything to Puerto Ricans," she said. "It didn't matter that I was giving up a job as a lawyer working for the president of the

Puerto Rican Senate." Vionette estimates that she sent out a hundred résumés and got two job interviews. She has a command of English but she speaks with a very heavy accent, which affected the way prospective employers looked at her. Finally, someone suggested she just take her law degree off her résumé. She got a job as a secretary and typed so much she began to suffer from carpal tunnel syndrome.

Vionette was bored out of her mind so she started to teach dance classes. They became the thing she looked forward to each day and she ended up starting a dance school. She used dance to empower women like herself who were struggling. Soon she extended her work to victims of violence. That led to a traveling theater. And then a book: *Detrás del Velo... Descubre la Diosa en ti* (*Behind the Veil: Discover Your Inner Goddess.*) By the time the book was finished she'd tapped a network of professional Puerto Rican women and found a job helping educate Latinos on housing rights.

CNN videotaped Vionette's book launch at the large Hispanic Business and Consumer Expo in Orlando that draws an estimated thirty thousand people each year. Vionette was over the moon that day. What a turnaround in just a few years. She is most proud of the fact that she did not compromise her ethnic identity to get to where she is. Her Spanish has ended up being more of an asset than her English. She is doing a show on Spanish radio and writes a column for *La Prensa*, the local Latino newspaper. This summer she will direct a monologue as part of her traveling theater project.

If Vionette's journey has taught her anything, it's that Latinos have to help each other. She is helping her office promote a program to help people buy foreclosed homes. "I am hoping I'll meet another Puerto Rican woman who needs help," she said. "That is the most important thing to me, to help people the way I was helped." She uses her English at work a lot these days and with each day her pronunciation gets better. "I'm fitting in here more and more each day," she says. "But on my timetable. For now I'm fine working with my own community."

The Business Expo is a reflection of how much the community has changed to accommodate Latinos. The local newspaper the *Orlando Sentinel* now has a section for Latinos and publishes *El Sentinel* on the Web. Telemundo and Univision have stations in Orlando. LULAC estimated "there are more than 12,000 Hispanic-owned businesses in Central Florida with almost $960 million in sales receipts. No business has centered on Latinos so successfully as the area's largest employer, Disney."

At that same fair, Vanessa Rosas is all smiles and corporate-speak. She is another Puerto Rican who relocated to Orlando. She was studying engineering with her then fiancé in Wisconsin. About eight years ago they traveled to a job fair in D.C. and visited the Disney booth. Disney hired them both in a short time. They moved to Orlando and bought a cute house with three big bedrooms so they could start a family. Then they had two little girls. They had the life they had always wanted.

We came to visit Vanessa in her sixth month of serving as Disney's ambassador. The designation is a major honor at Disney because employees have to compete in an *American Idol*–type contest for a chance to publicly represent the entire company. To Vanessa, Disney is a dream maker of giant proportions and she has become its chief cheerleader.

The day we go to interview her, everything is scripted as if we were seeking an audience with the Queen of England. Disney is like that. We are escorted by a legion of smiling "cast members" whose mandatory pins identify their place of origin and any special language skills. Vanessa's pin says "Puerto Rico" and "Spanish." To enter the area called Team Disney, which is backstage at the Magic Kingdom, you have to show ID, drive over a moat, and wait for a guard to raise a tiny metal security drawbridge. Once inside, everyone snaps into character and you begin hearing the constant background music of the various Disney theme songs. Yet for all the regimented appearances, there is always a sense of fun in the air. Disney employees are taught that their workplace is a theater, not a theme park. They are all actors in one enormous play and the estimated 200,000 people that walk across their stage every day are treated to a perfectly choreographed show. When you mix the easygoing manner of the Puerto Ricans with the intensely friendly Disney culture, you get Vanessa Rosas.

Vanessa arrives for our interview dressed in her "costume," which today is a cherry red business suit with patent leather pumps, a gold Disney brooch, and, of course, her name tag, which her PR handlers keep reminding her she is never to take off. She is all smiles and patience as my staff erects three high-definition cameras and lights of all sizes smack in the middle of a lawn in front of the main castle. We are traveling with three photojournalists, Dom, Greg, and Rich, who could be ripped right from the catalog of men who carry cameras. They have classic good looks and large muscles and tweak every light and lens as if they were fine cars.

Everything is timed like clockwork to be finished before the park opens. The carefully manicured lawn is brushed into shape, the walkways sparkle, the team assigned to us has made sure we are all in position and our gear and cars are tucked away so there is no danger a guest would see any mess. One of my producers, Kimberly Babbit, another perfectionist, has been working on this shoot for weeks. She is a very tall slinky blonde whose serious black suit can't hide the fact that her looks draw universal attention. Everything and everyone associated with this day is right out of central casting.

But when the time comes for all this to play out, one of the PR staff is failed by her GPS and gets lost. Instead of being guided in before the park fills, I arrive just as the crowds are pouring into the Magic Kingdom. I begin dashing off questions as everyone hustles into position. Kimberly has worked every angle of a production shoot to get it right and she is suddenly ashen from the stress. The PR folks are huddled around a monitor discussing how everything is going to look with all these unexpected people. Then things go from bad to worse. Neither Disney nor Kimberly is able to control the weather and the clouds bunch together above us as one of those unmistakably Floridian tropical storms begins pouring rain on everyone. I just can't stop laughing inside.

From here on, everything careens further and further off script. We abandon the interview and hop on a horse-drawn carriage to avoid the drizzle. Greg the camera guy hops aboard just as the cast begins belting out "Someday My Prince Will Come." We try to continue the interview over the loud clippity clop of the horses. Then the skies open and I am asking Vanessa about Puerto Ricans in Orlando in the middle of a major weather event.

Back at the setup, Dom seems to be the only one wearing rain gear, but he still looks like a wet puppy and a strong frown is etched on his face, his arms shielding tens of thousands of dollars' worth of equipment as Kimberly races around in stiletto heels throwing trash bags over everything. We do a loop with the horses and race over to the teacups to find shelter. There is yet another Puerto Rican staffer, who gets us into the ride, so we hop on with Greg spinning backward recording us as we lurch forward. The spinning usually makes me nauseous but I'm laughing at the whole situation.

Around and around we go in a giant teacup as I ask Vanessa to explain how she has devoted herself to shortening the lines and organizing food service, things you don't typically associate with engineers but that require near brilliance at a park so large. Her functions are truly critical. Her team invented the Fast Pass, which lets you jump the endless lines, priceless for any parent with crabby children in tow. We ditch the teacups and charge over to the train station, where thousands of visitors pour out despite the rain. Plan B is to continue our interview up on the platform, which is covered.

Vanessa was chosen by sixty-one thousand cast members for her ability to keep that smile beaming and she is doing a great job. There are Puerto Ricans everywhere and she is as proud of them as they are of her. Of all of us, she's the only one still looking good. "Every day you have a whole new conversation here about how you miss your hometown," she tells me as we duck for cover in a Germanic-looking bakery. Kimberly and the team have raced ahead to the platform to scout our next scene. My hair has gone totally limp and my black suit is hanging off my shoulders from the weight of being wet. My hairdresser Wendy has stopped following me around with a comb. The humidity is so strong that the air is wet between the raindrops. Vanessa and I chat and I compliment her on her clear English. Her accent is so slight, it is charming.

"How do you maintain your Puerto Rican-ness?" I ask her.

"We both speak Spanish at home. We try to maintain our Puerto Rican cooking. We buy cookbooks. My kids love eating plantains even more than they love French fries. They love singing to our music and dancing."

"What's the best and worst thing about moving to Orlando?"

"Being part of a Fortune One Hundred company that values diversity," she says, very much on script but with sincerity. "The worst, well, I miss my family, my friends. I miss the festivals. There is a festival in Puerto Rico almost every week."

The rain has now been joined by a gusting wind that pushes

the raindrops at odd angles. The Disney staff is suggesting every possible solution. I want to hug them for all their hard work, but we are clearly not going to have a formal, well-lit, sit-down interview outdoors today. Someone suggests we go to Vanessa's house and she eagerly agrees. Greg is soaked and wants his delicate microphone back before it is totally waterlogged. The equipment is scattered everywhere under plastic tarps. But the show must go on. So we jump into a caravan of cars and race away from the Magic Kingdom. When I hear about the tenth person wishing me a "magical day" I'm slightly in awe of how terrifically they run this place. I begin having fantasies about how they might manage my whole life for me. Maybe then I would be having a magical day.

Vanessa lives in a development called Heritage Place, not far from a few neighborhoods that are solidly Puerto Rican. Hers is a mix, but it looks a lot like Bayamon on the outskirts of San Juan. Some of the houses are painted in those soft Caribbean blues and yellows and, inside, she has prints on her walls of Old San Juan. Andrea, five, and Paola, two, are at a day care that has a pre-K program but their presence dominates the house. The bathroom is decorated with bright pink Disney princess curtains and pink bath towels. Toys are arranged very neatly in every corner. Picture portraits peek out from all the walls. The entranceway is dominated by some very large pictures surrounding a wedding picture in which Vanessa smiles that now familiar smile.

We settle in the living room, where a picture is hanging of a river in Barceloneta, where her husband was born. They were both Puerto Ricans making their way on the mainland when they met and came to Disney. As an engineer she was bedazzled by Disney's efficiency.

"This is a costume and we are all cast members," she says, referencing her own business suit. ". . . It's someplace clean . . . where you can escape reality and come into fantasy. It's a show and we are all part of the show."

We're hungry after our exertions so we order take-out Cuban food and the air fills with the smell of garlic and fried meat. But we have to let the food sit there and taunt us because we still haven't done the interview. So, about seven hours after my staff got up and a full fourteen hours since I boarded a plane from the West Coast to get here, we finally sit down for our formal interview. I'm hungry and a mess but Vanessa looks perfect. The only people checking to see how it looks are the Disney team.

Vanessa acknowledges Disney has had an aggressive recruiting effort of Puerto Ricans for years and says that's about its broader effort to keep its workforce diverse. It doesn't hurt that Puerto Ricans are U.S. citizens, absent immigration issues and many times bilingual and well educated. They have the right attitude, love the fun of Disney, and appreciate the warm weather. Disney is Orlando's biggest employer and a lot of Puerto Ricans have moved there with this dream in their heads that they would get a job there.

Vanessa's Orlando experience has been the flip side of Carlos's hard road. She senses no hostility and respects people's expectation that she speak strong English. She feels like Orlando welcomes diversity. She attends mass in Spanish and feels a sense of warmth and family around her that she needs. She feels free to maintain her culture in her own home. "Puerto Ricans. That is who we are. We have a heritage that is very rich," she said.

So she has taught her girls about Three Kings Day and how they will get presents if they put grass beneath their beds for the horses. They travel "home" once a year. She shrugs off her mother, who talks to her daughters on the phone and remarks that they don't have a proper Puerto Rican accent. She cooks plantains for them and reads books in Spanish. *"Pa'trás ni pa'coger impulso,"* she declares. Not going backward even to gather speed.

The storm outside has retreated back into the clouds. Vanessa is charming. This job and this place have given her the life she dreamed of having. She has been able to preserve the culture and language she loves so much and has not had one bad experience in this town. She is more nerd than automaton, truly accomplished and a great face for Disney. I like her. She is genuine in both her happiness and her commitment to her job and the life it brings. She is the living, breathing reason for why all those thousands on the island just up and left for Orlando. She represents the possibility of Puerto Rican portability, the notion of taking your culture "to go." We wolf down our heavy Cuban carryout because sometimes a Cuban girl like me needs a load of picadillo on a bad day. Then we head out.

We catch up with Carlos at his fiancée's apartment. He still hasn't moved in but he's slowly bringing his stuff over and insinuating himself into the place. His anxiety has grown at the same pace. Before even saying hi, he announces he really doesn't want us to tape him retaking his sheriff's exam. He is afraid he might fail. The last time he took it he says he scanned the room looking for a group of Latinos to sit next to but found no one. He got very anxious.

"I want to pass the test. I love this job. The security, the police, I want to be it again," he says.

"What's making you the most nervous?"

"I think it's the language," he says, his speech a smidge better than it was a few weeks back.

Carlos has been practicing diligently for months. His only time off is the time he takes to get to know his fiancée better and prepare for the baby. But he has no money and doesn't really know what to do other than be nervous and try to take care of Keila, who seems to be sleeping thirteen hours a day. She's getting cravings, waking up late and demanding he get her ice cream. She's very specific that it needs to be from Cold Stone Creamery, not the Baskin-Robbins closer to home. It's driving him nuts. She is rapidly growing their baby while he is intensely studying the rules for use of force, gang terminology, and quantities of illegal drugs needed to violate certain statutes.

The large empty living room feels like it's closing in on Carlos. He has four hours to answer 250 questions and he says if he spends too much time on any one question, it's curtains for him. Yet he is taking way too much time reading each question because his English comprehension is slow.

"Do you feel like you have a lot of stress on you right now?" I ask.

"Ah, yes." He inhales when he talks, as if letting out any breath makes it harder to talk English. If all this wasn't enough, Keila doesn't look happy and that bothers him. "Sometimes she feels like I do. That it's hard because she is getting a master's degree here and she can't work and get a good job," he says.

He was earning $24,000 in Puerto Rico, maybe $32,000 with overtime. A sheriff's salary would start at $39,000. She is fourteen weeks pregnant. If he fails the test, he can either give it one last try or give up and redo the entire police academy experience he had back in Puerto Rico. Neither choice is a good one, as it means additional weeks with no income and he's already feeling the pinch now. There is a baby on the way, he repeats again. He has to pass this test.

We follow Carlos to language class, where he begins by desperately asking the teacher if he would qualify for the intensive, faster class that meets several mornings. She tells him he's not there yet and his face falls. Today's topic is controversial issues, so they begin to recite phrases. "Let's raise the voting age," they chant. "Raaazing da boting ach." The Venezuelan commander looks more frustrated this time. He is very tired of being the pool boy and also wants to move up.

"If I can get a better level of English I'm hoping some doors open up for me," he says with a markedly reduced accent from just two weeks ago. Carol Traynor, the communications director for the college, tells me that some of these students are paying to take this class two, three, and four times. Everyone in the room is taking the course again after this session ends. The levels have optimistic names, like Intermediate Level A, B, C or Advanced Lower A. There are steps to climb in this process. Hundreds of students are taking them at any given time and the stakes are high for every one of them. I leave Carlos clutching a spineless workbook and calling out his drills with vigor.

That evening I book a room at a Disney hotel that is designed to look like a Polynesian village. You have to walk outside to travel between the many little buildings, which means walking in the aftermath of the morning's storms. The sprinkler system turns on automatically so it's fighting for attention with the rain. Small torches illuminate the walkways that are studded with these poles that look like totems. Everyone is walking around in flowery costumes that make them look like they might be in search of a spear. There's something uniquely American about dressing up working adults in funny costumes. The décor inside the rooms is very similar. Bedspreads with turtles and lamps with fake wood painted with the face of some sort of native.

The scene drives me to the bar for a Polynesian drink. Even the bars at Disney are full of children on vacation. The cacophony of voices with an undertone of children's music makes the place feel like it's humming. Even here, you see Puerto Ricans popping up all over the place. Either that or I've become acutely aware of Puerto Ricans in Orlando. They race around in Polynesian dress seating customers at the jam-packed restaurant or swiping credit cards at check-in.

This is one of the places Carlos has applied to work in case he doesn't pass his sheriff's test, in the massive hotel industry connected to Disney. His brother is already a chef at one of the restaurants.

They get a kick out of the costumes and the free-flowing laughter of people on vacation. They are silly guys and the silliness of all this stuff entertains them. I hope he passes his test, but it's a lot easier to picture him here rather than pulling over drunk drivers or muscling down a gang member.

⁓

The day he retook the test, Carlos already looked like a police officer. He was wearing his mirrored sunglasses and walking around with that confident cop swagger. But he was nervous, very nervous, and he was chain-smoking menthol Marlboro Lights.

Carlos had so much riding on this test he'd already failed once. He walked to the waiting area at the Volusia County Fairgrounds and stood apart from the other men and women. He smoked. He tapped his two number 2 pencils against one another. And he paced. He was an hour early for the 10:00 a.m. exam. He looked like a prizefighter about to enter the ring. When it was time to register he handed his glasses and cell phone to Kimberly, my producer, and said he'd see her in four hours before disappearing into the exam room.

The results were posted quickly, online. Carlos was almost as nervous as he had been the day he took the exam. He felt like he'd done better but bad news was pouring in like rain. Another potential job prospect at Disney had gone nowhere and he had not scored high enough on his English Pronunciation class to move to a higher level. His fiancée has her first sonogram in just two weeks. When the news came in, it arrived like those gray clouds that billow in the sky when it looks like it's stopped raining but really hasn't. Carlos had failed.

He walked somberly to tell his fiancée. Carlos needs a job. He needs to speak better English. Now he needs to take this test he's studied so hard to pass one more time. But there are some parts of his life that offer him certainty. He is staying in Orlando. This is where he lives now. He is not going back. Maybe he'll try applying for a job at Disney again. He's a sweet guy and his accent will matter less in a world where people are striving to have a magical day. I can almost picture him walking around the place, dressed in a floral shirt, and saying, "AH-LOH" over and over again.

4

the mexican in town

THE MORNING I drove to Shenandoah, Pennsylvania, the air was crisp with the end of winter. The mountains were brown and the trees were bare. Few mining towns are what you'd call beautiful, but it's especially hard when the earth is cold and colorless. Enormous metal windmills punctuate the empty landscape as you drive into Shenandoah and you realize you're not entering one of those picturesque American towns that sells taffy and still has rotating barbershop poles on Main Street.

Everywhere you look in Shenandoah there are signs of a better past: an arrow pointing toward a defunct Tastee Freez; a shuttered shop for precious antiques; out-of-date announcements for places where you used to be able to go dance. Today's town feels almost vacant. Empty front porches face empty front porches with broken stairs, there are few open businesses, and much of the town seems to have been painted and repainted in industrial white.

Shenandoah was settled by Eastern Europeans, who were drawn by the discovery here of anthracite coal. From the time it was incorporated in 1866 to the 1920s, the population boomed to nearly thirty thousand. The oldest residents still smile at memories of the prosperity of that time, when evening drew the miners down from the hills to greet their wives and children and have a drink. These are the kinds of towns journalists used to write about during the last economic decline: thriving U.S. towns undone when industries, like manufacturing, collapsed or went away.

Pennsylvania has many of these stories of wrenching endings: the death of steel in Pittsburgh; the closing of the Breyers ice cream

PREVIOUS PAGE: Soledad takes a walk around Shenandoah, Pennsylvania, with Lou Ann Pleva.

plant in Philadelphia. Shenandoah was decimated by the end of the anthracite coal industry after World War II. The mines shut down and the men stopped coming down from the hills. Shenandoah was once the most congested square mile in America according to Ripley's Believe It or Not! The population has dropped to just over fifty-six hundred in the 2000 census. Ultimately, migration killed this town.

I had come to Shenandoah to tell the story of how residents were so frightened by immigration that a young man named Luis Ramirez ended up dead. Ramirez came to Shenandoah looking for work and found the town friendly enough that he invited his mother to visit him from Mexico one year. He had distant cousins working at the local restaurant and friends close enough to be called "best friends." He was undocumented but he was making a life in Shenandoah. They introduced Luis to a girl named Crystal Dillman, who had just had a cute baby girl with soft brown curls.

I met Crystal Dillman at her two-story home in the center of town. Crystal has pasty white skin and reddish hair and talks like she's been through a few things that need mending. Hers is one of the repetitive houses with broken front porches and white paint. She says she rents the house with government assistance. We met just before Easter and the windows in town were decorated with plastic rabbits and colorful cardboard eggs. Crystal was collecting toy eggs from Burger King Kids Meals to give to her three kids as a surprise.

Crystal is a Shenandoah resident whose ancestors worked the mines, and she went to the same high school everyone else did. She says the town has been empty for ages. She told me folks on public assistance hang out in the emptiness looking for something to fill their time. Crystal was taunted in school about just about everything: she was too fat, too dumb, too alone. She spent a lot of time protecting her sisters, who also had few friends. She said she felt like her own mother didn't want her and now, she told us, her own father barely speaks to her. She has five sisters and three brothers and says it is a struggle to maintain a relationship with them.

At school Crystal rebelled and found friendship among the growing Mexican population. They were outsiders, too. She felt like her school was run by the football team, which was all white and had relatives who worked in law enforcement or in the town's few successful businesses, like Mrs. T's Pierogies. The teenagers liked to make jokes about the Latino kids, who were relatively new to town and had trouble learning English. Crystal and her sisters liked the newcomers so the other kids didn't like them.

When Crystal left school she got pregnant by a biracial kid who left her, she said, because he realized he didn't want to be a father. When Crystal met Luis she was a tough cookie with a loose temper who'd become exhausted by fending for herself. She looked at Luis and saw a guy with some fight in him but who was also surprisingly sweet and funny. Crystal was impressed by how hard Luis worked in a community where that was a rare quality. Here was a guy who would pick cherries one day, fix a roof another day, work all night if he needed to and was never without money, even though he couldn't legally work.

Luis started to treat Crystal's three-month-old daughter as his own. He learned English at a breakneck pace. She loved that he was Mexican and made silly jokes. He would play her Spanish songs and his mother, who loved Crystal, taught her Spanish. They had two more kids together, and one summer Luis and his white girlfriend dressed their three children in the colors of the Mexican flag for Shenandoah's Heritage Day Parade of Nations.

From early in their relationship, Crystal said, they wanted to get married but Luis didn't have the identification required to get a marriage license. Crystal says he began a process that took years, petitioning through the Mexican consulate, gathering birth certificates and documents. Crystal said he finally had an appointment at the consulate in Philadelphia in July of 2008 that would have made it possible for him to marry Crystal and begin the process to become a U.S. citizen.

On July 12 Luis was walking across the park on Vine Street in Shenandoah to meet Roxanne Rector, Crystal's sister, when six white teenagers, who all played football at the local high school, approached her. Roxanne is a wispy little brunette, very soft-spoken and not as tough as her sister. "The teachers all love these teenagers," Crystal said. "They're like the school heroes. They play on the football team." Roxanne remembers the teenagers asking her if it was past her bedtime. Roxanne just wanted to disappear. They challenged her for hanging out with this unknown Mexican guy. Roxanne said one of the teenagers told her to get her "dirty Mexican boyfriend out of here." Luis exchanged blows with one of the teenagers. Roxanne says after a few pushes, she and Luis walked away and called for help from their friends Arielle and Victor Garcia, who were close by.

Eileen Burke's house is right in front of where the attack occurred. She is a former Philadelphia police officer who left the force after her leg was pinned between her patrol car and a drunk driver in 1995. She got an injured-on-duty pension but couldn't live off $30,000 in Philadelphia, so she returned to Shenandoah, her hometown. Eileen is a strong woman with a square face who never felt like she fit in around Shenandoah. People treated her poorly.

That day Eileen had driven twelve hours with her roommate to get home from a trip to Myrtle Beach and was lying around her room being exhausted when she heard a group of teenagers screaming "the F word and saying 'Mexican' this and 'Spic' that." She had complained to the Shenandoah police about noise from the park in the past but they didn't treat her seriously. "Go get an AC," she said they told her. When she heard the voice of a woman screaming "stop kicking him, stop beating him," she decided to turn the AC off and stepped outside.

Arielle Garcia later told a CNN reporter that she arrived just as Luis was walking away. Then the kids started screaming racial slurs, like "Go back to Mexico." Luis got mad and came back. But this time the rest of the teenagers joined in and the fight ended up six to one, according to Arielle. "My husband tried to break it up. It happened so fast. My husband tried to get kids off of him," she said. Hers was likely the voice that alerted Eileen that something awful was going down.

From her window, Eileen says she saw this group standing in a circle around someone screaming ethnic slurs. She calls 911 and throws on some clothes. She says 911 in Shenandoah frustrates her. She reports a fight, begs for an ambulance, gets transferred. She finally throws down the phone and runs out. As she's stepping out onto her porch she hears this horrible sound.

"It was like a poof. Like when your car hits a pothole of water, really terrible. I'm a cop so I know what that sound is. You know how it sounds when someone gets a blow," she said. As she rushed down to see what's happened there are only two teenagers standing close enough to have delivered the blow, she says, Colin Walsh and Brandon Piekarsky. Piekarsky rushes toward her.

"He puts his chest into me but as a police officer I know I can't touch him. He looked totally startled when he realized that I know him and Colin."

The two of them run off and Eileen is left standing there with Arielle and Luis.

"I'm thinking the 'poof' sound was from his chest. Foam was coming out of his mouth. He was convulsing. We called it the death rattle when I was a cop in Philly. I just kept saying to him to please hold on. I didn't want to even try CPR because of his condition," she said.

Off in the distance she says she saw car lights coming down the street the wrong way. She says Colin kicked the door of a parked car and yelled to her "you effin' bitch." Down the street she says she also saw Brandon.

"The blondie is banging on the hood of a car and yelling 'you tell your effin' Mexican friends to get the hell out of Shenandoah,'" Eileen said.

She asked Arielle if she knows them and Arielle said that they are schoolmates. Eileen said police cars took a long time to arrive and when they did they were not from Shenandoah but from neighboring towns. She says she ran up to each of them urging them to get an ambulance there. Shenandoah Police Chief Mark Nestor says the response was quick and that he is proud of the job his officers did that day. He says small towns typically pool police resources and have whatever agency is available respond first. It's not unusual that officers from other jurisdictions would be the first on the scene, he said. He is satisfied that the Shenandoah officers who did work the case did their best that day.

"They kept telling me to shut up. It was unbelievable. They didn't even approach him and he's lying on the pavement obviously in a lot of pain. He is calming down. I'd say going deeper and deeper and all I get are these questions about whether he'd been drinking and if anyone knows how to spell his name," she said.

She says she heard neighbors talking about the teenagers needing to call their mothers. She says Brandon's mom works at a local bar and dates a police officer.

"No one is offering to chase the boys. It was unbelievable. I'm sitting on my stoop until two a.m. and there is still no crime scene, no one chasing suspects, no one even interested in interviewing me or getting a description. Luis just lay there. All the cops are in the park looking for something, talking on their cell phones. This was an open-and-shut case where all these kids should have been picked up and charged that night. I was sick. I couldn't breathe. . . . He's not an animal. It's human life."

What Roxanne remembers was that three of the teenagers were kicking Luis in the head over and over. She recalls his head banging against the asphalt and foam dripping from his mouth. His head was so swollen Crystal has nightmares about the way he looked as he died slowly in his hospital bed. The crucifix he wore had made an imprint in his chest. Crystal still has it. Luis Ramirez was twenty-five years old.

A day after the incident, Eileen says that Crystal came by with Luis's aunt and uncle to thank her.

"I didn't have the heart to tell them how much he'd suffered. That he was out on the street making a death rattle and no one was doing a thing. I could barely walk out the door and look at the spot the next morning."

Luis Ramirez was declared dead on July 14. The police criminal complaint signed on July 25 had an ominous description of the attack saying the boys had told Roxanne to "get your Mexican boyfriend out of here." They faced local and federal investigations because of the apparent racial nature of the crime.

At the time of Luis's death, Colin Walsh was seventeen and Brandon Piekarsky was sixteen, but they ultimately were made to stand trial on state charges of homicide and ethnic intimidation as adults. Derrick Donchak, eighteen, was charged with aggravated assault and ethnic intimidation. Frederick Fanelli, a lawyer for one of the accused, told CNN shortly after Luis's death that he would investigate whether Ramirez had a criminal background. He publicly questioned why the engaged father of three was walking on the street with his fiancée's sister. "Let's call it what it was: a street fight, a chance encounter with a tragic outcome," said Fanelli, who represents Piekarsky.

"They called each other names. The victim was calling them obscenities, vulgar names, and they said things back to him that would hurt him," Roger Laguna, a lawyer for Walsh, told CNN.

"It just means it was a foulmouthed argument, not ethnic intimidation."

Months later, Walsh admitted to knocking Ramirez unconscious and pled guilty in federal court to violating his civil rights. He will serve at least four years in prison under sentencing guidelines. Walsh testified against Donchak and Piekarsky, whose mother, Walsh said, lived with one of the police officers who investigated the case. Their defense lawyers argued in court that Ramirez was the aggressor and tried to pin the fatal kicks on Brian Scully, a fourth attacker who faced charges in juvenile court of aggravated assault and ethnic intimidation. Walsh testified that he shouted ethnic slurs at Ramirez and told him to "go back to Mexico."

Crystal didn't make it to the funeral in Mexico. Later, she rode buses for three days with three fidgety children to go see her fiancé's family in their small Mexican town. She still speaks a smattering of Spanish to her children. She can't collect Social Security because Luis was not a citizen, regardless of whether his employer paid taxes on him as a laborer, and Crystal lost her job shortly after he died and says no one in the town will hire her. She wants to move away from Shenandoah, because everyone accuses her of giving the town a bad name, but she has no place to go.

The walls of Crystal's house are decorated with pictures of Luis playing with his children. Crystal is homeschooling two of her sisters. Roxanne is one of them and little Eduardo lives on her lap. The other sister also helps with the kids. Crystal fantasizes about convincing her mother to give up custody of these two sisters so she can adopt them and move away. Her oldest daughter is developmentally disabled and she needs help taking care of her. Her youngest are shy, quiet kids, not old enough to say much. They're identical to their father, whom they still ask after. This is one very sad and disoriented young lady.

Historically hate crimes have brought tensions of race or ethnicity to a boil. They are signs that a debate over something else has gone too far. Emmett Till, a fourteen-year-old black youth, was caught flirting, it was said, with a shopkeeper's wife in the Mississippi Delta in

1955. Two white men, the shopkeeper's husband and a relative, were acquitted by an all-white jury of kidnapping and murdering Emmett despite eyewitness evidence against them. He was horrifically beaten and had his eye gouged out; his attackers shot him through the head and tied a seventy-pound piece of cotton ginning machinery, a fan, to his neck with barbed wire before they threw him into the Tallahatchie River. The anger over Emmett Till's lynching helped propel the civil rights movement.

Hate crimes have never gone away, but what they mean about a community and its motivations is no longer as clear. Our nation was electing its first black president, the son of an immigrant, just as the debate around Latinos and immigration had become fierce and racially antagonistic at times. Organizations that track hate crimes and study nativist movements say that KKK-type groups have shifted their focus from African-Americans and Muslims to Latinos. There was a 40 percent increase in attacks against Latinos from 2003 to 2007 at the same time the Latino population grew 16 percent, according to the most recent FBI statistics. Those numbers come from police departments that voluntarily report figures to the federal government and can define a hate crime any way they want.

The numbers of reported hate crimes are so few that they may only hint at what is really going on out there. The disturbing human stories behind these statistics are often not told by the press. Take Pedro Corzo, a Cuban-born immigrant with a management job with Del Monte who in 2004 was shot to death in Arizona by gunmen from Missouri, one of whom was sixteen. The two men shaved their heads and drove around Arizona looking for Mexicans to shoot. They are now serving life sentences for murder.

That same year in Tifton, Georgia, which is about 160 miles from Atlanta, a trailer park known for housing immigrants had been targeted for home invasions until one night a group of robbers went on a rampage. They murdered six Mexicans and beat five others. At first, the town came down hard. The district attorney announced he'd seek the death penalty and the mayor displayed the Mexican flag over city hall to honor the victims. The town was united against the killers until callers to the local radio station began voicing their resentment of immigrants.

In December of 2008, the public got a sobering glimpse at how vicious the attacks had been. At a sentencing hearing for one of the four people accused of the murders, Brenda Perez testified that after her husband had been shot in the head, she was raped multiple times while her baby daughter screamed by her side. She sent her seven-year-old son to call 911. The area where she lived had filled up with immigrants coming to south Georgia to work. The people who attacked them were black and poor. Jamie Underwood pleaded guilty to all four indictments against him and was sentenced to 120 years on three of them. The prosecutors wanted the death penalty against him and his codefendant, Stacey Bernard Sims, but the case has been delayed because the perpetrators have been too poor to mount a reasonable defense. The two female defendants were accused of transporting the men to the attacks.

In 2006, the Web sites of neo-Nazi groups tracked by the Southern Poverty Law Center carried exhortations that opponents of immigration should steal money from illegal immigrants, discourage their children from going to school and threaten them with physical harm. The Web sites they track reflect the direction the attacks are taking.

David Ritcheson, 16, testified before Congress about how a group of skinheads jumped him after he kissed a white girl at a party. He testified that he was called a "spic" and a "wetback." Two of the attackers broke his jaw, knocked him unconscious, burned him with cigarettes, carved a swastika into his chest, scalded him with bleach and sodomized him with a patio umbrella pole. David helped the Anti-Defamation League create an anti-hate program at his school, but months after the attack, he committed suicide.

I interviewed his parents following the attack and they were barely able to hold it together, they were so devastated. David's mother told me he was confined to a hospital bed and was so depressed he could barely say anything other than to keep asking "Why?" His mother told me she knew it was a hate crime.

"How do you put a swastika on someone or burn them. You have to hate someone to hurt someone like that." It was absolutely heartbreaking to talk with her. There are so many stories of beatings and taunts and fire bombings and cross burnings that I can't even digest them all. The attackers are almost always white, but they are sometimes black and even Latino.

Each attack is just more astonishing than the one before it. East Hampton, a place where New York swells go to vacation on weekends, was the site of a neo-Nazi skinhead attack on three Latino teens who were terrorized with a machete and a chain saw. The attacks in Suffolk County mounted until they struck the area near my hometown. A group of seven boys, who allegedly got together each weekend to intimidate Latinos, went on a spree of attacks that culminated in the stabbing death in Patchogue of Marcelo Lucero, an Ecuadorian immigrant who had lived in this country for sixteen years. The attackers, all high school students from Patchogue-Medford High School, face charges in eight attacks, including Lucero's murder.

The latest attacks against Latino immigrants drew media attention, but did not ignite passionate national debates over civil rights. Once the legal status of the victim is discovered, the crime itself gets overshadowed by the debate over illegal immigration. Towns like Shenandoah are left struggling to answer the question of whether the criminal actions of a few individuals against a stranger say something more profound about the town itself.

In 2006, Hazleton Mayor Lou Barletta attracted national attention for passing an ordinance to discourage hiring or renting to illegal immigrants by fining landlords who got caught. Several other U.S. towns copied the ordinance. Some piled on English Only laws. Lou Barletta became a notable figure in a backlash against illegal Mexican immigration that was played out each night on cable television and raged on the Internet. Civil rights advocates said the law led to racial profiling. A Puerto Rican physician in the town called in LatinoJustice PRLDEF (Puerto Rican Legal Defense and Education Fund), a civil rights advocacy group, because he was worried about how he would be treated after the ordinance passed. Puerto Ricans are U.S. citizens but he felt victimized by the ordinance because he felt it challenged his ethnicity, not his immigration status. That call led to a lawsuit by LatinoJustice saying the ordinance had denied due process to U.S. citizens and noncitizens who are both white and Latino as this town tried to enforce a federal law.

In Hazleton, the mayor and his opponents went back and forth. Mayor Barletta claimed Latinos had driven up crime rates. LatinoJustice presented figures that showed crime had fallen since the arrival of the newcomers. Barletta accused the new immigrants of stealing jobs. The local Chamber of Commerce credited immigrants with revitalizing downtown. The mayor claimed that the ordinance was a success because it had driven thousands of illegal immigrants from town. Business leaders pointed to shuttered stores and argued that was a bad thing. Barletta said landlords and business owners were simply asking for basic documentation. Latinos who are U.S. citizens complained to the ACLU that they had been singled out. In 2007, a federal judge struck down the law as unconstitutional, putting the debate on hold so an appeal can work its way through the courts.

Cesar A. Perales, president of LatinoJustice, said that the trial debunked the accusation that illegal immigrants were increasing crime with testimony that showed that four of 428 violent crimes in Hazleton in the last six years could be connected to illegal immigrants. He notes that the local Chamber of Commerce supported the lawsuit because the newcomers had helped the economy, not hurt it, even opening several new businesses that created jobs.

"What is clear is that this had been a dead town, shuttered storefronts literally, until Latinos revitalized the town. There are many of these East Coast towns like Hazleton and Shenandoah, particularly coal mining towns, where young people just left. The newcomers create jobs. They don't take jobs. Jobs went begging before they got there; there were undesirable low-paying jobs that went unfilled. That can't be refuted. Every time government goes in to look at the impact, they find the same thing: that there is a net positive in terms of the economy all around. But there is racial tension because you have a town full of very, very poor white people living in terrible conditions and they see other people coming in and moving into empty homes and opening businesses. The guys who killed Luis Ramirez were not irritated that he was taking their jobs; they were irritated because he was an older Latino guy walking down the street with a young white girl."

But Lou Barletta pointed to job data from around the country that showed that illegal immigrants do take jobs from white people when they move into a depressed town because they are willing to work for lower wages. He is such a popular mayor that he was a candidate for both parties when he was reelected in 2007, but lost a race for U.S. Congress in 2008. He has said he will take his case to the U.S. Supreme Court and has repeated his claim that he will remove illegal immigrants from his town. Back when the ordinance was passed Barletta wore a bulletproof vest to the proceedings because of what he called a surge in crime by illegal immigrants. He pointed to a 75 percent drop in business at Mexican restaurants as a sign he was getting rid of illegal immigrants. This is a politician who is clearly onto something.

⌒

Shenandoah is similar to Hazleton in some respects. It was once an empty town that filled up with immigrants looking for jobs, raw-handed worker bees who built a community. For Shenandoah, the last census recorded a nearly 10 percent drop in population and counted eighty men for every one hundred women over the age of eighteen. The per capita income in 1999 was $12,562. The average age was forty-five. Only a fifth of the population has children. These are the signs of a town still dying, a place that's emptying out. There's no daily newspaper in Shenandoah, no way to communicate simple information about day-to-day life and its challenges.

The school is a mirror of the community. The kids who play on the sports teams, like the accused teens, are lionized. Brian Scully said at the trial that he had known Derrick Donchak since they started playing Little League in the third grade. Over the years, they played baseball, basketball, track and field, and football. They are the Blue Devils and the football team is the Devil's Pride. They are winners at something in a town that is wanting for winners. The changing demographics in the town are reflected at the high school, of course. Twenty years ago there were 504 white kids, according to the U.S. Department of Education. There was not a single black or Hispanic teenager. In 2007, there were 461 white kids, 12 African-Americans, and 56 Hispanics.

In Shenandoah, Latinos filled some of the empty space and created opportunities. The town has plenty of cheap housing. As the economy has continued to sour, investors have snatched up three-bedroom homes for $15,000. I met more than one person who said they owned dozens of the two-story white houses that fill the town's center. The landlords need renters and they'd prefer someone who isn't relying on qualifying for public assistance to pay their way. Every afternoon in Shenandoah, carloads of Latinos in work shirts come home to the rental houses, just like the miners used to come down from the hills. The workers say the town has fields nearby with fruit to be picked and homes with roofs that need mending. They see the warehouses full of heavy boxes that need to be moved and the trucks in need of unloading.

The problem is that there are non-Latino folks in Shenandoah who would also like to work and bring the town back to what it once was, not what the town is becoming. In an editorial, the closest newspaper, the *Pottsville Republican & Herald*, described the new immigrants like this:

"Added to its melting pot of largely white European immigrants—Irish, English, Welsh, German, Italian, Polish, Lithuanian, Ukrainian, Russian, Slovak—who swelled its population to more than 30,000 during the anthracite boom of the early 20th century, are Latinos from various sources, blacks, Indians and Asians."

Some residents in Shenandoah simmer with the kind of resentment that keeps a guy sitting on his front porch cursing the guy who got up to beg for work that morning. It does something to your head to sit around remembering that things used to be better and not be able to bring them back.

In 2008, the Kaiser Family Foundation asked workers earning less than $27,000 whether they thought illegal immigrants take jobs from legal residents, and nearly half responded that they do. Eighty percent of the same population conceded that neither they nor their family had been affected negatively by illegal immigration. The more money folks earned, the more educated they were, the less they believed immigrants were a threat to them.

I interviewed a man named Joe Miller who lives in yet another of the repetitious white houses. Miller's front porch is filled with plastic toys and has a trifecta of flags flapping in the wind—the American flag and those of the Confederates and the U.S. Marines. He walks with the toughness of a mountain man but has a gentle way with his daughter. Miller had worked in a plant in Hazleton, where he estimates that 75 percent of the workers were working illegally, taking jobs he thinks belong to white people. He came to that figure because he dated a woman who was undocumented, and since she was, he assumed nearly all the Latinos probably were, too.

"It bothers me they're here illegally," Joe told me.

"Why is that so frustrating?" I asked.

"Well, for the most part they take a lot of jobs."

"Like what kind of jobs? What job did you lose to someone?"

"I haven't lost any jobs."

"What job did your friend lose?"

"My friends haven't lost any jobs."

"So who's losing jobs?"

"Sorta white people that can't . . ."

"Generally?" I ask.

"Generally. Blacks. Blacks. I would say for the most part."

"I smiled because the guy with the Confederate flag is defending the black people," I told him. "Is there an irony in that?"

"No," he says. And then we're both smiling.

Joe believes that Luis's death is an unintended consequence of the immigration debate, a street fight gone awry. If you talk to him long enough, you'd think it was Mexicans that closed the mines long ago. Joe has attended rallies where a group called Save Shenandoah has been wrongly branded as racist. Crystal showed up at one of the rallies and unfurled a Mexican flag, leading to a harsh verbal confrontation. Joe says she has shamed the entire county by siding with immigrants rather than Americans. Loud and provocative people like Joe who are willing to talk to the media have become the face of towns like this when most people think it best to be silent.

Lou Ann Pleva has refused to be quiet. She is gray-haired and stout, with a pretty face and an easy smile. She comes off as an essentially optimistic person. The day after Luis died, she picked up a flier at a supermarket asking people to pray for him.

"It was unthinkable. How could kids do this? How could kids who were raised in my hometown do this?" She asked herself, "What happened that night? What was this about?" She had lived through the pain of the town's decline after the mines shut. "It was like a domino effect. Everything, one thing closed, the next thing closed, our hospital closed, the employment office closed. That ran around for two weeks as fodder for some really good jokes."

Pleva's grandparents came from Poland and Germany. Her grandfather was a full-fledged miner at the age of ten, while her grandmother worked in a garment factory. Like a lot of people in declining small towns, Lou Ann moved away. She raised her children elsewhere, worked as a newspaper reporter for a time. She said she came back because "this is the only square mile on the planet that I love." To her, the windmills on the mountaintop look like installation art. The fact they stand where coal was once buried fills her with hope. Maybe someday Main Street will be full of proud people again, mining a new type of energy. Instead, she sometimes sees a town where a lot of people just can't let go of the tragedy of the past. She bristles that her town of hardscrabble immigrant miners is being recast as a home to hateful racists.

"Was this about hate?" I asked her.

"I don't think so. I don't think it's hate," she said. "I honestly don't think it's hate."

"Ignorance?"

"Ignorance. A lack of opportunity to travel in the world. To be among different cultures, all day, every day. To experience those things, when it's something new and it's the first new thing in generations. It's easy to say, 'That's too strange.' We don't want that here. We're trying desperately to hold on to what we were. We want to go back to what we were. We're not prepared for a future. We're reminiscing and nostalgic about our past. We want the past to come back."

In the days after the attack Lou Ann Pleva helped organize a unity rally. She told the Mexicans that they were welcome in her town. While she wasn't speaking in favor of illegal immigration, she drew ample criticism from her neighbors when the press interpreted it that way. She said that as a former newspaper reporter she likes to operate in facts, and sees the misrepresentation as typical of the coverage Shenandoah got in the aftermath of Luis's death. With no hometown newspaper, she thinks the townspeople operate on sensationalism and rumor. Presumptions become truths and lies get spread easily.

To understand the complexity of any crime, you have to be at the scene early enough to talk to people before some get fearful and clam up and others make up their own truth. Emanuella Grinberg, an eager young producer for CNN.com, went to cover the story of Luis's death in the early days, when most of the media wasn't paying attention. She discovered that Brandon Piekarsky is a National Honors student who made the varsity football team as a sophomore and works part-time at Sears. Derrick Donchak was the team's quarterback last year and was planning on attending Bloomsburg University in the fall. Michael Walsh described his son as a straight-A student who juggled track, football, and school.

"It's very stressing because you just don't expect it. If you had a child that's constantly in trouble, you'd say, 'Hey, well, this is coming any day,'" Michael Walsh told Grinberg. "Colin was a great kid and fell into a bad situation. He never really gave me any trouble. I feel sorry for the families and anyone who cares about Mr. Ramirez." Later his son would be the only one to admit guilt in the attack.

The *Pottsville Republican & Herald* reported extensively on a Sunday afternoon healing service attended by just fifty people:

"Resident Thomas F. O'Neill, speaking after his father, Shenandoah Mayor Thomas F. O'Neill Jr., said he had met Ramirez twice in passing, but never had a conversation with him. 'That's how most of the people in this town are viewing Hispanics,' O'Neill said. 'They're just there.' O'Neill said Shenandoah residents should take the time to learn about their Hispanic neighbors, and said the town's Hispanic population is 'vital' to its future and heritage." People in the town sounded very thoughtful in those days when the conversation was limited to Luis's death. Later, O'Neill would quietly resign.

When the conversation turned to immigration and tensions surfaced, the characterizations turned ugly. I asked Lou Ann if it surprised her that outsiders who had followed the case might ask in what kind of place do football players and honor students kill a total stranger because he is a Mexican escorting a white girl?

"It's easy to see how people could think kids in this town are raised with hate. It's very easy for just anybody to take a quick glance and say, 'That's what that's about,'" she told me. "But look deeper and you'll see it's not about that. It's about fear. It's about parents with kids who are facing possible life sentences in prison who are so afraid—that this is not the dream they had for their sons. That they'll say anything to defend their kids. Who could argue with that? Really, who could argue with them saying anything? Or not just with the parents but the people who feel protective of the kids."

The arrival of Mexicans, local lore has it, began with an Irish priest who invited some of them to his church from places like Reading and Hazleton. I found nothing to verify that tale but, like everything else in a small town, it gets repeated enough to become local wisdom. Townspeople talk a lot about the newcomers, as if there were so many, but officially the town is 97 percent white and 2 percent Latino. The 2 percent includes Carlos Ramos, a man of Puerto Rican descent who is dating Jenny Mease, a white woman. He came to Shenandoah hoping to buy up cheap real estate and flip it for a profit. The first time he rode public transportation with Jenny he said people made nasty comments. He says the issue is not immigration; it's basic racism.

"Some of them have never left here, they stayed here, they got jobs here, they've never been out of this town, so when they see a person of color come to this town or speak a different language, they lose it," he said.

Carlos is stunned how teenagers will say racist things to him as he walks down the street. Carlos thinks the claims of immigrants stealing jobs are baseless. He's seen no evidence that illegal immigrants have made life harder for people like him who are U.S.-born.

"If they read the newspaper there is a police blog in the newspaper and if they look at it and read it they will realize that ninety-five, maybe ninety-eight percent of the people that are caught dealing drugs—heroin, meth, cocaine, marijuana—they are all white folks," he said.

Carlos Ramos is about fed up with Shenandoah. He is afraid that what happened to Luis could happen to him, someone who has no connection to illegal immigration. He said he was making small talk with a white woman outside a Turkey Hill once when a guy tapped him on the back and said:

"What the hell are you doing talking to my woman, you freaking brown nigger, you freaking spic?" The man pulled a knife on him. Carlos did what Luis either could not do or chose not to do: he ran away. He said that days after Luis died, a group of folks dressed as Klansmen had a little rally in the park near his home.

Carlos and Jenny have two children and he feels like they will be associated with Luis.

"If you're Puerto Rican, Dominican, or whatever, you know to them you are considered a Mexican," he told me. "You don't matter, you're a Mexican. I can't tell you how many times I had people ask in the bars, 'Are you Mexican? Are you Mexican?' No, I'm not, I'm

Puerto Rican . . . they ask me for green cards and stuff like that. I say, 'Hey, man, I'm Puerto Rican. I was born in Puerto Rico and raised in New York City.'"

He says a city official told him they don't like his "kind" living in the town and pushed him about having an occupancy permit for his house so he could count how many Latinos are in town. He shakes his head for about the twentieth time during our short conversation. He is exasperated and emotional and is talking to me as much to vent as to express a different point of view. Carlos has simply had enough.

So much was lost in the asphalt on Vine Street. Crystal Dillman also wants to leave town. The youngest of her children looks just like Luis and all these months after his father's death, he still races to the door expecting Daddy to come home. Crystal is obviously depressed and getting very little help. Luis gave her a family structure and security that she didn't have on her own. Luis was her happy, hardworking guy, handsome enough to make other girls envious with his buttery skin and shiny dark hair.

The story line I saw focused quite a bit on angry white folks whose jobs were stolen by illegal immigrants from Mexico. There wasn't much discussion of what bred the anger in this vulnerable small town; no public debate about increasing economic development for the citizens who live here, improving their schools, providing cultural stimulation of any kind. The angry voices of guys like Joe Miller got more time than that of Lou Ann Pleva. Shenandoah was in trouble even before the recession and towns like this are erupting with frustration. When the media singles out immigration as the culprit, we give people a local face to attack. All that some folks in Shenandoah seem to really know about the Mexicans is that they're making trouble over in Hazleton and they're working places when most white people are not. And Luis Ramirez paid with his life.

⁓

The case was tried in the Schuylkill County courthouse just fifteen minutes from Shenandoah before an all-white jury of locals and a press corps limited to a dozen or so small local newspapers and TV stations. The county had decided to try Brian Scully as a juvenile and use him as a witness in the trial. Since Colin Walsh agreed to plead guilty, he would also testify at this trial. So Brandon Piekarsky and Derrick Donchak were left to face a public jury trial on their own.

The cornerstone to the courthouse was laid in 1887, when there was plenty of coal money around. It is a beautiful building. The walls are decorated by large and stunning black-and-white photographs of miners and mining. Presiding Judge William Baldwin, who has served for twenty-two years, said the courtroom he chose was the second largest in the northeast.

Baldwin was ready for the trial to be a big deal. But when it finally rolled around in April of 2009, it was quick and poorly attended. The large ornate room he had chosen was imposing for a trial that had teenagers as defendants and witnesses. Yet sitting in the wood-paneled room beneath the ceiling of bright stained glass were just the principals and their families, a smattering of supporters, and Crystal Dillman, with a lawyer from the Mexican American Legal Defense and Education Fund (MALDEF) and a representative of the Mexican consulate, Enrique Luis Sanchez. Their presence was often mentioned by locals as an example of outsiders who came to taint their town.

"I think by then people were scared and that's why we had to be here," said Gladys Limon of MALDEF. Limon says MALDEF sent her to monitor the prosecution, which she found to be lackluster.

"The local community, and especially the Latino community, feels intimidated by local officials and officers," Limon said. "They are very oppressive and corrupt. The community has learned through their own experiences that they should not speak out against them or be too public about their views, and instead they keep quiet. This is no longer a conversation. There is basically no protection by the local police. Community members view them as a gang."

The representative of the Mexican consulate did not speak to the press other than to say he was monitoring the case because one of his country's citizens had been killed on foreign soil. "If an American went to Mexico and got killed, wouldn't the U.S. consulate be on the scene?" he asked. Both said they had made no efforts to encourage protests or shows of force in the courtroom by local immigrants or Latinos.

The community did all it could to keep calm. The *Pottsville Republican & Herald* broke the story that administrators from Shenandoah Valley Junior/Senior High School were attending the trial to make sure none of the students were there. The superintendent threatened that they would be banned from graduation activities if they were caught anywhere near the courtroom unless they were relatives of the defendants. An editorial pleaded with anti-immigration activists from a group called Voice of the People to not protest at the trial:

"By demonstrating against people who are protesting violence and murder, VOP [Voice of the People] members will accomplish exactly what they claim they are trying to prevent. They will demonize themselves as extremists who condone violence against immigrants. . . . They will reinforce the stereotypical views of outsiders who see coal region residents as intolerant, backwater boobs." There were never large protests.

The county set up metal detectors and limited access to the floor of the courtroom to registered press and people attending the trial. The teenagers and their families were isolated in the law library on a different floor. Crystal Dillman and the MALDEF lawyers were kept in a room belonging to Victim's Services. The two sides never had to cross each other in the halls. Neither side said anything much to the press. Inside the courtroom, the case had enough drama and confrontation on its own.

The day the prosecution called Brian Scully to the stand it was not totally clear why this now eighteen-year-old man had ended up with a separate trial in juvenile court. He looks about the same age and level of maturity as the others. The night of July 12, 2008, he said, he had gone to Derrick's house on Coal Street to hang out with him, Ben Lawson, Josh Redmond, and Brandon Piekarsky. Their plan was to meet Colin Walsh and hang out at a spot in the woods they called "the Creek." They wanted to drink some Mickeys, a malt liquor the guys liked. They made a stop at a Polish-American block party and then left to go back to Derrick's house.

They were on the street where Crystal lives now, when they came upon Luis and Roxanne. Brian recalls saying to her, "Isn't it a little too late to be out?" Luis responded by saying something in Spanish, which prompted Brian to say: "Go back to Mexico." According to the trial transcripts, Brian describes the attack this way in a string of answers to questions from the prosecutor: Brandon and Luis run toward each other and end up wrestling. Brandon throws a punch that connects, then picks up Luis and throws him to the ground, as if he was tackling him in a football game. Brandon tries to kick Luis, but trips. So Derrick starts punching Luis in the head while he is lying on the ground. Luis tries to block the blows with his hands. Brandon gathers himself and kicks him multiple times. At some point Luis gets up, punches are exchanged and the group disperses. Brian recalls yelling, "Go home, you Mexican motherf'er" toward Luis. He remembers that Derrick says "f you" several times.

I must say it's amazing how everyone involved with this case is so shy about saying "fuck" but doesn't mind getting drunk and beating each other up. Brian says Luis hit him in the head and he pushed him off. Then Colin stepped in and punched Luis, knocking him out. Luis's eyes were closed and he wasn't moving. Brian testified that he tried to kick him but lost his balance and missed. So Brandon kicks him in the head and they run off into the park.

Colin Walsh's testimony followed a similar trajectory. The difference is that Colin owned up to his role in the attack. By the time he took the stand he had pled guilty. He said that the teenagers had been his good friends his entire life. Brandon and he had played football and run track together. He was now testifying against them at a murder trial.

"I was involved with a group of people that used force to intimidate this man who was a Mexican because of his race and because he lived in the community . . . resulting in death," he said on the stand.

Walsh's account also has the teenagers using racial slurs but he doesn't describe a fight. He says he was not scared of Luis because "he was smaller than us and six of us and one of him." He also recalls Luis walking away from them and says that Brandon "sprinted" after him with Brian. When Luis put his hands up in a fighting stance, Brandon tackled him. Then he says that Derrick punched Luis in the head "probably about ten to fifteen" times. After he is on the ground, "we are all kicking him," Colin says.

At that point, Victor and Arielle Garcia arrive and it looks like the incident is going to come to an end. But Colin says that Brian and Luis start up again and Colin punches Luis in the face. Colin describes the blow as strong enough to knock Luis out cold on the ground. Then, Colin says:

"I saw Brandon Piekarsky kick him in the head . . . it was a hard kick. He took one step and kicked him in the head." Colin said he was shocked "because it wasn't really right what he did, to kick a man when he's down."

The testimony from the teenagers buoyed the spirits of Crystal, who came to court every day. What the boys were saying sounded so brutal that she thought for sure the jurors would convict. Colin said that Brandon kicked Luis so hard his shoe flew off and that he had a piece of metal that he used when he hit him. That same day a police officer from a neighboring town testified that Luis's face was swollen and that he had a shoe print on his chest. Richard Examitis of Lost Creek Ambulance told jurors he found "an assault victim" who was unresponsive and had "snoring respirations." He never regained consciousness. He never opened his eyes.

"The one time I felt certain that there would be a conviction was when the doctors testified," Crystal said. "I was so angry and upset and I thought the jurors would find these people guilty."

The medical experts told the jury that a kick to the head had fractured Luis's skull, causing his brain to swell so much that it spilled out from his head. In pictures taken of Luis in the hospital the next day, he is unrecognizable. His face is so puffy it looks distended and his head is covered in an enormous wrap of bandages.

Gladys Limon said she felt optimistic about a guilty verdict after hearing the 911 tape of Arielle reporting the crime. Her words were punctuated by fear and panic. Limon remembered the sound of the tape long after it was played in court. But both these women hoped this case was going to end in a conviction on the highest charges.

"There was this general thing that these were these good kids, they never got into trouble. Well, they weren't good kids that night," said Crystal. "People changed their stories around. They stomped on his head and left him there to die while they got their stories straight and they tried to paint Luis as the criminal."

Then there was the testimony about how the teenagers met twice to get their stories straight, both the night of the fight and the next day. Josh Redmond, one of the teenagers, said they gathered in a garage after the fight at Piekarsky's house with one of the police officers and a number of parents in an effort to protect each other. Another boy testified that one of their chief concerns was that they would not be able to play football anymore. Their goal was to cleanse their account of any references to racial slurs, kicking, and the fact that they'd been drinking. The prosecution was left to convince jurors that the teenagers had somehow arrived at the trial ready to finally tell the truth.

But it didn't help them when Brian testified that he, Ben, Josh, Colin, and Brandon all gathered at Derrick's house. Brian says Derrick arrived in a Shenandoah police cruiser driven by Jason Hayes, a police officer who is identified as the boyfriend of Brandon's mother. What was discussed?

"That we should all have the same story," Brian testifies, and that they should leave out the part about the kick. On cross-examination, Brian admits that he told the other teenagers the details of the statement he'd given to police and assured them it was the lie they'd agreed on. The testimony went back and forth, with fingers pointing in many directions. At one point the prosecutor asks Brian why he is looking to protect the defendants. "They're my friends," he replies. "I didn't want us to get in trouble."

Colin's description of the gathering at the police officer's house is similar to Brian's. He also remembers Derrick riding up in a car driven by Shenandoah police officers Jason Hayes and Bill Moyer, whom he had known all his life. He identifies Hayes as the boyfriend of Brandon's mother. He had slept over at Brandon's house and knew Jason lived there. Shenandoah is a very small town. Colin says Hayes takes Brandon back to the crime scene while Derrick's mother ices his swollen knuckles. Colin says Brandon later calls from the crime scene and tells Colin that he told the cops only about the second part of the fight and said it was started by Luis. He adds that he left out the part about the kick.

So then the group gathered in the garage discusses how to square their stories with what Brandon has said. Colin testifies that Derrick and Brandon's mothers are there. Colin testifies that Tammy Piekarsky tells them that she has talked to Jason and "that this guy had to get life-flighted, and he probably won't make it and, if he dies, it's homicide so get your story straight."

Tammy Piekarsky has never spoken to the press about the case, nor has Jason Hayes. The fraternal organization that represents him did not return our calls. What the jury did not hear was how closely this scenario resembles the account of Eileen Burke. Eileen says she tried repeatedly to testify, even cutting short a vacation she took to get away from living in front of the scene of a homicide. She says the prosecutors kept putting her off. There was no testimony from Shenandoah police officers, either, but there were ominous references to witnesses being called in another case and reporters speculated that a grand jury might be hearing evidence in a case against the police for misconduct. The police officers who investigated Luis' death have refused to speak to reporters. The Shenandoah police chief said his town is so small that his officers frequently know the people involved in incidents they investigate. There is no way to avoid it. He said his department monitors investigations to make sure there is no bias and that this case was handled appropriately.

The trial was thrown another wrench when Roxanne Rector testified for the prosecution in a high, birdlike voice that she was uncertain which of the teenagers had delivered the fatal kicks. She looked distraught on the stand, maybe even scared, according to the CNN staff who watched the trial unfold. Roxanne, who is fifteen, affirmed the public defense that Luis was behaving inappropriately, secretly having sex with her and was planning to marry her instead of Crystal. After that testimony, the press stopped referring to Crystal as Luis's fiancée. She became the mother of his children and Roxanne became the fiancée.

Crystal was not in court that day, quite deliberately. The rumors that Roxanne and Luis had something going on had filled the town shortly after the confrontation. She said her mother disliked Luis and was taunted in the town after the attack. She believes her mother had pressed Roxanne to confirm the story. Crystal said she does not believe it's possible Luis and Roxanne could have had any kind of sexual relationship. There were not enough hours in the day, and the night of the attack he'd called her several times to say he was walking Roxanne over to Crystal's house.

"I know the truth and Roxanne knows the truth," Crystal said. "They acted like it was weird they were hanging out because he's twenty-five and she's thirteen, so he's some kind of pervert and she's this Mexican-loving whore. All of that is hanging on her. Why? Because she witnessed a crime. Her friends treat her differently. It bothers her. She looks so sad. She knew this would happen."

Several times, she repeats that she doesn't know what Roxanne said because she didn't attend the trial that day, even though she knows her testimony was widely reported. She clearly has doubts.

"What difference does it make? That makes it okay to kill him? They didn't even know him. They didn't know her," she says.

The story line that Luis was being punished for messing with an underage white girl was established in the minds of anti-immigration activists. Shortly after the attack, a newsletter called the "Minuteman's Militia," published by a group of border vigilantes, described the defendants as "teenagers who were apparently compelled to shield the 15-year-old female about to be violated." Copies of the newsletter were distributed at the courthouse after Roxanne testified. The testimony was supposed to speak to Roxanne's credibility, according to the judge, not try to suggest that the attack might be defensible if the teenagers were out to punish Luis for doing something wrong. But the effect of this story line was undeniable.

The facts just became more convoluted. Gladys Limon describes the situation. "Crystal was extremely upset by that testimony. She loves her sister and is taking care of her. She doesn't think it's humanly possible for Luis to have been two-timing her with her sister when he worked such long hours and had two children with her that he was racing home to see. It really messed with her head. But in any case it was so irrelevant. Say the guy was doing something that weird, they are going to kill him to punish him for that?" asked Limon.

At some point, Limon said, the prosecutor had offered to end the drama with a plea bargain that would have allowed the teenagers to spend just a few months in jail. One of the principals in the case was a part-time assistant district attorney named Rob Franz, whose wife, Sophie, is Mexican. He has salt-and-pepper hair closely cut around his forehead, and often has a shadow of a mustache, which makes him look gritty even in the dark black suits he often wore to the trial. Limon says Franz told her he had made a personal commitment to get justice for Luis, but she initially refused to even pass along the offer to Luis's mother. When it came time for Franz to call, he needed a translator, so she joined him on the call.

"He told this kid's mother he was doing everything to get justice but didn't even mention that the plea would mean these kids who killed him would be in jail for like three months," recalls Limon. She remembers this long silence before Elisa Zavala, Luis's mother, just

From left to right: Soledad's brother Orestes, Soledad, sister Estela, and cousin Kim (in white).

Soledad and best friend, Tricia, in the marching band representing the Smithtown Indians.

Soledad and her mom in 1997 at her sister Estela's wedding.

Soledad is treated to an impromptu concert by Willy Chirino and Lissette Alvarez and their children.

Soledad interviews Vanessa Rosas, ambassador for Disney, as storm clouds gather in the background.

Carlos Robles cramming for the Florida sheriff's exam.

Soledad meets Lupe Ontiveros, who tells her to please not "F" with the community.

Talking to Joe Miller in Shenandoah, Pennslyvania.

Soledad takes a walk in Shenandoah with Carlos Ramos and Jenny Mease while being videotaped by CNN photojournalists Jerry Santos and Cliff Hackel.

Eva Longoria Parker at the Childrens Hospital in Los Angeles.

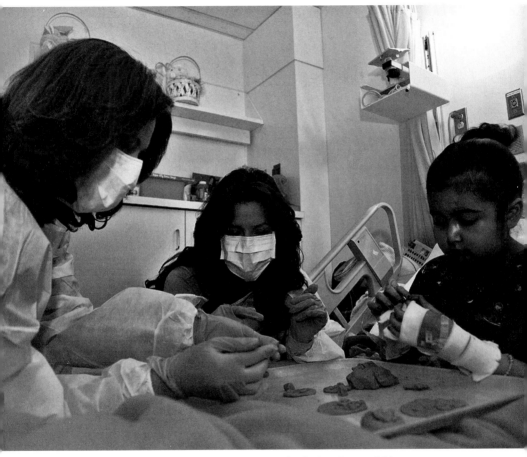

Eva Longoria Parker is the national spokesperson for *Padres Contra el Cáncer*.
Eva and Soledad visit the Childrens Hospital in Los Angeles.

Francisca and Xavier declare
their love in a heart-shaped
picture above their baby's crib.

Monica Garcia, president of the
Los Angeles Unified School
District Board of Education, in
the halls of Garfield High School,
which was made famous in the
movie *Stand and Deliver*.

Two generations of Ms. Pico Rivera, formerly
known as El Grito Queen: Mayor Gracie
Gallegos and her daughter Gracie Ray.

Pico Rivera's Latino families stick close. Mayor Gracie Gallegos lives with her daughter on the same piece of property as her parents and her sister and brother-in-law.

The author helps out with the Gracie Gallegos family barbecue in Pico Rivera.

Melinda Contreras holds a picture of her deceased sister, Maria Elena Hicks. Maria's death motivated Pico Rivera to crack down on gangs and turn itself around.

Erica Sparks, 13, outside her new home in Pico Rivera, California.

Erica Sparks and Soledad walk through Pico Rivera, California.

OPPOSITE: A member of the Together Car Club in Pico Rivera.

Taking a ride in a lowrider with a member of Together Car Club.

The Together Car Club's work on display.

Cindy Garcia and Soledad travel to Cindy's mother's shoe store in East L.A.

began repeating over and over again: *"Esto no está bien. No está bien. No. No. Mi hijo se murió."* This wasn't right. Her son was dead. So the case pressed on.

MALDEF discovered a picture on Facebook of Donchak at a Halloween party after Luis's death. He was wearing a shirt with an emblem on it that said "Border Patrol." Limon says she fought with the prosecutors to use it and they eventually did. But, she says, they were afraid to humanize Luis because it would leave them open to questions about his character. "The accused were referred to as 'boys' even by the prosecution and no one even mentioned that Luis was a human being with small children," she said.

In a wood-paneled room next door to the courtroom, about a half dozen local reporters filed stories each day chronicling the testimony. John Moser, a buttoned-down reporter with a square little mustache, reported the unraveling of the tight clique of teenagers for the *Allentown Morning Call*, one of the larger area newspapers. Four of the six teenagers testified at the trial, including the two teenagers not charged. The only place where their testimony was consistent was in confirming that all the teenagers, football players from Shenandoah Valley High School, were walking home from a block party and had been drinking when they came across Ramirez. There was testimony Luis had called several friends on his cell phone to ask for help with what was obviously going to be a fight. But there was a lot of finger-pointing among friends as to everything else.

By the time everything landed in court, the boys were barely looking at each other. The lawyers had presented conflicting accounts. Prosecutors said Donchak pummeled Ramirez holding a small piece of metal in his hand, while his attorneys said he was breaking up the fight. Scully said he'd used obscenities and told Ramirez to "go back to Mexico," which enraged him. But Walsh said Ramirez also said something in Spanish that they didn't understand. According to the *Morning Call*, he also said that the officers at the scene included Bill Moyer, whose son, the paper said, played football with the defendants.

By the time the case was wrapping up, the defense attorneys told jurors that the teenagers, "Divs," or Blue Devils, as they are called after the high school's mascot, were all saying whatever they needed to say to look innocent. What was in the papers was almost as important as what was being said in court. In a town where everyone has some connection to the school or the police officers, friendships and alliances were redrawn by this trial.

Gladys Limon said the prosecution seemed less than enthusiastic and noted that the local district attorney had to face an election that year. She said the absence of police witnesses was critical and noted that the one objective witness, Eileen, was not at the trial. She was visibly worried. The defense argued that this was a teenage brawl and nothing more. The prosecution kept pointing to the medical examiner's report as evidence of the ferocity of the attack, while noting that the six teens were not injured at all. Testimony was allowed about Luis calling friends to ask for help but none had arrived in time to intervene. This was six against one, if it was a fight. During his closing, prosecutor Franz showed jurors a picture of a fresh-faced Luis and the picture of Donchak in the shirt with the emblem saying "Border Patrol." There was no mention of Crystal and her children after the Roxanne testimony, even as she sat in the audience every day.

Jeffrey Markosky, Derrick's lawyer, began his closing arguments by declaring that the case boiled down to the credibility of the witnesses. The only credible descriptions, he says, are of a fight, not an attack.

"This case is not based upon racial hatred," he told the jurors. "This was a fight that developed spontaneously from the words that were being said at the scene," he said. The Halloween photo should be disregarded. "T-shirts are not evidence of crimes," he said.

Frederick Fanelli, Brandon's attorney, attacked the teenage witnesses head-on: "The problem here is that when each of these three kids sing from the same hymn book, now I decided to tell the truth, the problem is even after they made that—they had this epiphany that they're going to tell the truth after they've been rolled, they continue to lie . . . if you believe that any of these kids lied on any detail, you're free to disregard all their testimony. That's based on human experience. If you lie about the little stuff, you'll lie about the big stuff."

The prosecution's closing fell to Rob Franz. Franz told us he is a partner at a local firm that does workers' compensation cases. For thirteen years, he has also been a part-time prosecutor. At one point, he did defense work, too. He is thirty-eight years old and is a lifelong resident of the area, with a wife and children in the community.

"We are not out to take the boys down," he assured them before making his case. "We are not out to make an arrest at all costs." There was a reason that the medical examiner ruled this case a homicide, he said. "He was badly beaten. His skull was fractured in two spots. Fractured in two spots. Two injuries. And all three doctors gave consistent testimony that his brain was obliterated. And it wasn't just from one fall. It was from a direct impact to the left side of his head as well that took out, not just the front of his brain, but the whole left side of the brain."

There had been a lot of distracting testimony that he had to deal with. Arielle and Roxanne had both thrown wrenches into the trial because they were unsure who had been the kicker. The defense had harped on the fact that Luis called for help and that Arielle and Victor had another friend with a BB gun who had arrived at the scene of the attack. But keep in mind, he told jurors, that no one had been there in time to intervene. And after Luis lay in the street, the boys were gone, only to reappear at a friend's house to get their story straight with friendly police officers. Everyone was worrying about themselves as Luis's "head was split open. It was necrotic. And he proceeded to a brain death. That's the loser. That's the person who was assaulted. The boys had not one injury except for Derrick Donchak. And where was his injury? In his right hand, where he held a piece of metal and beat Luis Ramirez in the face. . . . This fight, if it was a fight, it wasn't fair. This assault, this fight, unfair fight, went too far."

The case went to the jury on May Day, which has become associated with pro-immigration rallies and protests. The teenagers' parents wouldn't talk to any of the fifteen reporters from the local newspapers and television stations that sat in the courtroom to await the verdict. They just paced and smoked and greeted the teenagers who came to show their support. Annette Holopirek, an alternate juror, was released after hearing the judge explain the charges and rushed out with a pained look on her face.

"He should not have worn that T-shirt," she said of Donchak's Border Patrol shirt. "I think there is guilt involved. That to me is a big ethnic intimidation." But Holopirek has a sixteen-year-old son who plays football. "If that was my son up there I would have been scared for him," she said.

Crystal went home at nine o'clock to put her kids to bed. "I had a feeling they would be found not guilty."

The verdict came down after seven hours and forty minutes of deliberations. The jury had asked a few technical questions and, even though it was past ten p.m., the judge kept everyone in the courtroom as anticipation was building. The young men, who'd been playing Uno with a crowd of teenagers outside, sat silently in their suits at the end, Donchak's leg bouncing nervously. Their parents, eyes red and grasping each other's hands, sat behind them. The room was divided roughly into three camps. The press all sat together watching on one side. The teenagers' supporters filled the center. On the other side were just three people: the MALDEF attorney, a Philadelphia lawyer who had come to keep her company, and Enrique Luis Sanchez, the representative from the Mexican consulate.

When the verdicts were read, they came in waves. "Not Guilty." "Not Guilty." "Not Guilty." By the time the third "Not Guilty" had been read the courtroom had erupted in cheers and the MALDEF lawyer was crying silently. The noise was almost too loud for the crowd to hear the teenagers convicted of simple assault charges and corrupting minors by giving them alcohol. The court officers stopped the parents from rushing forward to embrace their sons. Limon ran out with her cell phone to call Luis's mother in Mexico and Crystal. She shook as she recounted to reporters what she said.

"I had to just tell them that the teenagers who did this will not even have their lives interrupted by the consequences of what they've done."

As reporters asked her more questions, her phone rang. Crystal was at home, trapped there because her children were sleeping, and she was losing her mind with rage. "She just kept asking me why they had chosen to do this," Limon said. "She kept remembering all the details of what had happened."

Crystal boiled with rage that the jury had not gotten to hear much about Luis.

"He was a good husband and a good father. He worked two jobs to take care of his children and his family. He was proud. He was standing up for himself because he didn't think it was okay for people to talk bad. He had an appointment for the week after he died to get his papers together so we could marry and he would become legal and give his children a better life than the one he had growing up. He worked very hard for what he had."

Gladys Limon found her way to the lobby of the courthouse, where cameras awaited in a restricted zone surrounded by tiny American flags and the offices of the prosecutors, who paced the halls nervously.

"I don't know if there will be federal charges," said District Attorney James Goodman. "Who knows?" Rob Franz said he couldn't talk about the case because "there is still some activity." He says he doesn't rate his own performance as a prosecutor but he did the best he could.

Gladys Limon spoke haltingly outside the DA's office:

"Community leaders need to search their hearts and educate people in their homes and in their schools and make meaningful efforts to embrace diversity. . . . A message has been sent that you can kill a person, you can kick and stomp their head until they die and your life will not be interrupted because that person is less than a human. I know there are a lot of good people in this community but it is astounding to me that there is a segment of this community that is glorifying and cheering these defendants for having beaten a man to death."

Jury foreman Eric Macklin told reporters he was the lone holdout when the jury voted eleven to one for acquittal at five p.m., after deliberating for just two hours.

"I think it's absolutely horrible what happened to Luis Ramirez," Macklin said. "I was very, very close to finding them both guilty on every serious count, but due to the evidence presented, I was not sure beyond a reasonable doubt. I do believe that all four teenagers involved are racists."

Crystal locked her doors and stayed inside while all this played out. Friends called to warn her that people were driving through the town honking their horns and cheering, something that was later reported by the local papers. A few months ago someone had thrown a water bottle at her youngest son, nearly hitting him. She had seen people with T-shirts that said, "Fuck You Crystal. Your Day is

Coming." She had seen the teenagers around town many times. She was frightened.

After she got off the phone with Luis's mother, Gladys Limon could barely hold back her tears.

"How can I explain that her son was beaten so badly his brains fell out of his head and that the people who did this are guilty of nothing more than being involved in a fight. . . ."

Before she had finished, a wave of people raced down the stairs accompanying the teenagers and their families. Their attorneys stopped to tell reporters that they were too tired to say anything except to reiterate that they believed this was a fight gone bad and that they had won their case. But the crowds pumped their fists and shouted as they emerged into the night. "No comment," several yelled. "Don't say a thing." Others said simply, "Shenandoah got it right." The town was quiet that night, save a few horns being honked on Main Street.

Eileen Burke was at home when she got the call. "I couldn't breathe," she said.

"There is nothing worse than seeing someone die. They're supposed to be honor students and they killed him like an animal . . . I couldn't believe it."

She said her neighbors told her it was okay because he was not legally in the United States. Eileen had never thought about immigration issues before but she was shocked at what she was hearing in her own town.

"This is the twenty-first century. I knew this was very political. I think there was a police conspiracy. . . . They just didn't see him as human and they saw the boys as their boys."

In the days that followed, her car would be egged. When people went by to leave rosaries and candles at the scene of the attack, someone would pull them off the sidewalk in front of her house. She barely goes out. She dreads running into Crystal and the kids.

"They are two and four. When they are twenty-two and twenty-four and these punks are in their forties, I can't even think about it. I am sick for them. I can't step outside my house. I can't sleep. I can't stop thinking about their father lying on the street like an animal," she said. Her voice rattles when she talks, like a person in the middle of a nightmare. She cries easily. How can she walk out her door every day and see the spot where she saw a man die? she asks.

"No one will be punished for this?" she asks no one in particular. "How can that be?"

Crystal would later make plans to leave town altogether. "They don't want change in this town. They want to live back in the day when this town had one race. It's all about the color of their skin. They are focused on the Mexican. There are Puerto Ricans in this town [U.S. citizens], but if they're brown, they're brown. I need my kids to grow up in a place where they are proud of who they are, a place where there is diversity and people respect themselves and others," she said. She said it will be hard to go anyplace because she will miss her sisters and she has not been able to get a job. While her children were born in the United States, they cannot receive Social Security death benefits for survivors because their father was not here legally.

Gladys Limon drove into the fog for two hours to get back to her sister's house in New Jersey, even though it was well past midnight. She just wanted to leave Shenandoah for now. Crystal called her as late as one a.m.

"There has been this national campaign that has cast Mexicans like me as these social pariahs," she said as she drove. "I wonder sometimes how it has reached a place this remote." Hazleton flew by in the night.

"In bad economic times, immigrants always get cast as targets. There have been bad times here for a while. When people are fearful or threatened they have to affirm their identity, their own patriotism. This is a post-nine-eleven world and we only have this one big border to protect. The Latino community is very visible because of the sectors in which we work. We are the gardeners, we take care of children. We are in a vulnerable situation."

Crystal's front window looks out onto the street where Luis died. She knows all about being vulnerable. She is white but her children are Latino, and she wonders how she will look out the window with them and tell them how to live in this atmosphere.

"How can I explain to my children that their father was beaten to death because of the color of his skin? When I leave, the only people I will talk to here are my sisters and the people who supported me. Latinos here have been very supportive."

Gladys Limon's parents are Mexican immigrants, just like a lot of the people in that town. She went to Stanford. She laments that

Mexicans like her are not more visible so people can see some of the complexity of the community.

"The whole debate has become about an issue, not about the people. You look at Shenandoah and the trial and it was the same way. You barely heard about this person who died," she says as she drives rapidly away from Shenandoah, eager to see her own family and return to the West Coast.

"This trial had nothing to do with immigration. The problems in this community, the hatred, are so beyond that. Shenandoah is a town of immigrants. There are Latinos there who are not even immigrants. . . ."

Then the phone rings. It is Crystal calling again. Limon urges her to call the police if anything happens that scares her, or to at least call her back.

"That girl has to move out of there. She has to go someplace where she can build a new life in another community. It's just not her community anymore," she said and continued driving into the milky darkness.

⁓

Back in Guanajato, Mexico, Luis Ramirez's mother would spend weeks writing a letter to the judge that would be sentencing the boys who attacked her son. Elisa Zavala wanted them to know that Luis Eduardo, as she called him, had supported her family ever since he was a boy. When they were short of money, she recalled that even as a little boy he would "run and get his piggy bank and hand it to me."

Elisa didn't want her son to move to the United States but he wanted to earn more money and help his family.

"He worked in a potato factory, in a mattress factory, in a nursery, in construction and picking cherries. He always worked two jobs. He was my sole means of economic support. My family is doing very badly now without him."

She wanted the judge to know that the economic impact of losing Luis's income was only one small way the family had been affected by his loss. In her letter she sounds desperate and confused.

"Since he died I don't sleep. I cry easily and I'm depressed. I can't concentrate. I feel homeless. I only want to be alone because that's how I feel inside. I don't want the mothers of these boys to ever feel as badly as I feel because this pain is so great and this wound will never disappear from my life."

Elisa tells the judge she thinks these young men don't appreciate the consequences of their actions and worries about the message it will send to American society if they are not punished.

"There are moments when I ask myself how can I live without my son? I am no one without him. I worry that if Scully and the other boys don't get the sentence they deserve they could do the same thing to other people knowing that there would be no consequences.

"I don't understand how these kids can be so at ease with what they have done. They didn't kill an animal to feel so at ease with themselves. They killed a human being who was my son. I believe no one deserves to die like this simply because he was Mexican."

5

eva and lupe

THERE'S NOTHING LIKE interviewing Eva Longoria to make you feel a little unglamorous. I'm in the basement of Childrens Hospital Los Angeles, where a few floors above us there are very frail children fighting cancer. On a break from filming *Desperate Housewives*, Eva is going to pay the kids a visit as part of her role as the public face of a charity called *Padres Contra El Cáncer*, the only program in the nation that assists and educates Latino families whose children face cancer. But Eva's flight into L.A. is delayed and I'm sitting here in our camera setup fluffing and refluffing my hair, and crossing and recrossing my legs, while my producers check the monitors and tell me how I look.

L.A. is the bright, sunny, vibrant capital of Latinos in America. It's something of a relief from the complicated, dreary environment of Shenandoah, Pennsylvania. It is the most Latino county in the nation. There are 4.7 million of us here, nearly half the population. According to U.S. census data released in May 2009, L.A. also had the greatest increase in Latinos of any county in the country since 2007. If there is any town that's our town, it is L.A. Los Angeles is a town where Latinos have real economic and political power, where you have a sense that as a people you might just get a few things done.

Gladys Limon lives and works here. This is where she retreated after that dark night in Shenandoah. The Mexican American Legal Defense and Education Fund (MALDEF) is headquartered here, and this is where they launched a national campaign to get the federal government to go after the young men acquitted of murdering Luis

Ramirez. As an advocate for Latino civil rights, Gladys says that flying into L.A. gives her a sense of relief. She looks like she fits in here, with her sloping cheekbones and nut-colored skin.

Within days, MALDEF has a petition with twenty-five thousand signatures calling for federal charges for the young men, Gladys has done a string of interviews, and Latino organizations are issuing angry statements urging action. Brian Scully, the juvenile defendant, was sent away for ninety days of evaluations after the verdict with a promise that he'd be out in time for high school graduation. Pickarsky got six months and seven days minimum and Donchak got seven months minimum. Both have a max of twenty-three months. MALDEF expressed its indignation from L.A. and circulated a graphic created by an anonymous Shenandoah resident parroting a video game where you could practice killing Luis all over again.

There were plenty of things besides the Shenandoah case for Latinos to be angry about these days. One of the major pitfalls of working on a project so focused on your own ethnicity is you join this tiny circle that gathers you news of every triumph of your people as well as every slight. So these days I'm hyperaware of what's happening in and to the Latino community.

The outbreak of swine flu had started killing people in Mexico and had spread to the United States. To watch TV and read the papers you'd think all Mexicans carried horrible diseases. My colleague and friend Dr. Sanjay Gupta has been on CNN a number of times talking about how the outbreak has not actually become a serious threat in the United States. He has explained how transmission works and made it clear that U.S. travelers returning from vacation may be bringing home the disease. The swine flu is not something Mexicans in the United States just develop spontaneously in their bodies. But no matter. There seem to be angry folks everywhere who act like Latinos should be dubbed the Hex Mex.

Jay Severin, who worked at MSNBC when I was there, was suspended from his job at WTKK-FM radio in Boston when he said swine flu was the latest disease Mexicans were exporting, after venereal disease and women with mustaches. He described Mexicans as "the world's lowest of primitives."

"When we are the magnet for primitives around the world—and it's not the primitives' fault by the way, I'm not blaming them for being primitives—I'm merely observing they're primitive," he said. The guy wouldn't stop. "It's millions of leeches from a primitive country come here to leech off you and, with it, they are ruining the schools, the hospitals, and a lot of life in America," he said.

I wanted to call Jay and say, "Hey, remember we used to work at the same place. You knew me. I'm one of those people you're talking about." But what's the point? He will be off air for a while; then someone will let him back on.

Meanwhile I'm in L.A. worrying that I'm missing something weighty while I'm refreshing my makeup for a celebrity interview. I had gone into this project fairly certain we wouldn't be talking to any Latino stars. Celebrity interviews that aren't done for entertainment stories are really hard to handle editorially. Stars in general are taught (much like journalists) to remember they are always on stage when they are in public. They know from hard experience that saying anything remotely controversial can land them in the tabloids. Latino celebrities are no different and some choose only to emphasize their ethnicity when it promotes their career and to avoid it when it doesn't. But after I walked the red carpet at the unofficial Latino Ball following President Barack Obama's inauguration, I realized that reaching out to a few celebrities would help me tell an important story about the community. Latinos are born fans. They don't have hundreds of heroes in this country and they look to their few stars with enormous adoration. I walked the carpet just behind Marc Anthony and Jennifer Lopez and George Lopez and watched how people reacted to them. It wasn't just the usual celebrity fawning. Latinos look to their stars to find their place in this country, idolizing stars and talk show hosts and entire casts of the latest *telenovela* as cultural guideposts. To reach this community it was worth checking out the star circuit just a bit. The hard part was finding one of them with something interesting to say.

Eva Longoria seemed the right person to start with because she recently launched a documentary film project of her own called *Harvest*, about migrant workers, an updated version of Edward R. Murrow's *Harvest of Shame*. She has also supported United Farm Workers and the Mexican American Legal Defense and Education Fund. So I was hopeful I was about to talk to someone who had a real dedication to Latinos, the Hollywood establishment and her soaring career notwithstanding. And she was going to be a breath of fresh air after my time in Shenandoah.

When she finally walks in, it's clear that I have been wasting my time worrying about how I look. Even after sitting on a plane for three hours, Eva Longoria looks pretty darned hot without even trying. My assistant has freshened her hair and makeup, but she hardly looks like she needs the help. She has on tight Rock & Republic jeans, five-inch wedge shoes, and a plain yellow shirt with a white tank underneath. She is effortlessly beautiful, slim and tiny and totally at ease. What's more, she seems genuinely friendly. She says hello to each of the ten people crowding the small room, dumps a load of notes beside her chair, and begs someone to go grab her some chicken tenders so she doesn't collapse from hunger.

It doesn't make me feel much better when she divulges that she was her family's ugly duck.

"I cannot believe that you, as a nickname, were called 'the ugly one' as a child," I say.

"Yes, 'la prieta fea,'" she replies.

"Who called you that?"

"My mom, my sisters, my dad. I thought my name was Fea at first forever."

"No!"

"Yes, because growing up I was really dark. I still am pretty dark and have dark hair. And growing up it was, I guess, socially more acceptable if you were a light-skinned Mexican, and so I was a dark-skinned, dark-haired, dark-eyed Mexican, and my sisters were light. My sisters were very, very fair. And so, that's kind of where that was rooted from, and it was just a joke in our family. And now, you know, I get to go, 'Ha!'"

"Just call them and say, 'Ha'?"

"Yes. I send them every cover of a magazine just so they can see somebody thinks I'm pretty."

You just have to laugh at that story. But her looks are not why I'm here, so I get right to it.

"What do you think it means to be Latino in America?" I ask.

"Oh, I don't know," she replies, tilting back her head as if the weight of the question was too much.

"Everyone gives me a different answer so I don't know . . . ," I say.

"What does it mean? That's a hard thing to define. I think for me specifically because I'm from Texas and Texas, we think we're our own country already. . . . We think we're Texans before we're Americans. And then we're Texans and then we're Americans and then I happen to be a Mexican American. So it's always hard to define being Latino in America. It's funny because if I'm in America, I'm—oh, she's Mexican. When I go to Mexico, they say, oh, she's American. So it's kind of hard to have any identity anywhere because I'm a mutt of sorts. But I think I identify myself as American with a Mexican heart.

"We're ninth-generation Americans. We didn't just cross over. We're on the same land that we got in our Spanish land grant from our ancestors. We were Mexico and then the border moved and we were Texas, and then the border moved again, and we were America without ever moving. So my ancestry is kind of complex in that way, so I feel like I'm a native to this land that we call America."

I almost had to stop Eva when she dropped in the part about being ninth-generation American. Think about it—nine generations. In this country we are trapped in this endless, bitter national conversation about Mexican immigration. People are getting killed because they're considered the "illegal" Mexican, the foreigner, the threat. And here we have one of the country's leading "Mexican" American personalities who is nine generations removed from Mexico. Immigration as such isn't part of her story at all. She is one of those Latinos who are able to say "the border crossed us." After nine generations, you would think any person would have totally detached from their immigrant roots, even in this country of immigrants. But the Mexicans cannot.

Eva Longoria is in so many ways the living, breathing answer to what it can mean, maybe even should mean, to be Latino in America. She is firmly rooted in her personal and family history. She doesn't let other people or their prejudices define who she is. She believes that Mexican immigration stands out because it predates this country and will continue into the future. There is no outrunning the debate over Mexicans crossing the border, but she refuses to be defined by it and has chosen the role she wants to play in her own community.

Eva Longoria has chosen to take a stand. Sure, she has no reason to fear the Border Patrol or a group of Shenandoah vigilante teenagers who happen to be drunk. But it could cost her some of her hard-won status in Hollywood, and certainly a few fans. She has pushed past a powerful stereotype and has something valuable to lose if she gets trapped by it. She could jeopardize her career with her activism. Yet she is traipsing all over California urging Latinos to be counted in the census so they can be fully represented in Congress and have their schools and hospitals funded. She is advocating on behalf of organized labor. She is outspoken about one of the most controversial topics swirling around Latinos right now—whether immigration reform should include a path to citizenship.

"It's so funny that to people immigration is such a hot topic or an emotional button for people when we're a country founded on immigrants. I don't understand that. It's hard for me to understand as an American how we don't accept the idea that immigration reform is not only needed but it's going to be inevitable, you know, specifically with Mexicans. Not only do we share thousands of miles of a border with this country and hundreds of years of history, there's a cultural cross-pollination that's happening, and the United States houses the largest Latino population outside of Mexico."

There are not many prominent Latinos in Hollywood. There are even fewer who speak out about Latino issues, especially controversial ones like immigration. It's clear that Eva has decided to adopt a political personality. She campaigned for Obama and her documentary project makes a strong statement about her politics. *Harvest*, which is scheduled to be released about a month after this book, grew out of her work with the United Farm Workers, which has a foundation named after Dolores Huerta, who cofounded the union with Cesar Chavez. Eva said she was shocked to learn from the Farm Workers that children as young as eight are legally working fourteen hours a day in the United States harvesting food.

"Twenty-five percent of the produce we eat in America is picked by a child under fourteen. Twenty-five percent. This is something you think is happening in a Third World country. The United States has one of the strongest import-export laws regarding not accepting retail clothing from sweatshops, toys assembled by kids, computers assembled by kids, yet our agriculture in America is one-fourth picked by children."

The documentary is being produced by Shine Global, a nonprofit organization focused on publicizing the abuse of children, which gets its statistics from United Farm Workers estimates based on U.S. Department of Agriculture research. The plan is for cameras to follow five children, ages nine to fourteen, as they pick the harvest from April to November. Some of them are the children of U.S. citizens whose families ended up in the United States because they worked picking produce.

"So, this just goes on the same stereotype of 'go back to Mexico.' When they go to school and they have these special schools, and yet they have to be pulled out of school early and go to school late. So, they are inevitably set up to fail with education because they are always behind, and they can't catch up. But yet their family needs them for the income that they produce by picking. So we're hoping to, with the documentary, to humanize the issue, to put a face to the tomato that's on your salad today," she said.

"I imagine you get a lot of things across your desk," I say.

"Well, for me this isn't an immigration issue. *Harvest* is a human rights issue. And it's a labor issue. In 1935, the Fair Labor Standards Act was passed that gave us the forty-hour workweek and gave us overtime and all of this and it excluded agriculture. It said every industry but agriculture. And that has never been reformed. So we're kind of abusing this loophole in that act to keep children in the fields and so that to me—it kind of resonated with me. I do a lot with children's charities, whether it's children with cancer or children with developmental disabilities. So this just appalled me and I find myself pretty educated about labor issues and the fact that I did not know this. I don't think many people know this. And if they did, it's like, if you went into the store when you pay more for an organic piece of fruit. If you knew this fruit was picked by a child, would you pay more for oranges that were not picked by a child? I think you would do that."

"What's your goal to change?"

"The goal of the documentary is to humanize the issue that's happening in America regarding child farmworkers. It's also hopefully going to be used as a political tool to change the standards. And the problem is very, very tricky because we don't want to punish the families who have children because then you're taking away the income. The key is to subsidize them in some way, to give them an incentive to keep their children in school. To help these kids break this cycle of poverty."

Growing up on a ranch near Corpus Christi, Eva was the youngest of four girls. Her family worked the farmland that belonged to generations of family members before them. She has acknowledged in several interviews that they were very poor until she became a star. She received a bachelor's degree at Texas A&M University in Kinesiology (human kinetics) but wanted to be a model. A talent contest took her to L.A., where she was spotted and signed by a theatrical agent. Soon she became the popular "Isabella" on *The Young and the Restless*. Years later, her résumé spotlights not what she gets but what she gives, like the house she donated to a victim of Hurricane Katrina or when she donated one of her *Desperate Housewives* paychecks to Oprah's philanthropic show, *The Big Give*.

Eva's work has been recognized within the Latino community. She has won the Alma Award from La Raza, the national civil rights organization that honors Latino talent for creating positive images. She has won the Cesar Chavez Legacy Award and the Hope of Los Angeles Award given by the city of L.A. That is not exactly the work that reporters want to talk about. They are instead fixated on her appearances on "Most Beautiful" lists and her marriage to NBA guard Tony Parker, a handsome Frenchman with whom she often says she plans to have children.

Tabloids want to see the lives of Hollywood stars unravel. I see it a little on my end as profilers belabor questions of whether I can anchor television programs and raise four children. They ask what it is my husband does that allows me to do this. No one ever shouts a question on a red carpet about whether you're sharing your success with people in need. If philanthropy is not expected of public people in general, it is perhaps even less expected of Latinos. What is expected is a slower-paced, more family-centered life.

Just a few months previously, I had sat in a conference room in New York with Latino leaders and journalists inquiring about what topics they thought the *Latino in America* documentary should touch. The usual ideas were thrown out but one that was surprising was the issue of philanthropy in the Latino community.

"We need to become more giving. People are a bit too used to being on the receiving end of, well, being oppressed, of having difficulties, that they need to get rescued," said Maite Junco, who edits a Latino supplement to the *New York Daily News*. Maite talked about how the "big Latinos" needed to step up.

"We need them to set an example and create a model for giving. It's the only way we get past what's happening to us with education and negative stereotypes about immigrants, if the community steps forward to help itself." So, here I am interviewing some celebrities searching for that model.

"Do you like being a role model for Latinos?" I ask Eva.

"Absolutely."

"Is it exhausting?"

"No, actually because I like to walk the walk . . . I like to live by example, and if I'm going to be saying 'get an education,' I better have gotten an education. If I am going to say 'do community work,' I'd better be doing community work. So for me, it's not a difficult thing to be a role model. It's not this burden on my shoulders. I embrace it. I love the responsibility. And I try to find a lot of ways to be a role model."

But to be a role model in the Latino community is to feel a bit like Olive Oyl, Popeye's fickle flapper girlfriend in the cartoon who is constantly being kidnapped by Brutus and ending up as the rope in a tug-of-war. You feel pulled by competitive American culture on the one hand and by Latino family values on the other. What she is saying sounds too easy to me as I navigate flying from coast to coast trying to assemble a documentary while raising four young children. The stress of being a working mom of any ethnicity is plenty without meeting the special expectations of being a Latina. Does she ever feel as torn as all the Latinos out there whom I have met? Does she feel as ripped in half as I do some days?

"I felt pulled by my culture to get a job, not a career, to get married, have children. Like, my culture kind of, that's what defines me. And the American side of me was the go-go-go, obtain-obtain-obtain, achieve-achieve-achieve," she says.

"Was that a difficult pull?" I ask.

"No. It kind of went hand in hand because I feel like I've achieved a lot, whether it's my education or my job or my philanthropy. And at the same time I love being a wife, and I can't wait to be a mother. And I love to cook, and I love to clean, and I love to be that homemaker. . . .

I think the mold of being Latina is constantly evolving. I mean, from what my mom was to what I am to what my children will be is going to be different every single time. Even to the fact that I had to learn Spanish. I didn't grow up with Spanish in the household. My parents spoke Spanish, but not."

"They didn't teach it to you?"

"No. No."

"Why not?"

"Because it was a big thing to not speak Spanish. You were actually punished in school if you were caught speaking Spanish. So, my mom, being a teacher, constantly enforced English. She was like, English, English, English, English. And even my parents, they'd speak Spanish to each other but not socially, really. But my grandparents barely speak English, so, you see this shift in three generations, the difference of our evolution as a Latina."

"When did you learn to speak Spanish?"

"In college.... And I still have a lot of trouble. I went to Mexico, and I felt so disconnected from my own culture because language . . ."

"You were embarrassed because you didn't speak the language?"

"Very embarrassed . . . so I learned it."

Eva is very much the other side of the coin to so many people I've met on this journey. Unlike Luis Ramirez, whose skin tone played a role in his death in Shenandoah, and the millions of other darker-skinned Latinos, her skin tone was a plus. She can play a Jew or an Italian. She is learning both Spanish and French because it is an opportunity, something that provides flexibility. Just like Carlos Robles back in Orlando, she can tell folks she's an American, that her family has been American for generations. But, unlike Carlos, she sells her language skills as a perk while his are a hindrance.

"Let me ask a question about being an actor. Did you ever feel that being a Latino was beneficial, did it seem to hold you back?"

"You know, I was actually really lucky," she acknowledges. "I came in at the Ricky Martin, Jennifer Lopez, it was cool to be Latin kind of movement in Hollywood. So I never really encountered, you know, racism against—I can't get that role because I'm Hispanic. I actually got roles that weren't Hispanic."

"Because you would cross over?"

"Yes, you know, I was actually Gabrielle Solis on *Desperate*

Housewives, but before that, when I did a movie with Michael Douglas, that role was not Latina. You know, I think she was Jewish. You know? I've never played stereotypical parts. I've never played a maid. I've never played a gardener. But I find that the face of Hollywood is changing, too, and the image of Latinos is being reflected in movies and film and television and music. We still have a long way to go, but I find that Hollywood is making moves in the right direction."

On television, Eva plays Gabrielle Solis, a former supermodel who is married to Carlos, who begins the series involved in some moblike business dealings. Carlos is shadowed by his meddlesome, borderline sinister mother, Juanita, who is played by Lupe Ontiveros. She later gets run over by one of the neighbors on the verge of destroying Gabrielle over her affair with a hot Latino gardener who is a teenager. The Solises are clearly Latino but it's not particularly an issue. Over several seasons, the story arc has been more concerned with Gabrielle's journey overcoming her self-centered attitude and the fact that her bombshell looks seem to blur her judgment. She is catty quite a bit, coy, conspiring against anyone who threatens her.

When Carlos wants a baby and she miscarries, she refuses to try again until she extracts his concrete devotion. She toys with him, as Gabrielle so often does with any man she is trying to keep off balance. In one scene she fawns over a baby in church and Carlos asks, "She's adorable, isn't she?" Gabrielle cocks her head and answers, "She's okay." Whenever Gabrielle expresses any honesty or sincerity, it is usually in explosive moments. That same episode has her wrestling with a nun in the middle of church in a fit of jealousy over the sister's flirty friendship with Carlos. She then goes home and forces him to choose between having a baby and being her devoted husband. After he chooses her, she commits to trying to get pregnant again. That's not particularly Latino of her but it has slowly created this unpredictable character who seems obnoxious one minute and totally human the next.

In recent seasons, the Gabrielle character has taken a sharp turn. She leaves Carlos, only to discover that she truly loves him. Later, an accident leaves him blind and they find themselves penniless, forcing her to mature as a human being. She gives him the children he's always wanted and takes on responsibilities that once seemed beyond her. But the little girls are pudgy, round-faced, and look of Mexican descent. The former supermodel has to deal with children who fit a certain Latino stereotype.

"When you look at your character in *Desperate Housewives* . . . she [has] a lot more Latino characteristics, a girl who values her family, a woman who has two daughters—and children who she's concerned about their weight. . . . Is that anything that you pushed for?"

"No, actually, I've never felt like *Desperate Housewives* has had an overly ethnic line with me, a story line regarding Gabrielle or me. They've never been like, 'Come on over for tortillas.' We deal with issues that are universal. Having overweight children is not a Latino thing, it's an American thing. You know, we have the largest obesity in children in the world. Family issues, everybody has family issues. I always try to push Marc [Marc Cherry, the executive producer], I'm like, you know, we're Latin on TV. We should have more guest stars who are Latin because we should have that big family, you know?"

"Your cousins?"

"I should have cousins, and I should have, you know, sisters and brothers. And, I mean, Marc's been really great at just keeping Gabrielle a human being. She happens to be Latina, but he doesn't hit you over the head with it."

Eva now has her own production company. As satisfied as she is with how her culture has played out in her career, she does believe that Latinos have to produce more content if they want to truly increase and improve the images available of other Latinos.

"If more Latinos want to be in Hollywood, then more Latinos have to be the creators behind the camera, then write the Latin stories, then direct the Latin stories, then produce those Latin stories," she says. "To sit at home and go, 'There needs to be more, I'm an actor and there needs to be more Latinos on television,' well, then you do something about it. You know, create something for it. . . ."

Our time is running out and we've covered a lot of territory but we haven't even touched on why she's here. Eva is a national spokesperson for *Padres Contra El Cáncer*. When she began working with Childrens Hospital, 70 percent of the patients were Latino, yet there were no translators on staff.

"There are a lot of barriers that can be prevented, whether it's a social barrier of our culture not getting regular checkups, not having health insurance, not regularly going to the doctor because it's not in our culture to do so. Whether it's an economic barrier, obviously a lot of these families don't have the economic structure to support a child in chemo and drugs and all the therapies that they need," Eva says.

"So, is it a microcosm of Latinos in the country dealing with the health care system?"

"Absolutely."

Eva instinctively gets where this interview is going.

"This is why the census is so important, because people are here and we need to be accounted for because there are programs like *Padres* that need the funding, that need the grants, that need the support, but yet the old census says there aren't that many Latinos," she says. ". . . they're Americans. They were born here. We need to help the American children of today."

After she shares her chicken tenders with me, Eva invites me to visit Jessica Alcala, an eight-year-old, whom we find sitting in her room with her mother, Susana. To visit her we have to don sterile gowns and masks because her condition is so fragile. She is one of sixty-seven hundred patients *Padres* has helped over the years with everything from education and treatment to gas vouchers. *Padres* says that medical outcomes for Latino children lag behind other children with cancer because of language barriers and lack of education. Jessica's mother thanks us profusely. We're a good distraction from her day of uncomfortable medical procedures. She's young enough to find our cameras exciting, but she can't muster a smile.

As a mother, you know when a kid is sick. Their eyes are puffy and they look swollen and sad, as if this light inside them has gone out. IVs were running up and down her arms. She could barely move her arms as she played with Play-Doh on a plastic table. Eva sat there and made little pizzas with her. Her mother explained that her daughter was tired of being sick. She had the chance to go home but kept coming back because she got these infections. Her surgery to remove the cancer had gone well but she still kept getting sick. The hospital had done all they could to make the room look cheerful for a little girl and she had a big banner with pictures and cards and a photo of Miley Cyrus.

Eva didn't break her stride. She seemed very comfortable for someone with no kids of her own. She has obviously visited sick children before. Susana told us she was exhausted and had other children to care for. This little girl and her parents live a very different reality than the one occupied by either Eva Longoria or me. It's another one of those times as a reporter that I find myself saying to no one in particular, "I can't believe how lucky I am." I have four healthy children and that is a blessing when you know that can change at any moment. I've covered enough sad stories to know the truth of that. We offer each other one of those "good-bye for now" hugs and we're off into our separate rushes, traveling a fast distance from what we've just seen in that hospital room, knowing there are some things you just can't make better.

⁓

I race through Hollywood to the Four Seasons Hotel, where I have a date with my next celebrity philanthropist, Lupe Ontiveros. She played the role of Eva's former mother-in-law on *Desperate Housewives*. Lupe has spoken out forcefully about the abundance of stereotypical roles for Latinos in Hollywood, even though it's a stereotype she has helped create. From the moment we contact her, I am enchanted by her easygoing manner and her strong convictions. She is a Latina actor who came of age during what was a tough time in Hollywood for Latinos. She has deep roots in the community and has been willing to sacrifice her career by staying active with social issues that neither enhance her standing nor draw publicity. In many ways, she set the stage for women like Eva to take Hollywood by storm.

Lupe has had an impressive career but still lives just outside L.A. in a working-class city called Pico Rivera, which we've decided to profile for our documentary. We were intrigued by Pico because it is nearly 100 percent Latino, but most folks are many generations removed from immigration and are devoted to big Fourth of July parties and all-American-looking malls and housing developments. You don't hear a lot of Spanish spoken in Pico. In fact, residents complain when public signs and mailers have translations. Lupe raised two children here and refused to let fame pull her away. She calls it her Latino Beverly Hills.

Eva is thirty-four. Lupe is sixty-seven. A generation apart, they have very similar backgrounds. Lupe is the daughter of Mexican immigrants who opened a tortilla factory and two restaurants in her native El Paso. They were also poor, like the Longorias. Lupe received a bachelor's degree in social work but, unlike Eva, she lived in a time when Latinas living along the border didn't win talent contests or get to meet casting agents. For eighteen years she was a social worker, an activist and counselor, fighting domestic violence, educating people about AIDS, and working on health care issues.

Lupe worked with the Catholic Welfare Bureau and Head Start in East L.A. She dealt with child abuse cases in Pomona, special needs children in South Central, seniors and broken families and people who were very ill. She was frustrated and tired. One day she answered a casting call for "extras" and began a long acting career.

"I knew instinctively how to stand in front of a camera," she said. She had no idea of the power of that term "extra." Over the years she estimates she has played the nanny or the maid scores of times. She was asked to make *The Goonies* and knew it would mean a three-month move to Oregon that would jeopardize her day job as an eight a.m. to eight p.m. social worker. Then one day, when she was working with a six-foot-tall disabled boy, "he just walked up and clocked me," she remembers. "I got some medical leave and went and made *The Goonies*."

Having appeared so often in the background of TV shows and films, Lupe Ontiveros is one of America's most recognizable Latino screen faces, even though most people probably don't know her name. Those roles don't pay great, basic union day rates, and she clearly has not made the fortune that some of her costars, like Eva, enjoy. For some movie fans, she is reducible to being the heavily accented housekeeper getting harangued by Jack Nicholson in *As Good as It Gets*. In 1983, she played a maid in *El Norte*, a film about a newly arrived immigrant girl that reverberated in the Latino community for its powerful portrayal of the illegal immigrant experience. She was the maid in *Dolly Dearest* and the voice of the sleeping *abuelita* in *Maya and Miguel*.

Lupe played the murderer in a movie about the death of the Tejano singer Selena (played by Jennifer Lopez) so well that people stopped mistaking her for a maid, but began accosting her because they thought she was actually the killer. She has had trouble escaping the stereotype even as she publicly derides Hollywood for creating it. After all, she will tell you, she needs to get paid. In 2000, she was featured in *Chuck and Buck* in a role she says she took because it had nothing to do with being a Latina. For that role, she was nominated for Best Supporting Actress in a Motion Picture in the 2000 Independent Spirit Awards.

Lupe got a chance to play with the issue of stereotyping in 2003 when she played alongside America Ferrera in *Real Women Have Curves*. She is this portrait of the suffocating, oppressive Latina mom who talks out of both sides of her mouth. Latinos loved her, recognizing the complex Latina mom dynamic.

"You're not bad-looking. If you lost weight you could be beautiful," she tells her daughter, America Ferrera, as the waiters stand by for her dessert order.

"Stop it. You're overweight, too," America retorts. There is a silence as a single Lupe eyebrow rises accusingly.

"Don't eat the flan," she says slowly in a low voice. She and America won the Special Jury Prize at the Sundance Film Festival for that performance.

But for all the roles she has played, sitting down to talk to Lupe is like dropping by your aunt's house on a Sunday afternoon to ask what's up. She pushes her bourbon and 7Ups and enjoys an afternoon of light laughter. She has a face that is always smiling, hair that is streaked and arranged but not made up as if each interaction is a casting call. She can cuss and laugh out loud at the simplest provocation. I've gotten to interview plenty of celebrities between my stint with *Weekend Today* and CNN, and she is unusual. She comes off as frank and unafraid to speak her piece. She is constantly laughing at herself for not minding her tongue. Yet she is sweet and soft-handed.

The first time we meet she hands me a little pillbox as a present. She gives every woman she likes a small token. This "quick drink" is supposed to be our "getting to know you" moment but I am, as always, rushed. I flew in for the Eva Longoria interview, made poor Lupe wait because Eva's plane was late; then I am catching a red-eye to Miami to interview one of the Garcias, a Venezuelan chef named Lorena. Lupe finds none of this off-putting. I've carted along my coauthor and a still photographer who is capturing us for promotional reasons. We're surrounded by a bloom of fantastic flowers in the garden of the hotel, so he snaps a few shots of us embracing as if we're old friends. What's funny is it kind of feels that way. Lupe is ordering me water and food, urging me to eat and slow down before my flight. She wants to know about my children and how they survive my traveling as much as she wants to know what the documentary is about. She quickly establishes that my coauthor speaks Spanish and seems to make a mental note to debrief her about me in my absence.

I think I must have passed because that was the first of many conversations she will have with me, my coauthor, a number of my producers, and even the photographers working on the documentary. She must be the only Hollywood star on the planet who gives out her cell phone number to anyone and actually answers it and makes time to talk. She became quickly invaluable to the making of our documentary, making phone calls to get us access to people and information without concern for how it would help her. Lupe liked the project and is used to helping things she believes in. I knew she would from the hug she gave me that first day.

The next time we meet, I am back in New York and CNN has rented a Broadway theater so we can do an on-camera interview with Lupe. We are just a few blocks from the Winter Garden, where she made her Broadway debut in *Zoot Suit* in 1978. Even though she had been so cool, I expect her to talk nonstop about her career. That's what ambitious actors do when they meet journalists. Her fond memories of *Zoot Suit* put her in a wonderfully crazy mood. She recalls hearing the terrible reviews while sitting at Sardi's restaurant with the cast. She was thrilled to see Andy Warhol in the room and was satisfied knowing she'd put a spotlight on issues of race and ethnicity. But it wasn't about her for very long.

Like Eva, Lupe frantically ticks off her causes, searching for ways to get them attention. She also is obviously trying to interest me in investing time in any one of them and I am intrigued. There is her work with the deaf. She has sons with hearing problems. So she worked with the city to provide more services. Now they have deaf interns. She has multiple projects in the schools. She works with the Latino Commission on AIDS, which has brought her to New York for their annual fund-raiser. There is a part of her, she readily admits, that is still a social worker. She tells us she has recently begun "working with" a family where a daughter has diabetes. "This is what I do, a little bit of everything and I love every minute of it, the relationships I've formed," she says.

She lives across the street from the elementary school her sons attended when she was not a public figure. The children there used to speak a lot of Spanish and she viewed it as an opportunity for them to learn. Now the kids all speak English, and one day a little girl knocked on her door and asked her to talk to her class. Lupe went. She rarely says no. She brought all her awards and ended up visiting four classes. The teachers told her that the presence of someone successful in this working-class Chicano neighborhood is life-changing. She also visited the local high school.

"When I speak to the little tykes I address their obligations to their homework and school and self-esteem. A lot of that lack of self-esteem has been projected from the parents and yet you have some enormous numbers of success stories. . . . I'd rather talk to the parent than the kid to say to them, 'Where are you at? Are you guilty of projecting your own insecurities?' When I talk to high schools, I say, 'What do you think is important right now?' I normally walk around them and look at them face-to-face . . . and I'll ask the girls, 'You think pole dancing is important?' I'm very confrontational in that respect."

None of this is hard to imagine. An eyebrow always rises when she is punctuating her points, so you can almost picture her sharking around a teenager evoking the specter of pole dancing.

She knows all about self-esteem and openly admits it's been a struggle to preserve her own when so many people in Hollywood view her through the prism of the Latina stereotype. She has begun playing a millionaire on *The Reaper*, which is being shot in Vancouver to air on CW. When she first walked onto the set and saw her wardrobe she asked the director, "What is this?" There were nice clothes. "We didn't tell you that you're supposed to have money?!" she remembers him saying. The house where they were shooting had beautiful artwork. "I can get used to being rich. I don't even have to get into character. Ha ha ha!" she said.

Lupe recently shot *Southland* for NBC, where she plays the matriarch of a drug gang with real-life gang members being rehabilitated by a program in South Central L.A. I'm quite certain her agent would like her to plug the show but she gets too excited pitching us a story on the rehabilitation program. The guy who plays her son had to be replaced because he was sentenced to jail time. Her opportunity to promote a good program helps alleviate her frustration with being asked to play yet another negative stereotype. "I used to literally have to walk Hollywood Boulevard to get cast," she says. "I did it so much a guy once propositioned me!"

"How many times do you think you've played the maid?" I ask her. "*Ay, dios mío!*"

"In a movie? On a show?"

"You know, I kind of stopped counting . . . I'm still playing them. I'm still playing them."

"So when you stopped counting."

"I think I was a maid. Although they said, 'She's a family member, a friend of the mother's.' But I knew because I was—"

"Cleaning!" I finish her sentence and we both laugh.

"Cleaning the kitchen!" she adds. "So I knew I was there for a purpose."

"How many would you guess? A hundred?"

"Oh, I would say. Mmhm."

"A hundred times."

"Yeah. Television shows, films, major films—and they paid off. Let me tell you, I wouldn't change anything about what has happened in my career. I'm very, very happy to have been able to explore the different types of women that provide a service."

"But you're also frustrated by it."

"I'm very frustrated."

"You talk about it. You talk about loving these women who you play and being frustrated by having to play those roles."

"Well, I think every actor gets to a point that they know any example of any good actor that you think, my god, I've never seen them like that, and they surprise everybody—because we all train and we train for various roles. And to me just the housekeeper, the maid. They try to assuage your anxiety, or whatever, agitation at it, by saying, 'Well, she's been with the family forever, and she's the confidante of the alcoholic white chick with the mansion, or the kid that's on drugs' or what have you. But nevertheless, it comes to a point where they automatically just say, 'She's a maid.'"

Lupe recalls auditioning for a role in an episode of the TV show *Veronica's Closet* and being told they wanted her to have a foreign accent because it's exotic. She can laugh about it now. Back then she played with the producers by doing a formal Spanish accent of an upper-class Spaniard.

"They said, 'Well, we don't want a Mexican accent.' What the hell do they know about a Mexican accent? Or a Peruvian accent or a Cuban accent? Come on, give me a break. You know what I'm saying? When you're only English-speaking, monolingual, then you don't really know what different accents sound like. Latinos, let's talk Latino. But I went in and I said, 'Okay. It's get-back time.' And I give them a Spanish accent. *Espaaaaaaaña*." She says that last word with a flourish and begins to laugh.

"Is it changing?"

"I think so, very slowly, very slowly. I think with the young talents that we have right now, like our America Ferreras and Eva Longorias and, I'm talking the feminine, the women. And the guys, you know, Jesse Garcia and all these kids that are—Freddy Fernandez and Jay Hernandez, and these young men that are coming in. They're bringing a whole different generation and a smarter, more in-tune kind of very Americanized style of acting. They're just as good as any other good actor. And they are given these good roles and I am happy for that."

"Did you help knock down the doors for them?"

"Well, I don't know that I knocked down the doors, but I refused to let the door knock me down."

I love the phrase and make a mental note to keep it in my head. I owe a debt of gratitude to Lupe, just like all those actresses do. She was once asked to change her name and briefly called herself Elia Monte. That morphed back to Lupe Ontiveros. Women like her are one of the reasons I can roll my eyes at a guy that wonders if I'd drop the María de la Soledad business. She is not bitter and that means a lot.

"I cannot complain. The world had opened up for me. If I had resisted it. . . . I'm glad I wasn't a raving beauty. Because I certainly wasn't a raving beauty. I'm still not a raving beauty. Anyway. It's just—that would have taken a toll, because many of my friends—I lost so many—many of my friends along the road. It was very painful for them to have to go continuously fighting against, against, against. They got tired of it. And their dreams vanished. And that's not fair . . . I'll work against it, and if not, then I'll work with it."

In fact, Lupe worked with the guy who asked her to change her name.

"I didn't even know what the hell he was talking about. In other words, he was saying, I think, 'You'll never be somebody interesting' or whatever. He just made it sound that way. Which you might equate it to being a maid. Because the system, the establishment, is not gonna ever accept you for anything other than [she ticks off on her fingers] a Latina, *chaparrita*, shorty, stubby, chubby, with an accent. You know?"

Oh, yeah. I know.

That weekend she is transported out to Fire Island by a group of gay men who have adopted her while she's in town to help with the Latino AIDS fund-raiser. Ever since her role in *Chuck and Buck* she says she has appreciated the generosity and good humor of gay men. She sits in the cold night at a wooden beach house joking about the lack of carbs in everyone's diet and tries to educate them all about immigration laws. Several of the men are from Latin America so they nod their heads in agreement when she shakes her cocktail glass in the air and condemns that *"Pinche pedazo de papel,"* that silly piece of paper that is a green card. She worries aloud that immigration is stratifying the community by levels of victimization. She had just been in Guadalajara for Eva's birthday and says it filled her with joy to see a generation of women so free from the burdens of the past but so up for the fights of the future.

The next night she wears a strapless ball gown with golden glitter and works the room at the AIDS fund-raiser. She tells the audience that in a previous life she was a man and she enjoyed every minute of it. They laugh hysterically. The event is in an ancient city building with a towering domed ceiling and dangling chandelier. She is like something out of a black-and-white movie.

The Latino Commission on AIDS was founded in 1990 and works with Latino communities in forty states and Puerto Rico. There are over 200,000 Latinos in the United States with HIV or AIDS. They are the fastest-growing ethnic group in the United States with AIDS, accounting for 14 percent of the U.S. population but 20 percent of

AIDS cases. Lupe's goal is to put a spotlight on that crisis, and that night's event has drawn together people from all areas who do not know that AIDS is the fourth leading killer of Latinos.

Phil Rotter, who is a young white orthopedic surgeon who looks like he's about twelve, is sitting in the audience. He saw five patients that morning and two were HIV-positive. He did not expect to treat people with HIV when he was studying orthopedic surgery but the medications needed to keep people with HIV alive are ruining their bones. At the podium with Lupe is Dennis DeLeon, the organization's president, whose face is mottled and marked from the effects of AIDS treatments. Dennis has been HIV-positive for twenty years and suffers from heart disease and diabetes brought on by his medications. The idea of Dennis on AIDS medications for so many years causes Lupe to shake her head as if she's angry at something. Phil has been stuck by needles twice and had to take the medicines as prevention. "It was the sickest I've ever felt in my life," he says. "I just can't imagine taking them every day."

Lupe has come to this event before. She sees it as a continuation of the work she did as a social worker long ago. Even though the event has a very somber purpose, she is in the best of moods. She has been asked to do some work for Planned Parenthood and is using the night as an opportunity to introduce some of their leadership to Latinos. The zipper of her strapless dress has disconnected almost to the top and is holding her together by a thread, so she's decided to stay at her table and beckon folks to come over. Rosie Perez is also sending folks her way, and Lupe looks both immensely proud and flattered that this saucy young Latina is in her camp.

Onstage, the lead singer of the band Bacilos has donned one of those small brimmed caps that reporters used in old movies. He is Jose Villamizar, a Colombian guy with a thin dark mustache and wispy black hair. The group won a Grammy with its Spanish rock album, *Mi Primer Millón* (*My First Million*). Young Latinos and their Anglo friends go wild for that sound of classic American rock mixing with a Latin beat. They have transformed Latin American groups into big multimillion-dollar stars in the United States. The crowd jumps onto the dance floor as Lupe's face breaks into a broad smile. Her shoulders move to the beat as Jose leans over, as if he's singing his popular lyrics to her. The song is about dreaming of making your first million by scoring with a big hit song. That's exactly what Lupe needs, a hit.

The following night I am invited to join the *50 Mas Bellos*—the 50 Most Beautiful—at the *People en Español* party thrown in their honor. It's my second event in twenty-four hours, so I shoehorn myself into a tight black gown and a pair of high heels I bought at the last minute. I made the *People* list in 2000 and the list of *People en Español* in 2004. But this is 2009.

It's intimidating on that runway. I wasn't exactly raised to be overly focused on my looks. It's not a thing of value in my family. And I didn't feel all that beautiful much of my life, with my kinky hair and smoky look. My hairdresser, Wendy Evans, travels with me everywhere I go, drying and styling my hair into the familiar layered anchor look but with a hint of style. I have an extensive wardrobe for these events. I can flash the toothy smile required of women on runways and I work out every morning at dawn. But I really don't care to do this stuff. It's just part of my job at this point.

My mother and father are there, sitting on tall stools inside surrounded by skinny people with tiny dresses. I decide to join them and navigate the catwalk later in the evening. The event is at the Edison in Manhattan, where the walls have black leather upholstery and everything has a shimmer to it. In one corner, women are dancing in silhouette and in the other, two guys in Panama hats are rolling cigars. Little pieces of raw fish on crackers are circulated through the crowd and the liquor flows freely. My mother has terrific rhythm and you can see by the way she's moving her shoulders that she could dance to this salsa music if she were up for it.

At some point the event reaches some kind of New York party climax. The crowd outside has become very large and traffic has slowed to a stop. The paparazzi are numerous and they hang over the rope line yelling in both Spanish and English. Mom is finding the whole thing highly amusing. She has on a red turtleneck with stripes and a white blazer but she looks totally at ease among the beauties. Dad has on his happy smile. It's really loud inside but they seem to be enjoying themselves. I realize that my parents are just happy to see me these days, to check in and make sure that I'm okay. They sound somewhat interested in what I'm doing but mostly they couldn't care less. What they want to hear about are

Brad and the kids. They want to talk about family—theirs, mine, and ours.

Eva walks the catwalk outside and it is the highlight of the event for the paparazzi and gawkers. Her hair hangs dead straight like some weighty expensive fabric and has that supermodel shine. There is not a line in her skin. She is wearing a beige dress and beige pumps by Blumarine with what my daughters would call sparkly things. It is a minidress that cuts off just below her hips to give her short body the look of having long legs. She flashes the anticipated smile but looks a bit like I do, like she's working.

Eva answers questions in respectable Spanish, then switches to English. She tells the editors she's flying to Cannes that evening and can't stay. She is asked how she feels being one of the most beautiful people in a Hispanic market, since it's the Spanish-language edition of the magazine. They point out that she speaks English and she "belongs to the general market."

"I definitely think I belong to the Mexican community more than any other community. So it's nice to be honored by the community I grew up with," she says tactfully. There is a look in her eyes that says "bye" and she is off in a flash.

I venture outside after she's done her walk and pull my parents to the corner of the red carpet so a photographer can take my picture with them, too. I can't tell really, but my mom looks like she's genuinely smiling. I have become used to doing a lot of events, but it's not like you're standing on a red carpet being snapped by paparazzi with your daughter every day. That makes the entire late-night event and the humbling experience of being surrounded by twentysomething beauties totally bearable. My mom's cheeks are puffing from the smile she's holding in and that feeling around her is always priceless.

My parents are getting on in age and it makes me feel good to make them happy every so often. They know some about the documentary and this book but they don't really ask a lot of questions. Some parents would want to comb every page, inspecting how they are represented. They had a chance to sit with my coauthor tonight for an hour, meet the publisher, and take in the event without me. They didn't really care to hear a thing. They just spent the night craning their necks for a sight of me. That's what makes them special.

They are like my personal L.A., the place you can retreat to where you know you'll fit in. The bar where everybody knows your name. They do not measure my success in how many flashbulbs pop or how my last piece of work is developing. They are just happy to spend time with me. They search for humility in the way I present myself in a crowd, want to know what I've done to help the world around me. They couldn't care less if I'm pretty. They know that. I'm their Soledad.

As I walk to my car with my arms around them, I feel fully centered. On the way home, my mother is looking at me like she's concerned. "It's so nice to see you," she says before we arrive at her home. The documentary is really exhausting. It's coast-to-coast flying. I have a lot of stories to keep track of and a big staff with a range of talents. The project is very important to the network, but even more so to me personally and I want it to do well. My mom skips past that and asks about Brad and the kids with even more concern. She gets that all this flying around means they are at home without me. She refers to an upcoming family reunion like a subtle reminder of family. I like that I'm sitting in the backseat like some kid with my arms around my parents.

My relationship with my mother is not always smooth. Even these little exchanges have a subtext. She expects a lot from me. She expects priorities—and Brad and the kids, my siblings, my parents are those priorities. Then comes my community and my faith, and the need to give back. Her expectations line up like planes on a runway. She also wants me to be successful and smart and studious. But those other things come first.

"Get some sleep," she counsels me.

"I can't sleep," I tell her. The difficult balance she is unearthing is very real. It is why I can't sleep. There are so many forces pulling me in so many ways. Like Eva, like Lupe, like so many other Latinas, I can't just see trouble and walk away. I want to do a good job and be a good mother. I ache over some of the things I'm learning on this journey through Latino America. I fight to balance what makes me happy with what makes me sad. My mother looks at me through one side of her eyes and pats my hand.

"Then get up and say your prayers," she says.

6

morir soñando

I TRAVEL TO the South Bronx on one of the first sunny Sundays of the year to meet fifteen-year-old Francisca Abreu and her mother, Isabel Valdez, and the baby they are bringing up in their apartment. The pulse of merengue music mixes with the traffic noise outside their home, the second floor of a spotless two-story Section 8. The neighborhood says Latin, from the smell of butter at Sindy's Bakery around the corner to the boys neck-high in smocks getting shape-ups at the barbershop. The Bronx is half Latino, half its residents speak Spanish, and half of those were born outside the United States. Yet they are living in a place that is very much American in nature. In fact, the Bronx is America gone extreme.

The South Bronx inflicts modern urban American stresses on its people in a way that only a poor, blighted U.S. city can. The South Bronx has been the recipient of wave upon wave of revitalization, most recently $3 billion invested by the city in 2002, that has improved the situation so much that community groups now complain about gentrification. But that has not changed the fact that the neighborhood is densely populated and plagued by high rates of poverty, substance abuse, and health crises, together with double the national average of teen pregnancy and a historic housing crisis.

From the time Irish and Italian bootleggers ran its saloons to the arrival of the Caribbean Latino immigrants who now make up half its population, the Bronx has been a place people work immeasurably hard to prosper. There is an energy here that makes me want to root for the home team, just like folks are hollering for the Yankees, who play in their brand-new stadium just a few blocks away. There is a

Francisca Abreu, fifteen, all dressed up for a fund-raiser for the Puerto Rican Family Institute, where she spoke publicly for the first time about her struggle with depression.

constant laughter in the streets, a sense that everyone is getting up every morning and giving it their all. The Bronx is a place where everyone seems to be smiling and playing ball outside, whatever may be going on behind closed doors.

When I enter their house, Francisca and her mother are dressed and pressed. I know they view me as this important TV personality but they seem to exhale slightly when I explain that I'm late because I have four little kids fussing because I ran out on breakfast. Kisses to the cheek are exchanged and I'm offered drinks and food and then we settle down to chat. The living room is as neat as they are, polished wood tables and chairs aligned just right and sofas set against the wall at a ninety-degree angle. The few pictures on the walls are carefully squared and there is not a toy in sight. No one really wants to talk about why we are here, so there is a lot of playing with the baby and comments about the apartment.

Five people share this small apartment that has three bedrooms carved out at the end of the hall but still feels roomy and neat. Isabel sleeps with her youngest son, Eddie, thirteen, in a room where the beds nearly touch. Her oldest, Rafael, nineteen, has a room that barely fits his twin bed and a dresser, and Francisca shares a room with her daughter, Destiny, who is five months old. Everyone in this house is Dominican. Xavier, Destiny's father, is a seventeen-year-old Puerto Rican kid who comes over and races around doing everything that could possibly be expected of a new father, including making *arroz con pollo* while we're chatting about him all of five feet away. The conversation is filled with pauses as people admire the baby's latest gurgle or smile or get up to attend to one of her needs. "It's all about her," says Xavier, who Francisca calls Savi. "She's like the center of everyone's attention."

She really is not. The birth of a baby to a girl so young has clearly thrown this family off balance. But the real tragedy in this family is what was swirling around in Francisca's head long before her teenage pregnancy. This very troubled young lady had decided she wanted to die. There is no quick way to open that conversation but you can tell from the way everyone is acting that it's already in the room.

Isabel's attention is equally divided between this new little girl and her own little girl. Isabel sometimes looks at Francisca as if she's the toddler and could fall down at any moment.

Francisca is in the throes of being a teenager. She sits fidgeting on the fringes of the conversation between the adults even though we are all here to talk about her. She has a shiny row of braces that accentuate the fact that she sometimes mumbles and giggles when she speaks. Her body is shapely, a combination of adolescent bloom and the fact that she delivered a baby five months ago. She is dressed in pink like her daughter but a more subdued tone, and she has the same dark shock of hair, except long and settled carefully behind a headband. Her hands fold neatly into each other on her lap as her legs arrange the way a proper girl's should. Her eyes wander from Destiny to her mother to her boyfriend, as if waiting to see who needs something from her next. The baby has dark frying-pan eyes with thick lashes. Destiny's skin is the color of caramel and has that furry baby feel that adults just love to touch.

Isabel finds her new granddaughter delightful and comments on how much she has warmed up the house. Yet there is no denying by Isabel's looks how little she wanted to see her sullen fourteen-year-old daughter with a baby. Isabel speaks very little English so our communication about her daughter is halting. Finally she sits down next to Francisca and hands me the baby, as if to communicate the weight of what she's facing. We both stare alternately at both girls and there is really no need to say anything more. She gets up quietly, walks into the kitchen and pours condensed milk, frozen orange juice, and ice into a blender. We each get a big glass of this sugary Dominican milk shake that has a name rich with meaning. It's called *Morir Soñando*—to die dreaming. And as soon as Isabel has a few sips, she begins to tell her tale.

Isabel was raised in a small town in the Dominican Republic by her very strict, very religious parents. She had a sister and brother and they played with what seemed to be an endless stream of cousins in the constant heat. Their weeks were marked by trips to church and school and evening meals with large groups of relatives. The men worked and the women were devoted 24/7 to their husbands and children.

"If a child coughed at night, it was the mother who got up, then made breakfast hours later, then took care of the house and the kids and the food so her husband could come home and rest," she remembers.

The kids all married young and made their own identical homes. No one was earning enough money, not enough to buy new clothes or enough food or do anything but watch the children play in the dirt all day.

Slowly, the extended families found ways to gain entry into the United States and left. Isabel's parents went, then her brother and sister. Soon, she found herself alone with her husband and three children in the town where she was raised, repeating a life her mother had decided to flee. Her parents obtained green cards and got jobs that earned them enough money to come visit. Isabel felt like nothing more than a twenty-nine-year-old housewife.

"My children ran around without shoes, playing with dirt on the patio," she said in Spanish. "I wanted to work. I wanted to give them something better. If you saw where I used to live it was obvious that any good mother would want more." She dreamed of being something more than a housewife.

So she left. She remembers the day she handed over her kids to her husband and a neighbor who babysits. Immigration restrictions wouldn't allow her to take them and promises spilled from her mouth about how she wouldn't be gone long and planned to bring all of them back to New York with her. Francisca didn't buy it. The three-year-old was hysterical, begging, clinging. The separation was heartbreaking. Isabel arrived in the Bronx with just a suitcase and all her family's pictures. She lived with relatives and got a job very quickly, despite knowing little English, and immediately found herself raising money to go back.

"I worked for plane tickets," she said. "Francisca missed me so much and I couldn't bear to hurt her like that. I went back and forth so many times. She stopped believing me when I swore I would come back. She was so upset that when I called she refused to talk to me on the phone because she said I lied." Isabel pulls out pictures of Francisca, her "Franny," and her brother when they were little. Big smiles reveal rows of perfect teeth. Then she shows me a picture taken of them on one of her visits home. "See how the little happy faces just became so sad," she says, her voice cracking painfully from the memory. "They didn't understand that I was doing this for them."

Isabel received a letter from U.S. Immigration granting her an appointment to consider a visa for one of her children. She couldn't understand why they would only hear the case of one child and not all of them. She brought all of them to the immigration office and got down on her knees and begged. "I remember my son had to get some shots and he screamed from the pain and Franny wanted so badly to come with me that she kept begging the doctor, 'Please give me the shots. Please let me go with mommy,'" she recalls. It was four years before Francisca was given permission to go.

The day Isabel brought her children to New York it was snowing and her sister came to pick them up. "I told them, here I can take you to the park. I can buy them fresh fruit. Back there we had no park, just weeds," she said. In the snow everything seemed very cold and unapproachable. As soon as they were unpacked, Isabel went back to work and the children were left with different relatives. Francisca was disoriented and lonely.

The noise in the Bronx was overwhelming. Francisca's brothers had an easier time adjusting than she did. Eddie, who was six and is now thirteen, cried when they asked him to speak English in school, yet in no time he had no accent at all. Rafael, who was twelve then and is now nineteen, began working almost immediately and now works in a supermarket. They became these delightful, curly-haired guys. Francisca was the exception.

From the time Francisca arrived in America she was sullen. She liked the new challenges that starting school brought and tried to make new friends. But she was shy in school and didn't quite feel like she fit in. She went from missing her mother to missing her father. She wanted desperately to do well and behave herself. Lots of kids spoke Spanish but they still seemed foreign to her. The TV shows, the language, the attitude was so different. The boys responded by becoming more brash and Isabel and her family commended them for being outgoing and mature. Francisca was told not to be outspoken and flashy like the other girls. She was reminded every day that she was not to dress like them and be out without permission.

Even though Francisca was surrounded by family it wasn't the family she knew. Although everyone was giving her directions, they worked long hours and had little time to spend with her at home. Isabel worked two jobs and sometimes a third on weekends. Francisca felt like her mother was never home. Isabel felt like she was trying so hard.

"I'd get up early and come home to eat when they were asleep and then go work, then weekends I would work. I was with them but I wasn't with them. I really was seeing them a few hours on the weekend at most. They had come all the way to be with me and they weren't with me," she said. At first, Isabel was a home attendant caring for the elderly. Then she cared for children. She was caring for other people's children but she couldn't care for her own. The irony destroyed her. She knew the whole thing was unwinding. She could see the unsettled look in her children's eyes, their anger building.

Francisca says she felt completely at loose ends. Her mother was working so hard so she wanted to please her. But her mother's expectation that she would be a quiet, studious teenager who stuck close to home just didn't connect to the world she was now living in. Her new friends were "crazy," she said.

"They didn't answer to anyone. We would skip school and no one would even notice. If I wanted any attention at all in class, I had to be really aggressive and that wasn't me. I didn't fit in anywhere. My mother was only there for long enough to tell me to behave. I was lonely. I was sad. I was confused." She started to feel pain behind her eyes, headaches that were unbearable. She would fight with her brothers and fight with her mother. She could never be the girl her mother wanted her to be yet could never be the girl her friends expected her to be. There were days she would just sit in her room in the darkness and cry.

When Isabel sensed something was wrong at home she worked fewer hours, and only when the kids were at school or asleep. She wanted to be around when her children were home.

"I came to this country because I wanted the best for them and I knew the way to get it was to work, but I had to try to be there for them," she said. But even when she was home, Francisca barely spoke to her. "She would write by herself, almost never came and talked to people. I would ask her what was wrong and all I'd hear is how much she missed her father," she said. "She really adores him." Isabel made an effort to bring the children's father to the United States, but he was indecisive and the four years of separation had destroyed their relationship. "All of this here would not be so hard if you could split the work in two, but with just one of me it was really difficult," she said. "I could see that Francisca had some problems but all I knew about dealing with problems in teenagers was to discipline them."

One day a counselor at school called and said that there was an emergency with Francisca at school. Isabel said she expected to hear that her daughter was making trouble, so she went in angry. When she heard what the counselor had to say, she was speechless. Her daughter was suicidal. She looks away when she recounts that story as if there is profound shame in what she is saying. She recalls how angry she was when the counselor told her they could not share personal information with her about Francisca. "What personal information? Here they value the children more than the parents. They are on their side. There is no personal information about your children. They are your children," she says angrily. The counselor said they had called her only because Francisca had revealed something they were required to report. Isabel said the school hadn't even noticed she wasn't there, when she had plenty of opportunities to try to hurt herself.

The school told her that in February of 2007, when she was just twelve years old, Francisca had written herself a note in science class saying that she wanted to die. The teacher confiscated the note and called the guidance counselor, who called Isabel. Francisca said she was hospitalized from March 5 to 9. She began counseling at the Puerto Rican Family Institute, a nonprofit health and human services agency that has been working with Latino families for nearly fifty years. Isabel is still not totally clear on what had happened.

Isabel says Francisca had spoken of two "attempts" at committing suicide while she was twelve. Francisca told us that she had taken some of her mother's pills and all they did was keep her awake. Once she had also cut herself with a knife. She had told her friends she was a very depressed person and "didn't want to live."

By the time Francisca resumed school she was taking medication that helped lift her spirits. Her grades began to rise. Even as her daughter's depression was slowly lifting, the mental health treatment process was a mystery to Isabel.

"In my country, if a kid is depressed you give them a good slap and tell them to get with it," she said. "Here they send you to a doctor for everything. . . . What do we gain by confronting those things or confronting the people? You just draw attention to the problem.

Here, everything gets fixed with a call to the police or a call to the doctor," she said. "That's not how we are."

Isabel wanted to believe that everything was getting better. Francisca was almost thirteen and had gotten her period. She was looking less like a child and more like a teenager. Isabel noticed Francisca had stopped hanging out with some of her girlfriends, girls whom Isabel considered a bit loose. She had also begun spending time with a boy named Xavier, fifteen, who seemed very sweet.

Isabel remembers the day: April 10, 2007. Francisca said she was going to the park to meet a friend, but to her mother the story didn't make sense. Isabel headed for the park and as she walked across the grass she could see her daughter from a distance, sitting on a bench next to Xavier, the two of them hugging. It was just a hug but Isabel knew exactly what this meant. This was almost as bad as the suicidal thoughts and the warnings from the counselor. This was her thirteen-year-old daughter, the girl whose heart she had broken by going away, the girl whom she cried over all those years. She was working hellish hours raising someone else's children so Francisca could have a place to live and food to eat. But she was never home for her. The sense of guilt pained her. Isabel stopped by a tree to steady herself. Then the tears came and she had to inhale a few times before she could muster the will to confront them. She knew what that hug meant.

Francisca's mother begged her to not be with that boy. "I don't want people talking about you like you are one of those other girls," she said between tears. Francisca had been seeing him all of sixteen days, but it was the best she'd felt in such a long time. Francisca remembers how angry her mother was but also that she planned in her head how she would be able to keep seeing Xavier. "I missed my father. I missed having a family. No one was home. His family was really big and really warm. He was so funny. The boys in his house would write songs and they'd all sing together. His family is crazy. It was nice how they were always together."

Francisca began skipping school to be with Xavier and she'd have her friends cover for her. They began to have sex and he told her he didn't like condoms. She told me that he wanted her to get pregnant. She worried about getting pregnant but felt powerless to do anything about it. On March 2, 2008, on her birthday, Francisca woke up dizzy. She read a book that said her breasts would be tender if she was pregnant and they felt funny. Xavier's aunt gave her a pregnancy test and she went to a clinic to confirm the result. Francisca and Xavier put the pregnancy test down on Isabel's dining room table and waited for her to come home. Francisca expected her mother would scream at her, hit her, and send her to the Dominican Republic. "My mother is very strict. She has a temper. I knew this was going to be very bad," she said.

Isabel thought it was a bad joke.

"Then I had a minor nervous breakdown. I really just caved," Isabel said. "I couldn't eat. I just cried. I'd wake up hoping it wasn't so. We fought a lot. She wanted me out of her life."

Isabel's parents are Pentecostal, deeply religious people. Isabel is a Catholic. No question about it, Francisca was going to have the baby. Isabel forced herself to prepare, trying to support her daughter even as her anger consumed her.

"It's easier here to have a baby. They help you. In my country you might as well jump off a bridge. Her high school has day care. They think it's totally normal for them to have kids and still be in school. In the DR, they have kids so they can escape home and get a different life. Here they do it for pleasure. I kept telling myself that at least he was a nice boy. She's fallen in love and chased his kisses. All I could think was that now she would spend her days cooking and cleaning," Isabel said.

Isabel had left the Dominican Republic to give her children a better life, so they could go to school and have a future, and now her daughter was facing motherhood at fourteen. Isabel consoled herself by deciding she would try to teach her to be a good one. "She is not just a woman because she wears a skirt. She needs to learn how to run a household now. I told myself that I would teach her what this meant. Here, being a woman means having a man. That's what she'd done. She'd become an American woman. Well, in the DR you are responsible for more than that. She needs to learn how to be a woman now, a person who takes responsibility for what she does."

Her story echoed in my head. I remember my mother's voice: "Where did I get all these little Americans?" Her anger seemed recognizable to me, the kind of over-the-top anger you reserve for someone you love in immeasurable amounts. My mother could never be fully satisfied with me even if I did all the things that seemed to satisfy mothers in general. Her disappointment was always laced with anger. I was succeeding on American terms, the terms she had laid before me and my siblings. Yet at the same time she was a proud black Cuban woman. So what did she expect me to be? And how could I be two so different things?

Here was Francisca, pulled from both ends but with none of the many resources I had. She was pushed to be close to a mother who seemed so far away. And she was asked to succeed in an American environment while living in one that was so clearly Latin American. Now she'd done something that was so clearly wrong by her mother's standards while fighting off a feeling that she was so inadequate all around. And she was in trouble for not acting like the obedient child she was yet being asked to act like an adult to deal with the consequences. How devastating the day Francisca told her mother she was pregnant must have been all around.

As Isabel is telling the story, she looks over at Xavier, who is chopping chicken for the *arroz con pollo* and half listening with that smile teenagers get when they think they know better. Xavier has been in and out of trouble a few times and says he used to run with a tough crowd. Meeting Francisca gave his life a new focus. He took night classes to obtain a GED and started to work days, most recently at an auto shop. He wants to quit school to become a security guard. By the time Destiny was born, Xavier was seventeen. He wants to marry Francisca and have more children. He is very proud of being a family man. He has no regrets about getting Francisca pregnant. He wanted to grow up fast and is very dismissive when anyone asks him if they are too young to have a family. He seems very much in charge of what he is doing.

"They think like children," Isabel says. "They come home every day and play family." Isabel watches Xavier change and feed his daughter. I ask if I can meet his mother and he says, "You already have met her, the Dominican version," and smiles at Isabel.

Francisca is not as attentive to the baby as Xavier is and is more than ready to hand her off when it's time. She's frustrated that Destiny seems more attached to her father. She seems a bit distant from Xavier herself and she confides that he overwhelms her a bit. He doesn't leave. It hadn't occurred to Francisca that he was going to be around like this. Xavier keeps talking about some faraway future and about other children. Francisca asked Xavier to use a condom for the first time about six months after her child was born. Then a doctor offered her a shot of Depo Provera, which threw her period out of whack for months.

I ask Francisca how things are with her mother now that she is a mother herself and she smiles. "I get her now. I really do. I understand how she must feel about me." Isabel and Francisca spend a lot more time together now, and Isabel says, "I can't be away from her ever again. I don't care what I have to do." Francisca responds but talks instead about her own daughter. "My daughter will never be left anywhere without me. I don't even want her in day care. My mother can be with her."

The dynamic between the two is a back-and-forth of unrealizable expectations. Isabel wants Francisca to be a sweet, obedient, pious girl, grounded in faith and family and looking to fulfill the future her mother has set out for her. Instead she is depressive and a teen mother and Isabel hasn't changed her expectations one bit. Francisca wants a mother who is attentive and happy, lighthearted and understanding of the culturally different environment in which they now live. Instead, Isabel is sour from lack of sleep and a tough disciplinarian who acknowledges she knows only one way to raise a daughter, the way her mother raised her back on the island. Now there is this baby between them who both unites and divides them further. They share a love of her and a responsibility for her and their power struggles are halted by their dependence on each other. Their fights now end in silence as often as they end in hugs.

Just as Destiny is beginning to show signs of needing a nap, I say good-bye. Isabel and Francisca can pick up their sacred Latina mother-daughter dynamic once again. I know their love-hate tension so well. I've seen it in so many Latinas like me. But what I did not know, and what weighs me down as I walk out of their home, is seeing how it bears down on people of scant resources. A dynamic that gives Latinas so much good can also create stresses that can break a young woman and blur her judgment. I walk over to Sindy's Bakery around the corner to buy my children some sweet flan from the Bronx, the kind of food I would be able to cook if that particular Latina gene had made it to me. I think about how they will smile when they see that Mommy brought home a treat. Thank goodness they don't know the story Mommy was reporting when she went to buy it.

There is no way I can understand this part of the story without thinking about my own mother. There have been days recently when she just stops talking to me. Usually it boils down to the fact that I didn't call or I didn't call often enough. I think it's curious to punish me by just shutting me out altogether. But it makes perfect sense on some level if you're the child of a strong-willed Latina.

There is a woman in the Bronx, Dr. Rosa Gil, who calls the Latina mother-daughter relationship the "Maria Paradox." This Maria knows exactly what she's talking about. I am neither the Virgin Mary nor Mary Magdalene. I'm another Maria in between, the Maria who can never be what my hardworking mother who sacrificed everything for me wants me to be. Whatever they may be, and I'm not quite sure what, these expectations are unreachable. Would it have helped had I been dunked fully gowned in the baptismal font of a sacred Latin American church? I don't know. What if I'd danced with a court of well-dressed teenagers at a traditional *Quinceañera*? Perhaps things would be different. We weren't at all like that as kids and no one explicitly asked us to be. How can your mother expect you to be *that* girl if you live in a place like *this*? When you live in this country of short skirts and sexy music lyrics and parents who are much more detached than my own?

I was an American kid, speaking English and dating boys of every color. When I went to college I made an effort to be regular. Rather than being thought of as special I wanted to be known as someone who worked hard, the girl who could realize her dreams, who could balance the two Marias. In many ways, we Latinas spend our lives striking this balance. We celebrate the Latin things about us that bring us comfort and happiness, the smell of our cooking and the large family gatherings, the optimism and good humor, the way we connect with other human beings from a place of humility and warmth. We try to reject our insecurities and our feeling of discomfort and not fitting in. We try to thank our mothers for their guidance, even for the pressure they place on us that comes with mountains of good intentions. And we try not to buckle from the weight of their expectations.

I went back to the Bronx on another weekend to meet Dr. Rosa Gil and some of her patients. I wanted to explore further the world of the Marias who live on the brink, the Latinas like Francisca who are overcome by the emotional weight of what's expected of them and what is so out of reach. The journey itself says so much about the way Latinas live in this country, split by a socioeconomic divide. I live in Manhattan, an island of great successes, where downtown is mostly home to the wealthy. I take the number 3 subway up to a section of the Bronx far north from where Francisca lives. My train emerges onto an elevated line at Jackson Avenue, exploding into sunshine, graffiti, and public housing complexes with small rows of windows covered by child safety bars.

As I make my return to the Bronx, everybody begins to look like me and Spanish fills the air. The building that houses Dr. Gil's program was put up in 1902, right by the subway line and down the block from the entrance to the Bronx Zoo. "They used it to house women out of wedlock who they wanted out of the way," she explains as we step into the institutional green halls. Her program, Life Is Precious, gets money to provide family services. They host domino tournaments to attract the fathers and food and conversation to engage the mothers. They are trying to build an Internet café because the teenagers live on MySpace. Their logo is two hands caressing a heart. They advertise pet therapy, knitting and horticulture, mask making, jewelry class, and art. There is nothing written or displayed anywhere that would spell out their mission: trying to reduce suicide attempts by Latina teens.

In this building decorated with delicate hearts Dr. Gil is treating a lot of Franciscas. One is a girl who speaks to her mother long after the woman's death. "To an Anglo that may mean she is hallucinating but in our culture it's not uncommon to believe in spirits," she explains. From the grave the mother continues to press her daughter to be humble and to have *pudor*, a great word for being chaste. The girl feels like a disappointment. Another girl feels like her mother works so hard that she can never be perfect enough to justify the sacrifice. You hear that story often from Latina teens and it's an immigrant thing.

Something dreadful is coming of this dynamic among Latina teens. These girls have been referred to this program because they have either tried to kill themselves or talked so much about it that someone got very scared.

"Latino youth are most likely to report feeling sad or hopeless at 36 percent overall and 42 percent in Latina girls," Dr. Glenn Flores, a professor of Pediatrics and Public Health at the University of Texas Southwestern Medical Center, reported to the Centers for Disease Control and Prevention in a 2007 study. According to Dr. Flores, one in six Latina girls ends up actually attempting suicide. "Indeed, in the past year," he said, "one out of every 25 Latina teens made a suicide attempt that resulted in an injury, poisoning or overdose."

These are breathtaking numbers of children so depressed they think of ending their lives just as they're on the brink of becoming adults.

Dr. Luis Zayas is the director of the Center for Latino Family Research at Washington University in St. Louis. He has been studying two hundred Latina teen suicide attempters, the largest study on Latina youth and suicide in the country, research funded by the National Institute of Mental Health. According to 2000 data from the National Household Survey on Drug Abuse, the teenagers most likely to attempt suicide are U.S.-born Latinas age fourteen to fifteen (22.6 percent), giving Latinas the terrible distinction of being more likely to attempt suicide than any major ethnic or racial grouping.

In the mid- to late seventies Dr. Zayas worked in mental health clinics in the Bronx. He says he saw girls in the emergency rooms and outpatient clinics who had attempted suicide and a high number seemed to be Latinas. He wasn't sure if it meant something so he began to do some research and found no information. He began calling other clinics and asking other doctors. Everyone had seen the same thing. He finally turned to the CDC for data. "In the 2007 survey we had fourteen percent of all high school Latinas reporting that they had made a suicide attempt, fourteen percent compared to roughly nine to ten percent of African-American girls and eight percent of non-Hispanic white girls." The peak was in 1995, he says, when the rate was twenty-one percent versus ten or eleven percent of black youth girls and white girls.

Dr. Zayas is a handsome man with hair speckled with gray and a soft goatee. He speaks the language of a researcher who knows the answers he seeks could be the key to saving lives. Dr. Zayas believes that the relationship of a Latina with her mother is the determining factor in how they handle adolescent distress. He suspects that Latina teens are particularly at risk because Latino families are heavily invested in a culture of family unity that runs in conflict with American values. Latinos expect their children to show deference, they want their girls to guard their sexuality, and they exact authoritarian discipline on children who reject their values.

"The girl is out in our society attending school, watching television, being exposed to very different models about what girls should do and can do and are permitted to do. And so that's where we begin to see a level of conflict emerge," Zayas said. "Now we have to put this in the context of what happens to teenagers. What we do know about teenagers, and this is the overarching idea, is that adolescence is a period where the young person struggles between how free I am, how autonomous I am as a person and how much I stay connected to my parents, or my family."

Zayas's profile of the typical Latina who attempts suicide, that fourteen- or fifteen-year-old, is likely to be the U.S.-born daughter of immigrant parents who are low-income, have limited education, and are not adapting to this country as rapidly as their children. The profile is very similar to Francisca. But the teenage daughters of other immigrant groups have not been affected the same way. What makes Latinas different is their particular way of centralizing family in their lives. While some immigrant families celebrate their children meeting American teenage milestones, Latinos relate every step their children take away from them as a rejection of the family unit. Where some teenagers may be applauded for getting a driver's license, Latinos don't understand why their child would want to go anywhere without a parent, sibling, or cousin. Where are they going that they'd need to drive themselves?

In his studies, Zayas calls it "familism," quoting a word from Dr. Gil's research, this need for the family to be the guiding force of every girl's life, to create intense attachments to relatives and be primary in the teen's self-identity and social world. To stick so close to family, Gil said, girls have to avoid sexualization and brashness, they need to be "passive, demure and hyper-responsible for family obligations, unity and harmony." If a girl feels she has breached family integrity, the stage is set for her suicide attempt.

In this country, Zayas says, families are experienced quite differently than in the mother country. American girls are bombarded with a popular culture that views them as sexy and expects them to be assertive. Independence comes hand in hand with the U.S. adolescent experience. Schools are very child-centered. Teens get more privacy, more rights, and more privileges as they get older. Latina teens who try to embrace that culture get angry and frustrated and act out because their parents, particularly their mothers, hold to a culture that expects them to contain their anger and show deference to their parents.

"Familism is a very strong bond between the parent and the child and among family members. So the girls that we're talking about are socialized in that and they do appreciate the level of familism and the sense of togetherness the parents are trying to instill in them. There's never been any hint that they're opposed to it. But what happens is that familism faces an adolescent who is changing, who is becoming this freer or more independent person in a context in which there are other social contexts in which there are other prevailing values, such as we see on television in the U.S. and our different take on the family and on how adolescents should and shouldn't behave."

That complexity is not only evident among girls who attempt suicide. Look at how high teen pregnancy rates have soared among Latinas, despite prevalent Catholicism and intense supervision. The rate of teen pregnancies for Latinas in 2004 was twice the national average. The National Campaign to Prevent Teen and Unplanned Pregnancy estimates that 53 percent of Latinas will be pregnant at least once by age twenty, compared to 31 percent in the general teen population.

"Here in the U.S. our emphasis on what you want to do when you grow up is to be a lawyer, a psychologist, a social worker, what have you, and the emphasis in many Latino cultures is when you become an adult you're going to be a parent. There is a subtle difference there but it is about what adulthood means," says Zayas. The teen pregnancy rates and birth rates are higher than they are for any other racial or ethnic group. So much for *pudor*.

"The family is the core of the Latino experience," says Dr. Gil. "We ask girls who their role model is and no one says J.Lo. They all say a struggling woman in their own family. It is clear immediately who these girls are failing to please."

Dr. Gil escorts me into a conference room where teenage Latinas are eating snacks with their counselors and parents. Every girl looks out of the corner of her eye to her mother, as if asking for permission to even breathe. As I accompany them to a discussion session in the next room, two moms whisper under their breath to the daughters. *"Cuídate,"* says one. Take care of yourself. *"Ten cuidado,"* says another. Be careful.

Dr. Gil glances my way. "Back in 1998 I already knew that Latinas had a high suicide rate," she tells me. "Then it went from ten to fourteen percent and I was like 'where will this go?' The girls are no-shows in the mental health clinics. The staff doesn't know the nuances of a Latino family, that you don't seek help for these things. And the schools don't help. They see something wrong and they complain to the mothers and here are these mothers who went through hell to get here and now they're being told their daughters are a failure. Girls are not supposed to speak up when things go wrong. They are supposed to express humility." Dr. Gil talks about the Maria Paradox and tells me about a woman she knows, a brilliant thirty-seven-year-old Wall Street lawyer up for partner who dreams her grandmother is telling her she was supposed to have ten kids. "Everyone talks about machismo," she says. "This is Marianismo."

As we follow the girls, Gil and I smile at each other like we both know what we're about to hear. When people used to tell my parents we were so great, my mom used to say, "Well, there's this list of things that aren't so great." The expectations of us were so high. Yet to get my mom to say her kids all went to Harvard was so painfully hard. Humility was so important. But in this country, I always thought, humility doesn't work.

All nine of the girls in the meeting have a drama unfolding inside. I decide not to use their last names even though their parents have signed release forms. These girls have enough going on.

The first girl to talk is Alex, who is sixteen and of Puerto Rican descent. Her mom died when she was two and she now lives with her seventy-six-year-old grandmother. "She grew up in the thirties or forties and I'm growing up in 2000," she says. "She wants me to be some proper young lady." She is slinking down in her seat, a T-shirt with fading logo wrinkling into her tummy. Her hair is everywhere. She is a large girl who looks like someone who feels very small.

Next to speak is fourteen-year-old Stephanie. Her parents have split. She says her mother doesn't tolerate a speck of dust in her house and rides her about her grades. When the teachers called her mother about a D, her mother wanted to sit in her classroom to see what was going on. The other girls look aghast at the idea of a mother sitting in their classroom in front of all their peers, but Stephanie's mother thought it was a normal thing for a mother to do when her daughter's future seemed at risk. I tell her about how my mother used to wear this weird hat that looked like a skunk with circles and how she taught at my high school and was always around. Everyone nods knowingly.

Then comes Ashley, fourteen, with an Ecuadorian mother and a Dominican dad. Her mother had her when she was sixteen but Ashley can't have boyfriends. Her mother shows off her baby picture to her girlfriends and tells other mothers when she has her period. She can't understand why you don't do that here. The girls look horrified. I decide it's time to take the conversation beyond teenage angst and cultural divides. "I know that one of the reasons people come here is because they've tried to commit suicide. I know that some of you may have felt that way." Natalia is fourteen but she is the only one to fill the silence that follows my comment. "Coming here to start a better life is really difficult. They want a better future for us," she says. Stephanie pipes in. "They expect their children to do better but they come to a whole new lifestyle here. They don't understand their kids." They are all talking about their parents to avoid talking about themselves.

Ashley jumps in and suddenly it's very painful to listen. "I tried suicide," she says, and even the most fidgety of the girls falls silent. The words just hang in the air. I bow my head toward her. She is a beautiful girl, her hair with highlights that only happen naturally when you're a young girl. She is small enough that she still looks like a child, young enough to play. "I got tired of having dreams and hopes and they just get destroyed. You prefer ending it than suffering it. It's hard to see other people succeeding. Our mothers are more aware of their daughters." She has not been alive long enough to have given up on any dream she may have at this young age. But she seems so certain that she won't get there. In her world, opportunities come and go in the blink of an eye. The counselor writes me a note that Ashley's mother has also tried to commit suicide. Says she is not doing well. I stop asking her questions.

Then Alex speaks up. "We can't talk to a lot of people about our problems. Our parents aren't from here and they won't understand." Somewhere nearby a heavy door closes and the conversation just rolls to a stop. We return to the room with the mothers and the girls file back in and sit in chairs next to them. The mothers' eyes follow them as they enter the room and then they put a protective arm around each of their shoulders and resume eating junk food and cake.

Dr. Gil is studying how mental health service providers can better treat the Latino community. She said that she has learned over and over again the depth of the importance Latinos place on family. "In the process of acculturation and assimilation, the stress that is put on the family nucleus breaks it down," says Gil.

"Something happens in the tenth to fifteenth year of being in this country to the family structure that it begins to buckle." It's ironic that Latino immigrants achieve a better economic life here but find the strength of their families eroded. Gil has watched this play out in rising dropout rates, teen pregnancies, drug use, and incidents of attempted suicide—problems many of these families did not experience in their homeland. The fewer resources women have to cope with life's stresses, the worse the problems.

Gil began her career giving therapy to professional women.

"The Maria Paradox was based on successful, educated women," she says. "I didn't see women who were thinking of suicide. What I saw were women who were very depressed, who struggled with gender issues, who were having trouble balancing the expectation to be good mothers and good wives versus their desire for mainstream, professional success. They became conflicted." Her clients were not easy to reach. Their gut told them that they were not well and should see a doctor. But they do not naturally trust doctors who are disconnected from their family structure.

"We were taught to keep a physical distance between ourselves and the patients but that doesn't work. I'd put my arms around them and say, '*Qué pasa*,' and the other doctors would say into the waiting room, 'Mrs. Garcia, I'm ready for you.'"

One year, Dr. Gil was assigned to work with Puerto Rican mothers in Brooklyn whose elementary-school-age children were acting out. She gave them appointments to show up at one p.m. and, as each week went by, fewer of them would come. After four weeks she had lost them all. So she decided to do home visits. She found most of them eating lunch and watching *telenovelas*. Not dissuaded, she suggested they eat and watch together. "They started by talking about the *telenovela* and in a few weeks they were talking about their own *telenovela*. One of them now has a master's degree and every one of them has a good job or has graduated from something. I realized working with them that if their kids had a problem it was because they had a problem. But to get at that I needed to be able to have *familismo* with them, to make eye contact and have physical moments, to be part of their world."

When she began working with teenagers, Dr. Gil saw similar stresses and tried to address them in similar ways. But the teens she met didn't have the resources or educational levels of her past clients.

"Poverty and class is superimposed on immigration and acculturation issues. That is what is affecting the young Latina," she says. "When you are living in a one-bedroom apartment with ten people and your mother works all day and the school is complaining about you . . . what makes them different [from other poor teenagers] is that they very much need a community within which they can deal with this and this is one community of color that does not hold together well. We have Peruvians and Puerto Ricans who don't feel like they are the same yet they are all Latinos in this racist society. We do not melt into the pot easily. We don't even talk about assimilation. There are too many of us for that. We talk about acculturation because we are walking in two worlds."

The suicide attempts themselves are another thing we don't talk about. *El Diario La Prensa*, the nation's oldest Spanish-Language daily newspaper, commissioned a series by reporter Elaine Rivera in 2006 that was lauded by the *New York Times* as having uncovered this terrible phenomenon, yet so little other press shed light on the crisis.

"I had been seeing these statistics about Latinas having high dropout rates and Latinas having these high pregnancy rates and then I saw an article about the suicide rates and I began to ask myself whether there was something going on with Latina teenagers as a group," Elaine said.

"As I asked people in general and mental health people, they confirmed everything that I'd suspected. There was this one demographic and it existed in places all over the country of these first-generation Latinas or who came here little. They were in denial about suicide, denial and emotionally all over the place. You could see them getting agitated just talking about it. It was easier for them to talk about everything else, teen pregnancy, fighting with people, everything but suicide."

In Lansing, Michigan, I meet one of our Garcias, Noelle, a tall, pretty girl with long dark hair who had suffered from depression and thoughts of suicide. Noelle is very serene, quick to smile, and has a calming manner. She is clearly sincerely religious and seems centered and mature. She plans to marry this summer. She shows me photos from when she was twelve, thirteen, and fourteen. She's right when she tells me she dressed like a forty-year-old frump in roomy dresses. She looks much older than her age, twenty-five. She also looks unhappy. I point that out to her and she agrees. You can see it in her eyes. Her mouth is smiling but I've analyzed my own kids enough to know she's not smiling; she's putting her mouth into a smile.

Noelle's mother is white; it's her father who is the Latino. He is Mexican and has told her that he's faced some very real racism along the way. She felt a little unloved by her parents, who adopted Mexican children. She felt like maybe she wasn't Mexican enough.

"I always ask my dad why he never taught me Spanish," she tells me.

"You don't speak Spanish?" I ask.

"Not very well. I can speak enough to get by, but my dad never spoke it to us growing up and he said the reason that he didn't is he fought all his life to lose his accent because it was constantly, you know, discrimination, discrimination, and he said, you know, if they had an accident they automatically assumed that because he was Mexican that he was uneducated, or lazy."

Noelle's father had the best of intentions and she ended up feeling like she had fulfilled them by learning to speak good, unaccented English, yet still missed the mark by not learning Spanish. It was such a familiar story line. She takes me from one issue to another with her father and his unmet expectations. A lot of them are about being tortured over not being the right kind of Latina. At the same time she hated her body. It didn't fit the image she had of how she should be. Noelle began to cut herself. She was suicidal and depressed.

"There's a lot of pressure in the Latino community to look a certain way, I think that's a big thing, you're struggling between cultures and Hispanic culture to an extent. Your family is so close. So everybody knows everything unless you're hiding in the closet, which is what I did. Everybody knows everything about you, there's no real escape. And I think that there's such a pride in the Hispanic community to not get counseling, to not get help," she said.

Religion has lifted her out of this dreadful funk that caused her to maim her own body and hate herself. She sings beautifully and dreams of counseling Latina teens on how to get past their demons.

Someone suggested we take Noelle to the Bronx to meet some of the teenagers we've interviewed. I laugh thinking about the image of her meeting Francisca and walking around the projects of the Bronx, this squeaky-clean girl who comes from Memphis and sings inspirational music to wash her blues away. Francisca might think she is wonderful. Or she might think she's a nut. Noelle's fiancé is half Puerto Rican and she is clearly in love. Francisca could relate to that feeling of being transported by your emotions to some new place, of meeting someone who might just rescue you. But for Noelle it's a mature love. The way she looks at life now is from the vantage point of a grown-up, a person who embraced her God and got herself to a place where she could cope with what ailed her.

"I'm going to feel good about myself. I'm going to get it together. I'm going to realize that me blaming my appearance on other people or just feeling so trapped with something that I could get out of, that I could work on that. It was within my control to a certain extent," she declares. "And just that feeling of empowerment would come so much later that at the time I just couldn't see that. I couldn't see that eventually one day things were going to get better."

The next time I see Francisca and Isabel it's Mother's Day. I want to see what Mother's Day looks like in this very vulnerable family. My own children have wrapped bathroom things like soap in Christmas paper and we have had a happy breakfast together. Here in the Bronx children walk the streets with cellophane balloons and bundles of red roses in crisp white paper from the corner bodega. To mark this special day, Isabel's parents have come to visit. Her father is a quiet guy who spends the afternoon watching the Yankees play Baltimore. Her mother, Altagracia (high grace), has dressed in a sharp red dress and has her hair perfectly combed into a neat bun atop her head. Francisca is out with Xavier walking baby Destiny, now six months old, around the park with bottles of formula at the ready.

As soon as I walk in, Isabel begins mixing up another round of *Morir Soñando* and begins talking about her day. Francisca and Eddie gave her red roses and Rafael gave her $100 to replace the cell phone she had lost. She remarks that he presented it in a card that cost $5.41, which she considers a waste of good money. As she passes round the milk shake, she begins to talk about "that boy," Xavier. Francisca is still having postpartum depression and he is asking about moving in, she says. Her daughter has just begun to take Zoloft to deal with life's stresses. "He wants to live here but I have enough kids already," she says. "Him living here is not the same as him being here all day. He buys everything for the baby now. But if he moves in, the next thing will be that I'll have to support the baby and him, too. Francisca doesn't want him to move in either and I really don't want them to get married."

Isabel's father yells over his shoulder between innings in the game. "Gringos kick their kids out as young as possible," he says, referring to Xavier, whom he considers a gringo since he and his parents were all born in the United States. Then he drifts back into his game so Altagracia is left to finish his thought.

"We hold very tight to our children," she explains. "My children, I give them love. We are a nest. We worry about each of them when they have problems. Their problems are our problems. Their happiness is my happiness. There is not a day that goes by that I'm not in touch with what my kids are doing."

Her life philosophy spills out easily as it is something she is deeply proud of. It becomes clear that Isabel, who has left her husband and works full-time, is living a Maria Paradox of her own. "In our country the fathers work and the mothers don't work. That doesn't change here, because even when the mothers have to work their children are still their chief accomplishment, not their job," Altagracia says, staring at Isabel, whose daughter was pregnant at fourteen. Isabel dips her head as if in shame. "When my children misbehaved, when they even thought about misbehaving," she says, "I'd make them kneel. I'd hit them and they would go off someplace to sit where there is no TV. There is a line that they may not cross."

Isabel stares across the room at her mother and says to me: "If I had come home pregnant, she would have killed me. In the DR, it would have been so hard for Francisca. A life is more possible here. Maybe that is why the girls come out pregnant. Because they can. There they say you should get married before you have sex. Here they learn they should have sex and someday they may get married."

Altagracia says that back home children could fear and love their parents at once. "You respect your mother, you worry about what she'll think, you worry if what you say might give her a heart attack," she says. Isabel replies that "every mother sacrifices because they want everything for their children. Something happens and you think the world is going to fall in. I was embarrassed to tell the neighbors about Francisca being pregnant. I was embarrassed that anyone would know and think it's my fault. I was most embarrassed to tell my mother."

Just before I'd arrived, Francisca had let her grandmother feed Destiny before taking her out for a walk. She sat on the couch, next to her mother, her daughter, and her grandmother, four generations of women together on Mother's Day. While Francisca's mother and grandmother chatted in Spanish about Destiny, she turned to our producers and declared that her Mother's Day wish was never to be as unkind to her children as the mother sitting next to her had been to her. Isabel ignored the comment. Francisca said, "I'll never tell my daughter I wished I'd never had her." Isabel turned to her with a look of anger and guilt at the same time but didn't say a word. Altagracia was the one who cut in. "Feed the little baby that your mother is raising," she said and handed Francisca nine pounds of pure responsibility and guilt.

Later, when she is out, the women don't stop talking about Francisca. We sit at the dining room table to eat cake and Isabel tells me how Francisca has become much more social. She talks more. Her anger concerns them. Isabel has embraced the concept of psychotherapy, which she found very suspicious, and is even supportive of Francisca taking antidepressants. "I want her to graduate from school. I want her to continue with Xavier and hopefully they will grow up together and someday be married."

I ask her if she blames the influences of this country for what has divided her from her daughter and created so much stress.

"It's not what this country does to us, it's what we allow our children to do in this country. I need to be the one to put on the brakes. They have their laws and I have mine. In this home, I'm in charge, not American culture. My children do what I say and they will respect my customs or they will go to the street."

Her voice is firm and not without anger, though it's not clear what or whom she is angry about. I have opened up some kind of door with my question. She feels like she needs to assign responsibility for Francisca's depression and her subsequent teenage pregnancy.

"She missed her father. She felt like she'd lost me when I came here and then she lost him and her friends when I brought her to join me. I asked her what was wrong and that's all she'd say. So now she's with this guy and if he keeps showing this nice face then maybe they'll be a family. But right now they are so young. She believed that she could come and go with him as she pleased and she wouldn't talk to me about it," she says.

She outlines for me the work schedule she has had since Destiny arrived, making a case for having spent a reasonable amount of time with her children. She only babysits during the day a few days a week when the family needs her and she is driving people to work in the evenings, but that doesn't eat up as many hours as her earlier jobs. She is still out very late and up very early. She stops when I ask her if life is hard. "The worst has already happened," she tells me. "That is what is hard."

"Has something about the way people live here made it harder?"

"I think so," she says and her tone escalates. "I ask one thing of my children. One thing. I ask that my kids be humble. They should work hard because that is a good thing to do in this country. But above all, the most important thing we want of our children is humility. Humility is what I will never ever allow myself to lose and I can never allow them to lose."

"If there were ten American women sitting around this table and I asked them to name the qualities they want from their daughters, I assure you none of them would say humility."

"My daughter may have gotten pregnant but she asks me permission to go out late. She doesn't go to parties. She is still a good girl. *Buen hijo, buen esposo, buen vecino, buen amigo*. Humility. It is too dear a value to give up. It is not something I can concede. People here could use so much more of it."

Good child, good spouse, good neighbor, good friend. Isabel begins to sob, full tears streaking down her face.

"Why are you crying?" I ask her gently.

She can barely speak. Her mother gets up and passes her some paper towels. Isabel's mother makes a case for her culture, as if it had been tarnished by Francisca's challenges. "I used to open the doors of the patios on both sides of my house in the Dominican Republic," she recounts with a smile.

"The kids would run in and out in the breezes and laugh. Being with your family, the humility of simplicity was lovely. Life was not stressful. Here women live their life in a rush. As soon as you get up you're in a constant rush. You rush for the bus then you rush for the train then you rush to work and rush back home to rush to the super or the doctor or to make dinner. Life is lost in the rush. I always feel a little ill when I come back from visiting my country. It's the rush."

I feel the color in my face as she is speaking because my life is all about that rush. I rush away from my kids to work on a Sunday and rush back to see them before they sleep. I rush to get ahead and rush to not get behind. I rush through life and sometimes I rush past it. I fully understand why Isabel is crying. It's not because her daughter is pregnant or suffers from depression or because this smug teenage boy is moving in on her family. It is because she feels the weight of what she has lost in the rush.

Humility may clash with what classic American values are about at this moment in time, competitiveness that borders on aggression, that turns life into the rat race we supposedly disdain. But it is humility that keeps a Latina grounded, that reminds her of what is important in life. Isabel had trouble keeping in touch with it before Francisca ever did and her efforts to keep it in her daughter as she rushed through life have had great consequences.

When Francisca comes back home I ask her to take a walk and we watch the sun set in bright orange on the hilltops around her urban landscape. Old men are playing dominoes in alleys near her house. Girls her age sit on fire escapes listening to music. The boys are all standing out on the sidewalks teasing everyone who walks by. There is a minor-league baseball game being played at her high school down the street and the bats crack every so often before a wave of Spanish voices gathers into a cheer. The next day she has to be at school by eight a.m. She often comes in late because she oversleeps. A few times a month she just skips class to help her mother take care of the four children she is babysitting.

The only thing that ensures she will get up and make it most days is that Destiny cries and wakes her up and Xavier often spends the night. She says she has mostly eighties and nineties in school these days and likes writing and English the best. She has decided that she wants to be a social worker so she can help troubled kids. Xavier lives in a very tough neighborhood not far away. His building smells of urine and tough guys hang around outside. She likes him to stay at her place. But he can only stay the night. She has an appointment with WIC tomorrow to pick up vouchers for food for Destiny and she was hoping he would come along. She is counting on calling her mother to come help her with the baby.

Boys whistle and chatter as she walks by and she dips her head and walks straight past them. She is having migraines again, she says. She feels this weight in her head and admits she suffers from depression. Having Destiny has brought her great joy, she says, and it has made her closer to her mother. She is an easy baby and she adores her. The night is closing out the day so we begin to head back through the electric feeling of the city streets. Neon signs are blinking on and mothers are calling their children home to eat.

Francisca is relieved that her mother is leaving for work in a few minutes and she can be home with Destiny and Xavier. I ask her who will take care of Destiny as she tries to graduate and make a life with her boyfriend, whom she now says she plans to marry as soon as Xavier turns eighteen and won't need the permission of his family. She looks at me like I've asked a question with an obvious answer. "My mother will take care of her," she says. "She's great with her."

7

lowriders in mayberry

AS SOON AS I meet Bob Spencer my first impression is that he reminds me of my dad, except younger. It's not just that he's Australian; it's his wry sense of humor and the way he extends his hand warmly in your direction even before you're close enough to shake it. He has kept his accent and has my dad's closely cropped hair and buttoned-up way of dressing. He wears his smile like another piece of clothing and searches for places to lob soft little jokes into the conversation.

Bob Spencer is an immigrant who blends in easily without any pressure to assimilate. Perhaps that's one of the advantages of being an Anglo immigrant to this country. You're not really an outsider at all. In some ways you're welcomed as the force that built this culture in the first place. No one worries that the Aussies are taking over the United States; they're these charming cousins from the old country who've come for a visit.

At first it seems funny that Bob's the guy who is going to give me a tour of Pico Rivera, California, a town just east of East L.A. where 92 percent of the residents are of Mexican descent. But Bob the Aussie with his infectious boosterism totally fits in here. Pico residents think they've created a Latino Mayberry, a place so removed from immigration and the acrimonious debate that the residents get insulted if you assume they speak Spanish. I like Pico for our documentary because it's a window into what the future might look like.

Bob Spencer is the town's public information officer. He doesn't speak any Spanish. Bob left Melbourne in 1987 with plans to swing in a hammock behind some tiny shack of a house on a Hawaiian beach. Instead, he ended up cleaning the inside of 747s and decided the island life wasn't for him. He searched for a job in a mainland American town and got hired as the public information officer for Pico.

"I wanted them to give me the title Public Information Manager Person so I could put PIMP on my safety vest, but they wouldn't go for it," he quips. While the large Latino population makes the place interesting, for Bob its most defining characteristic is that the housing is so expensive he has to commute from many miles outside the city.

"I'm the only Australian working in this town. Thank God they speak English here! My division is in charge of publications, newsletters, the TV channel [Bob anchors the local news]. One of the amazing things here is the population gets really upset when we run stuff in Spanish. They like to call us and remind us they speak English, thank you! We only do emergency publications in Spanish. It's all English because that's the way they like it."

Bob and I hop into a white City of Pico Rivera van to tool around the nine square miles of densely populated low-rise housing developments shared by Pico's sixty-five thousand residents. My team has rigged a lipstick camera to the dashboard to film me and Bob in the front seat. The audio device and monitors are sitting behind us in the large empty space where the seats have been removed. One of my producers, Catherine Mitchell, and my coauthor are banging around back there monitoring equipment and taking notes. An SUV trails us with two photojournalists and their video camera, a still photographer, and an associate producer. The plan is for one of them to videotape our car and the things we see on the tour via the SUV's sunroof. You work in TV long enough and sideshows of these proportions seem utterly normal.

The first thing I notice is how much Pico Rivera looks like Smithtown, where I grew up. A lot of small American cities that sit outside a major metropolis have this feel to them. My Smithtown had a Chili's and a Crown books and a lot of ranch houses. Pico has a Chili's and a Borders and plenty of bungalows. It's clear the people here care about their homes and communities and that business is putting up a healthy fight against a bad economy. The lawns appear combed and the gardens tended to. Municipal success has been defined by the presence of a big-box store: there's a mini-mall with a giant Lowe's and a couple of Starbucks and a Payless Shoes. The parking lots are full of shoppers and teens hanging out.

Our van swings around the wide corners on Pico's broad streets, sending my producers and equipment sliding across the back floor of the van. Bob and I are melting because the high noon sun is beating down on the wide front window and we can't turn on the AC because the buzz will ruin our audio. Bob describes the residents to me.

"These are generally third- and fourth-generation Latinos. Most have no contact with Mexico. They've never been to Mexico." Yet Bob says Pico has had to fight to attract new businesses because of the negative stereotypes some merchants attach to Mexicans. Pico tried to lure an Outback Steak House and they declined.

"When some of these places look at the cold demographics and see it's so Latino, what they think is that people won't spend money," he says. "But this is a middle-class community."

The town had similar trouble attracting a bookstore. "They acted like Latinos didn't read," he said. Borders opened up a large store after Pico used a federal redevelopment grant to pay them a $10,833 monthly subsidy for fifteen years. They placed a big Spanish books section there and it became a required stop for Latino authors, and that Borders is now the chain's top seller of Latino books.

"So not only do Latinos read but they read in English and in Spanish?" I ask.

"Exactly," he says, breaking into this proud Aussie smile as we swing past the bookstore.

"Is it a Latino community?" I ask.

"It isn't really. It's a fiercely American community."

Pico Rivera had its fiftieth anniversary last year and they celebrated by publishing a book with classic black-and-white photos that Bob presents to me as if it is a sacred document. Pico is bordered by water on three sides, the San Gabriel River and Rio Hondo on its east and west sides and the Whittier Narrows Dam to the north. The book tells the story of how the land was called the Rivera, literally "along the river," and was developed by two men who thought it had great potential for commerce because the Santa Fe Railroad was coming through. They named the town for the last Mexican governor of California, Don Pío de Jesús Pico, whose country house, El Ranchito, was built along the San Gabriel River.

The roots of Pico Rivera tell you a lot about the history of California's relationship to Mexico. Pico Rivera sits on a piece of land called *Rancho Paso de Bartolo Viejo* that was given by the Mexican governor José Figueroa to local people. It eventually ended up in the hands of Governor Pío Pico, who sold it off in pieces to various white pioneers. Píco Rivera's anniversary book shows that when the town adopted the name of the Mexican governor, it was mostly white.

The people farmed the land and called it Maizeland for a while because of its plentiful corn. The railroad changed everything, and by 1947 the town was divided into Pico and Rivera by groves of orange, walnut, and avocado trees. The book's photographs show impressive mansions studded by tall palm trees, and white mustachioed men wearing long black coats sit next to somber women in broad skirts.

The two towns were joined to make Pico Rivera in the late 1950s, and it's at that point that the faces and names in the picture book change. Boys on the 1959 flag football team have the surnames Rios, Castro, and Herrera. An American GI Forum was started to address the issue of discrimination experienced by Hispanic veterans. When the first high school opened its doors in 1952, the white student body named it El Rancho to reflect its heritage, and the local school district is called El Rancho. The American Institute of Architects awarded the school as the most beautifully designed in the nation and its halls filled with teenagers.

The Ford Motor Company opened an assembly plant in 1957 that employed three thousand people and the town boomed. When the Ford plant closed in 1980, the property was sold to Northrop Corporation. They developed the B-2 stealth bomber, but then they too shut down and the community began the lengthy process of turning the property into an industrial park and commercial center.

"So this used to be Northrop Grumman?" I ask as we roll through this expansive mall.

"This used to be Northrop Grumman."

"What's in this shopping center now? Marshalls, Staples, kind of the basics."

"Yeah, it's a lot of good all-American stores. Staples, Wal-Mart . . . Wal-Marts are everywhere, of course. In fact this one is one of the busiest Wal-Marts in Southern California."

"That's saying a lot for Wal-Mart."

"Yeah, it is. Actually, they estimate about twenty-five thousand people on a Saturday alone come through this Wal-Mart."

Just as the face of business was changing in Pico, the face of its population began to change, too. The Pico of the 1960s had a legendary high school football program that was named the best in the nation, and Latino boys were among its stars. By 1973, a girl named Donna Tafoya was the reigning Pico Rivera queen and her court had both white and Latina girls. Yet just twenty years after people of Mexican descent overtook the town, it's not easy to find a *Quinceañera* in Pico Rivera. We looked but all we found were Sweet Sixteens. The town prides itself on its large Fourth of July fireworks festival but barely notices Cinco de Mayo. Little League and football have won over soccer.

"The residents here will tell you they're Americans. When you drive around this community, you don't see many flags of foreign nations here, but there are lots of Stars and Stripes," Bob says to me as we roll past every U.S. food chain imaginable.

"Do you think that people telling you that Latinos will not read books, so we're not going to put a bookstore in, is that basically racist?" I ask him.

"It's certainly not good to generalize like that against any particular ethnic group, I think it's shortsighted on the part of people, particularly those who should know better. And those are the booksellers and companies. Same goes for companies and restaurant chains that may say that Latinos don't eat this style of food. People just think it's Mexican restaurants and taco restaurants."

"We've passed a lot of Chinese restaurants."

"There's a lot of Chinese. And we just opened up our first Thai restaurant recently, which is very well patronized, and there are lots of different types of food. We've got tons of pizza stores now. And we have some of the major national brand companies that are starting to look for space here. And unfortunately it might be too late because there's not a lot of space in Pico Rivera."

"They should have made their move when they had the chance."

"And we certainly offered it to them, but they look at that ninety-two percent Latino on paper and think it's not gonna do it for us."

"But what does that mean, they look at that ninety-two percent on paper and they think undereducated . . . low income . . . impoverished, don't speak English?"

"All of the above."

"Don't identify as Americans?"

"Certainly all of that, I think, has factored into their thinking."

"Was that frustrating for you, or did you think, hey . . . you know what? Then someone else will take your slot. Then Borders will move in and make money."

"Right, it was very frustrating for us when that was happening."

One of the charming things about Bob is that he is so identified with Pico Rivera that he can talk about how Latinos are treated and say "us." That is another way that he reminds me of my father. He's a part of the tribe he's with. We wheel around and take our tour group back to the government center to say good-bye because we have a meeting with the mayor lined up.

I half expect Mayor Gracie Gallegos to be a traditional West Coast Chicana with a middle-class perspective. But Gracie is more Bob Spencer in spirit than she is union leader Dolores Huerta. Gracie was once named the *El Grito* Queen ("the Scream Queen"), like being Miss Pico Rivera, and she's blond and spunky and an irrepressibly cute cheerleader for her town. (El Grito is the celebration of Mexico's independence from Spain.) She is tiny and curvy with the energy of ten people. Gracie fits not one stereotype of Latina I know, except that she is all about her home. She loves this small city with its pretty gardens and tidy people.

"A lot of the stuff I report, I get this sense that there's this giant fear about Mexicans coming to America, and if you look at the statistics, the fact that Latinos are going to be the majority population as we head into the next decades," I tell her. "Is Pico Rivera a lesson in that? Is there a takeaway that it works just fine?"

"I think that Pico Rivera is one of those cities that instead of catering to where people come from, it's retained its Americanism. I call it Pico-Rivera-Mericans, because other cities that cater to immigrants, you know, to their culture, which is beautiful, it just doesn't work in Pico Rivera. In Pico Rivera, everything is done the American way. You'll have ten thousand people at the Fourth of July celebration. Cinco de Mayo, oh, 'Let's have a Corona and we're done,'" she says and breaks into peals of laughter. "So you know, I can see it as a model city."

I meet the mayor at her home, which is on an acre and a half of land she shares with her parents, her sister, and an odd assortment of animals. Her mother is a Mexican immigrant and her father is a New Mexican of Spanish descent. She says her family looks at this country as a place to succeed and has aggressively Americanized. She is the single parent to her nineteen-year-old daughter, whose academic awards line the living room walls: highest grade in math, highest grade in social studies.

"Most of my friends were Hispanic but everything was about being an American. We celebrated and had traditional Mexican meals. My dad raised horses and rodeo is very popular in Mexican culture. So I was raised with those roots," she explained. "But being here is all about being American. When I went to high school, I went to a private high school, it was diverse. We never talked about being Mexican. We always talked about being American. I don't even look Mexican. I'm very light so you would never know I'm Mexican. There was always, 'Don't forget your roots.'"

At some point her sister pulls up on a Harley with her jet-black hair with fine gray streaks blowing around her neck. She has darker skin than her sister. Gracie and she are like salt and pepper and she remarks that her sister's experience of being Latina has probably been quite different.

"So you speak Spanish?" I ask Gracie after hearing her banter with her family.

"Yes, I speak Spanish fluently, but I didn't realize it until I was about twenty-one. I was working and a gentleman came in and he spoke nothing but Spanish and I realized that I understood what he said and I could respond to him, but we never spoke Spanish in the household."

"Why not?"

"My mother wanted to make certain that we'd mastered the English language. She's very proud to be an immigrant and to be here in America and she wanted us to be American and she wanted us to have proper grammar before we learned Spanish."

Gracie's mother came to the United States knowing no English and now teaches bilingual education.

"My mother was the same way," I tell her. "I speak horrible Spanish because her attitude was you're American, learn English, I speak Spanish because I'm from Cuba but you're not from Cuba. In Pico Rivera, do most people speak Spanish, or only English, or both?"

"I think a lot of the older generations, they speak Spanish. But many people my age really don't. You know, you have third and fourth generation, so they really don't speak it. They speak the George Lopez Spanish, the funny stuff and probably a lot of the bad words, but no. My mother always enforced that if we were going to speak it, we were going to speak it correctly. So, I would say predominantly the older, the seniors, they speak Spanish."

"Is it a point of pride to not speak Spanish because you're in America and you're Americans, or . . . what is it?"

"I think it's a point of pride in assimilating, being American."

But the city's own statistics show that 70 percent of Pico's residents are speaking a second language at home and it's probably not a stretch to guess that language is Spanish. Even Gracie, after insisting how fully Americanized she is, launches into a celebration of her Mexican roots. She talks about her big family dinners and how nice it is to have her family's houses right next door. They sing Mexican songs in the backyard at family parties. While I'm there, Graciela, her mom, is cooking up beans and *carne asada* and Gracie jokes with her sister that it's "car-nay ass-adda." Gracie is a ball of energy. She likes being Latina. Her city council is all people of Mexican descent. She said there wouldn't be much chance of seeing a Caucasian on the ballot since the town has so few of them. They don't think about or know of any significant population of illegal immigrants in their town so it seems funny to her that they'd be associated with them. It's only people from outside Pico that make those connections.

I think about all the slurs you can hear about Mexicans.

"Especially during the swine flu scare, people would just go off on radio about dirty Mexicans and the insults I could not repeat on television, they're so unpleasant. Does that affect you? Do you feel like, why are you saying this about my people? Is that ignorance? What is it?"

"I think that is ignorance," says Gracie. "It does offend me because I think about my relatives, I think about my mother and how hard she had it when she came here. But I also think about how stupid they are because they have no idea how we thrive and what we do and what we're all about. And it is offensive. There was a radio station, and when they found out about our tax increase here in Pico Rivera, they said on the air, 'Who cares, it's just a bunch of Mexicans.' And I really wanted to call in and say, 'No, we're Americans, dork!' You know, we are Americans of Mexican decent or Hispanic or whatever it be."

Smack in the middle of this town lives its only celebrity, Lupe Ontiveros, who tipped me off to this town in one of her early interviews with my producers. She is a transplant, moving to Pico as her acting career took off. Traveling from Texas to California was a tougher transition than she had expected. In El Paso, she'd grown up in a very multicultural environment, going to school with Jews and Syrians and Mexicans and Latinos from all over. Everyone spoke Spanish and people moved easily back and forth across the border and there was always a connection to Mexico. In California, people were much more focused on integration. They wanted to make sure their children spoke English with no accent.

"Well, that's bullshit!" she exclaimed. "I always tell people you've got such a beautiful accent, I love it and to me if I can feel their background through their accent, it's a point of interest and a person always likes to be asked, 'Where are you from?' That opens the doors immediately to that other human being."

"How long have you been there?" I ask her about living in Pico Rivera.

"You know, I've been there about forty years. My children were born there, they were raised there. Nobody's ever bothered us."

"How come you don't live in Beverly Hills?"

"What for?"

"Because you're a movie star, that's what for!"

"No, no, no. That's not me. That's not me. You know, I think Beverly Hills, it's too expensive, too! I mean even the parking tickets are expensive! No, thank you! You go to buy a cup of coffee and it's twenty dollars? No, I don't think so. I'm not crazy. But no, I go to Beverly Hills, in and out, do my business, I have friends. But I'm just a person of the earth. I'm just a real person, and Pico Rivera is *mi gente*."

"Your people?"

"And I don't have any pretensions of any sort. And plus they consider me their most famous resident."

"In Pico."

"In Pico Rivera. Lupe Ontiveros."

"So you won't leave."

"In Beverly Hills they'd probably ask me to clean their house," she says and we both laugh.

Her home in Pico Rivera has a stunning garden. It is a modest house, one that fits into its neighborhood. She has made herself a part of this town, where she reports that the Latino identity is a subtle one. When she first arrived it was still a very Anglo town with a growing Latino population and she has seen it evolve into a Latino town that is fast becoming Americanized. Her first neighbors were Anglos, working-class people like most of the people in the town. She sent her children to parochial schools and they went to college, like most of the kids they grew up with. The town became much more middle class but didn't adopt pretense. There was always a new cycle of young Mexican-American families moving in. The place always felt like home to Lupe, affordable and familiar. She could walk through the Target and get recognized by her fans. That made it feel like her town.

"Does it feel Mexican-American?"

"Very much so."

"How so?"

"It feels like home. It feels like you're with, amongst your own. Not that I'm afraid to live anyplace else. I don't mind. I paid for my house. Right now I don't have to worry about anything. Why would I want to move to a place where I'm gonna have to worry and not sleep because I gotta pay a ten-thousand-dollar [payment] or something like that and try to keep up with the Joneses. I think we paid twenty thousand for our little house. Can you imagine that? And we were afraid when we had a hundred-and-nineteen-dollar payment that we would not be able to make it. We were a young couple then. Been married forty-four years. Can you imagine that?"

"That's amazing."

"Pico Rivera."

Lupe has adopted a new pet project that she says grows from her roots in Pico, which she sees very much as a town built on immigrant roots, regardless of its Americanized state. She is trying to raise money and political clout to help pass the Development, Relief and Education for Alien Minors Act, or the DREAM Act, a bill introduced just a month before I visit Pico Rivera. The legislation would help undocumented immigrant students obtain legal status if they go to school and stay out of trouble. Lupe believes that by helping the best and brightest immigrants succeed and stay in this country, you will get more Pico Riveras. These kids, after all, have spent most of their lives here and succeeded in an American system.

Lupe introduces us to a girl who is graduating from UCLA but cannot get a job because of her legal status. She's one of California's top students but we can't even use her name. California's public colleges have their version of the DREAM Act that allows kids in her situation to study, but they can't do anything for them when they get out. The young woman is raising money a few dollars at a time in hopes of going to graduate school because she can't qualify for loans or scholarships. She didn't even know she was undocumented until she was five.

Through this student I'm put in touch with Nancy Guarneros, another high achiever who was accepted by both Harvard and Brown but couldn't go because without a visa she is not eligible for loans or assistance. She hopes to go to UCLA if she can pull her finances together. California is like an oasis for undocumented kids. There are lots of stories like theirs, Lupe says. Lupe has rallied her Hollywood friends and neighbors in Pico Rivera to support these kids. Not surprisingly, she has found support for the DREAM Act in Pico. She has met no one who simply thinks these high-achieving young people should just be sent home to a country they do not know. That attitude is what makes her stick with Pico.

"I am able to go to work, do my work at the studios or party or go to the theater downtown, and then come back to my little part of the world where I feel my privacy and it's home, and I'm at peace."

"You described it in an article I read as the Beverly Hills of Chicanos."

"Oh, that's what I call it! The Beverly Hills of the Chicanada," she says, laughing one of her hearty laughs.

"Chicanos are Mexican Americans, and it's a slang word for describing ourselves. But Mexican American is most appropriate. But I call it my little Beverly Hills. What the hell, you know? It's mine. It's just my little safe haven."

It's an attitude that's in sharp contrast to what I've encountered in other parts of the United States.

Just a few weeks ago I had been driving on a desert highway outside Tucson to see Isabel Garcia, who is Pima County's chief public defender. This part of the country looks like the beginning of a movie about the old Wild West that begins with a rattlesnake sizzling across the steamy hot highway. There are brilliant cactus in wild shapes spiking into a serge blue sky from a land that is a kaleidoscope of red, orange, and brown. Fast-food joints and Circle Ks and small churches flew by me as I passed and it was clear I was entering a part of the United States with a personality all its own.

Isabel's house has wiring under the back gate to keep out the rattlesnakes. It occurs to me that people who fight off rattlesnakes are probably pretty tough. She and I take a walk around a community that has a little over a million people, about 30 percent Latino. Unlike Pico, the issue of Latinos transforming the place is nowhere near settled in these parts. This chunk of Arizona was bought from the Mexicans in 1853 and has Native American reservations dotting a sparse landscape with Tucson, a real city, as its apex.

Mexican immigrants have moved back and forth across this land forever but have not always been welcome. Illegal immigration is a topic of constant debate in this area, in shoutfests on radio and TV, on the editorial pages of the newspaper, and among regular folks living and trying to make a living in a troubled economy.

Isabel has been fighting a trend in that state toward criminalizing illegal immigrants. Crossing the border illegally is often treated as a civil offense, something that causes the Border Patrol to send people back to the other side and taints their record with U.S. immigration authorities.

Isabel has become a foil to Sheriff Joe Arpaio in nearby Maricopa County, who created a national sensation by rounding up illegal immigrants, usually a federal function, and corralling them with criminals in tent cities in nearby Phoenix, where temperatures can reach as high as 150 degrees. Arpaio paraded his detainees in front of cameras in pink underwear and put female prisoners and juveniles in chain gangs. He sees schools struggling with an influx of Spanish speakers, exploding numbers of people in emergency rooms or seeking social services, increases in crime—and points to the Mexicans. Arpaio has been featured in reality TV segments. He appears as a guest on *Lou Dobbs Tonight*, which airs on my own CNN.

Sheriff Arpaio is a hero to those who demonize illegal immigrants. He is being attacked by an alphabet soup of human rights organizations, like the ACLU, ADL, Amnesty International, and many others. He spends a small fortune defending his town in court because of unexplained accidents, incidents of abuse and even deaths. He has had reporters arrested after they criticized him. The *East Valley Tribune*, the local newspaper, revealed that his focus on catching border crossers had allowed other crimes to thrive and led to racial profiling. The reporters Ryan Gabrielson and Paul Giblin recently won the Pulitzer Prize for their coverage of Sheriff Arpaio's efforts.

Isabel Garcia is the only non-Mexican to win the *Premio Nacional de Derechos Humanos* from the Mexican government, a peace prize for her work with the Coalition for Human Rights in Tucson. Her father's activism on behalf of Mexicans is part of that country's history. She is as far on one side of the immigration debate as Arpaio is on the other. She wants the borders open and considers border enforcement an abuse of human rights. When I talk to her I feel like I'm talking to a radical. She let her anger boil over at one of Arpaio's book signings in Tucson and joined a group of people beating up a piñata in his image. She claims she was dispersing the crowd but local radio shock jocks painted her as a communist and joked about her being raped. Local police officers said she's crossed the line to irresponsibility.

These two forces ran into each other about a year ago when the Arizona Department of Public Safety raided a Panda Express restaurant and arrested eleven workers, chasing some down to their homes and handcuffing them in front of their children. The workers were charged with felony identity theft for using Social Security cards to get low-wage jobs. The company, Panda Express, was not charged with anything despite the fact that twelve of its fourteen employees were undocumented and working with fake Social Security numbers.

Marlen Yobana Moreno-Peralta, twenty-four, was snuggled in bed with her eight-month-old baby, Freddy, when they came for her. She had been in the country since she was a kid but had never obtained legal status. Araceli Torrez-Ruiz, twenty-five, had been in the United States since she was seven and had worked for Panda Express for seven years. She was arrested with her coworkers at the restaurant so she never got to say good-bye to her three-year-old, Giselle, who is a U.S. citizen. Although none of the workers was earning more than $8 to $10 an hour, they all told their lawyers they loved their jobs.

Isabel Garcia stepped in to represent all of them. She claims the fake Social Security numbers belonged to no one so it made no sense to call it identify theft. It's how immigrants commonly get jobs where employers can pay their taxes. Her clients were in jail next to murderers and thieves, but unlike them were not allowed to post bail under new state laws. Six were returned to Mexico, while others await deportation. Marlen, Araceli, and another former Panda employee named Omar petitioned to stay here as all three have children who were born here and are U.S. citizens. Their cases are pending. Local activists finally raised money to bail them all out.

By the time Marlen saw her son again, he was a year old and had no idea who she was. Araceli's daughter is angry and doesn't understand why her mother vanished for so long. The Panda Express group has twelve young children among them, most of them U.S. citizens. The group pleaded guilty to the lesser charge of criminal impersonation and a judge ruled the infraction a misdemeanor, sentencing them to time served.

Just two months after their arrest, immigration authorities tried to use the same statute in Iowa after raiding a meatpacking plant in Postville and arresting nearly three hundred workers from Guatemala. They pled guilty to document fraud charges to avoid serving long sentences and admitted that they were using made-up Social Security numbers. Most went to jail for five months and were deported. Immigration advocates like Isabel were outraged that what they saw as the common practice of using a fake ID was being turned into a federal felony.

The case of a man named Ignacio Flores-Figueroa, a Mexican citizen, was taken through the court system all the way to the Supreme Court. He had used a fake Social Security number that didn't match that of anyone to work a job at an Illinois steel plant. He turned himself in to his employer and pled guilty but was sentenced to seventy-five months in prison, fifty-one months for working illegally but an additional two years on top of that because of the use of the identity theft law. Last month, more than a year after the Panda Express case, the Supreme Court unanimously rejected the use of this tool by prosecutors in immigration cases. Conservative Justice

Samuel Alito said it made no sense that someone who picked a random fake Social Security number that happened to be real would be punished more severely than someone lucky enough to have picked a fake Social Security number that belonged to no one.

When I met Araceli Torrez-Ruiz she fluctuated between acting tough and being vulnerable. She was wearing a T-shirt and jeans and her hair was cut in a long bob. She looks younger now than she does in the middle and high school photos she shows me, where she looks overwhelmed by hair and eyeliner and dark lipstick. She has an accent and is clearly more comfortable in Spanish. Her answers to my questions are different depending on which language we use. In English she is not so worried about her immigration case. In Spanish she is worried, even angry. She didn't even know she was undocumented until years after arriving in the country, when she figured it out for herself.

"My mom was a single mom so she had to do everything twice, do everything double. She would have two jobs, paid all these bills and all, whatever she had to do. So it was difficult for her and I did ask her, 'How come I can't get my documents to go to work?' And she said, 'Well, we just don't have them. We're just waiting.' We were just waiting at that time."

While she was waiting, Araceli went to school like the other kids and grew up with little recollection of Mexico. She felt very American and had a baby here with an eye toward living a regular life. Araceli has trouble talking about the day of the raid. She just gets too emotional.

"What was going through your mind?" I ask her.

"My daughter."

"You thought about your daughter."

"Yes."

"And how old was she?"

"She was three."

"Is it still upsetting to think about?"

"Of course, yeah. I think that it will be for the rest of my life. Because separating from my daughter is . . . she's just everything to me. And I think it would be for every mom."

I point out that Araceli knew her immigration status was illegal but since she came here as a child, she feels like she has committed no crime. She never made a decision to cross the border. She is just here and was raised here. Her daughter was born here and because of Araceli's status, she has been afraid to seek benefits for her. While she was in jail, her daughter got sick and her family took her to Mexico to see a doctor because she doesn't have health insurance.

I ask her why this country should let her stay.

"We were all honest people. We are just hardworking people, and I think we all deserve it to stay here," she says of her friends at Panda Express. "We come here to contribute a lot to this country, and we work hard. We work hard. And we do the minimum wage. We do all the lowest things that everybody else gets. I think that the government should do something about it because, I mean, we contribute a lot. What could the United States be without us?"

"Your daughter's an American citizen."

"Yes."

"Your mother's a resident."

"Uh-hm."

"Your uncle?"

"He's a citizen."

"Your sister?"

"Citizen."

"Who do you know back in Mexico?"

"Nobody."

"You literally know no one?"

"No."

"What do you think your chances are?"

"I think they're . . . I dunno, I think they're good. I wanna see them good."

"Do you feel like you're an American?"

"Yeah."

"Mexican American?"

"Well, I think that I'm more American. Honestly, if you asked me if I wanted to go back, no. Maybe to visit, but it will not be the first thing that I would do."

There have never been immigration problems that anyone can remember back in Pico Rivera, even though most people you talk to have someone in their past who came as an immigrant. A lot of them, like the mayor, only need to go as far back as their parents. They associate immigration from Mexico with a golden period when Pico became predominantly Mexican and all the houses were bought up. The schools filled with children and the town was moving from working to middle class.

Pico did encounter problems down the line, after the children and grandchildren became the dominant force in the town and crime, drugs, and violence began to soar. If you look back five to ten years ago, people in Pico tell you, the place was beginning to get a reputation as a *cholo* town, a term for Mexican gang members.

UCLA did a study on assimilation that looked at L.A. and San Antonio. They focused on Mexican Americans, Chicanos, over four decades and examined them on every level of assimilation, how they did in school, as breadwinners, with language proficiency. They even looked at how well they mixed with Anglo neighbors and whether they got involved in politics. They found that by the second generation, Chicanos have learned English, are becoming more educated, and are fast improving their quality of life and earnings and seem to be integrating with the Anglos in their lives.

Yet as they get further from their Mexican roots, something terrible begins to happen. Their educational levels drop. In some cases they are even lower than the generation before them. Their economic status follows the same pattern. There was a period in Pico where things seemed to begin to fall backward. The town was having trouble attracting businesses. The city's walls started to fill with gang tags, those unintelligible swirling multicolored sprays of graffiti that mean so much to angry teenagers when they're at war. Pico had 78 percent home ownership and the town hunkered down against the gangs. In 2006, the city had a per capita homicide rate of 12 per 100,000, double the national average. The place looked sinister, even by Bob's account, and he's the PR guy. Traffic slowed to accommodate tattooed men in lowriders who cruised the streets in search of trouble.

Bob drove me by the place where it all came to a halt. One night in August 2007 a fifty-seven-year-old grandmother named Maria Elena Hicks saw a man tagging a section of a forty-foot cinder-block wall at San Gabriel River Parkway and Woodford Street. The

wall had always been clean. Then one day the spray-painted letters
PV showed up. The city tried to paint it and ivy grew but the tag
kept coming back.

Maria Elena had lived in Pico her entire life, just down the street
from her mother and across the street from her daughter and three
grandchildren. She had also raised a son in Pico and had six other
grandchildren. Her friends called her Quita. She was from the
Quintero family, the daughter of Ruben and Elena Quintero, who
raised her in a stucco house with a shrine to St. Teresa out front.
She had a lot invested in this town and was fiercely proud of her
neighborhood. She was the neighbor who remembered to water
everyone's lawn when they were away.

Maria had spent the day at the home of her sister Melinda, playing
with Michaela, her three-month-old daughter, and driving around
picking up stuff for a yard sale. Maria had a wonderful time playing
with her niece. "She was saying, 'We had so much fun together,' and
it was her last day. That was a tearjerker. Michaela was only three
months old so she won't remember her," Melinda said.

Maria had to drive by the four-way stop on her block to get
home. That's where the wall is and a man was defacing it just as she
approached. Maria began flashing her headlights and honking. As
she drove by, one of the tagger's companions pulled up behind her
and opened fire on Maria's car. The bullet hit her right in the back
of the head.

Maria's daughter, Melinda Wall, was driving home just after it
happened but couldn't get onto the block because the police had
taped the area off. She took the kids to dinner and they got back late.
She remembers her son and her niece yelling that the police were
at Grandma's house. They recognized Grandma's car on the street
but Melinda told herself it couldn't be her mother's car. She began
calling around trying to find her.

That night in the hospital her children just sat there waiting for
Maria to die.

The four people arrested were all young Latinos, who are currently
facing trial. Police believe they belonged to a gang called Brown
Authority that claimed the territory around the wall they were
marking. They saw graffiti from a rival gang called Pico Viejo and
planned to mark a warning. The gang was estimated to have just

forty-eight members and one mile of territory but had a reputation for shootings and thefts. The gang was like a twisted version of a Latino family; many were related by either blood or marriage and they got together for big parties. A lot of them were members of the Tafolla family, who had raised their children not far from where Maria and her family lived. They went to the same schools but had moved in a drastically different direction as kids, commandeering the local Little League fields as territory and pursuing crime as a way of life.

Melinda was devastated to find out her mother had been murdered by the children of her schoolmates. In court, she said, the Tafollas would blow kisses at each other and show off their gang signs. No one showed any sign of remorse. She still can't believe that all this happened because they wanted to cross out the graffiti of a rival gang on a simple concrete wall. She was equally blown away by the reaction of Pico Rivera.

"It was, 'That's not what we're about, not how we represent ourselves.' Especially the Hispanic community, there are stereotypes. People were just outraged that, over voicing an objection to defacing public property, it was okay to take a life. That got people upset. My mom was a really good person. She touched a lot of lives when she was here," she said. "It was overwhelming, the funeral and candlelight vigil. It was way bigger than anyone would have expected. The town was just outraged and just upset."

Maria's death had come toward the end of a year with a string of particularly appalling gang attacks, each chronicled in the Whittier newspaper for the community to read. Early that year a man had been shot while driving an SUV and careened into a car driven by sixty-seven-year-old Marlene Johnson. She died and her daughter was injured. Then local gangs crashed a house party, shot one man to death and injured several others. A few months later a man was found dead in his car. The city was filling up with graffiti and residents were becoming disgusted with the gangs. Maria Hicks's death wasn't even the end of violence for the year. Not two weeks later, an eighteen-year-old was shot to death on the sidewalk outside his home. The city didn't record its final homicide until three days before the end of the year.

But it was Maria's death that seemed to hit some kind of cultural nerve in Pico Rivera. You don't go shooting someone's *abuelita*.

Everyone seemed to be talking about this grandmother who finally got fed up. The political leadership of Pico and surrounding towns was in an uproar. Gracie Gallegos says it was a real turning point. "I always say that Maria Hicks, she didn't die in vain because that drew national attention."

L.A. Supervisor Gloria Molina, who was born in Pico, found $400,000 for a Graffiti Enforcement pilot program that teamed up deputies with prosecutors and probation officers. The teams zeroed in on offenders and tried to recover the costs of graffiti abatement from the offenders or their families. If they did not have the money, liens would be placed on their homes. Instead of jail time, the offenders and their parents have the option to join intervention programs. The teams arrested 168 people in the first six months. A database was started to identify areas targeted by taggers.

"When we see graffiti now we take a picture and it links up through a satellite. We use a GPS system and we're able to pinpoint where all this graffiti is taking place," said Lieutenant Steve Sanchez of the Pico Rivera Sheriff's Department. "For the most part these individuals are doing it within a certain radius. Using this system we're able to pinpoint how many of these monikers exist. If your moniker is 'Dopey' we'll go to the schools and find 'Dopey' and apprehend him, then prosecute; then the city goes after the parents to pay for restitution."

The plan seems very simple, superficial even, targeting the gangs by working to erase their calling cards. But it's been extraordinarily successful.

By the 2008 celebration of Pico's fiftieth birthday, the city was experiencing sharp reductions in crime. Gun incidents had fallen 71 percent. The drop in crime also dovetailed nicely with a resurgence in development. The industrial park had opened as an industrial warehouse complex and a shopping complex, one of three with chain stores and restaurants. The city got a fitness center and a large theater complex. Home ownership continued to be high regardless of the housing crisis. On my tour with Bob, he showed me a large condominium housing development with half-million-dollar homes not far down the road from where Maria Hicks died. The city faces the same deficits and budget issues facing all American cities during a recession, but there is unanimous agreement among its leaders that it has escaped the worst.

As things improved, the focus on graffiti expanded to include an attack on the gang culture itself. Lieutenant Steve Sanchez had grown up with his grandmother in East L.A. The Maria Hicks murder reminded him of the environment he was trying to escape. Sanchez's best friend, Eddie, had become a drug user, having several children, some of whom have ended up in prison. Steve could have gone in the same direction. He remembers the strong grip the gangs had on his neighborhood. He didn't want to see that in his new home. He helped begin a program called PRIDE that targets kids drifting into gangs or beginning to use drugs. He wouldn't work with kids already in gangs because those kids had no choice but to move somewhere else. He tried that, but eventually the gangs would hunt the kids down and kill them.

"That's what we tell these kids, once you're in, you're in forever. Once you come back, your friends will turn on you and kill you," he said.

Steve likes taking the kids in PRIDE to the pathologist so they can see what gangs can do, the dead and the drug-addicted victims of their work. The group also works with clergy. There are parenting classes for the parents. Gracie's mother is one of the parenting instructors. There is an aspect of the program that feels a bit like helping the kids discard the stereotype of the urban Mexican gang banger for that of the devoted family-centered child of immigrants. "I think that a lot of us, we have a lot of pride in our culture, but by no means do we carry that," said Gracie. "I think that culture is, your culture where you come from, your lineage, it's definitely a beauty mark, but it's not who you are. You are what you make of yourself."

The day after I meet the relatives of Maria Hicks, I visit a barbecue in a parking lot where ex–gang members have gathered to show off their lowriders. The lowrider is a creature of the car culture of half a century ago. Where white kids jacked up the suspension in the back of their cars, Chicanos rode their cars low, practically sliding along the wide boulevards of L.A. They started in with Chevys in the 1940s and moved on to the wide, long cars of the decades that followed. Unlike the white kids whose cars spoke to rebellion, these cars embraced the religious iconography and formality of their grandparents. They were a form of social protest against Americanization.

The guys formed the Together Car Club that reacted to Maria's death by working to discourage kids from joining gangs. The guys wear wife beaters and shorts with knee socks. Their heads are shaved and most have a goatee or a mustache. If you were casting a movie about gangs, this would be a great casting call. One guy has "Together" tattooed across his upper back. It's so thick with hair around it that it almost looks like a crown. Another has the word settled into the fatty ripples of his lower back. There are tattoos everywhere. Their bodies are canvasses for naked women, swirling serpents, and those hands clutching torches you see everywhere these days. I am so glad I am wearing black today because I blend.

A guy named Hector Avila comes up to greet me and show off the collection of lowriders that bonds these guys together. Even though he seems like the nicest guy he looks pretty scary and mean. Hector was fourth-generation White Fence, one of the gangs you don't want to meet on a dark street, but he chose to leave. Instead he goes to car shows and shakes hands with police officers and donates the proceeds of his winnings to the PRIDE program and a scholarship in the name of Maria Hicks. Hector is disdainful of his father, who was in and out of jail, and he hasn't spoken to him in fourteen years. He says a lot of guys join gangs to replace their broken families but he chose to have a family of his own.

Together gathers each weekend with wives and kids in tow (wives can't join and only watch) to polish and inspect their cars. Hector loves the fact that they've co-opted lowrider culture and used it to reinvent the whole gang look.

"I always say, 'One Sunday let's get the kids together and take them cruising on the lowriders, show them they don't have to be in a gang to have a lowrider. We're all working men, but we work twice as hard because it's an expensive hobby. I put in almost twelve hours a day, seven days a week. I work my butt off so I can do both of them. We try to send that message to kids. You just work your butt off," he said.

Hector says his car has $10,000 in additional stuff. These men are fiercely proud of these vehicles. The moment one of my photographers pulls out his camera, fifteen guys automatically grab chamoix and start rubbing down their hoods. There are incredible cars with shiny chrome muffler tubes sticking out in odd places. They are sparkling new with colors so dramatic and in such pristine condition that they rent out for weddings and win awards. The hydraulics are operated by switches that can make the cars go up and down and side to side. One car has a plasma TV that folds in and out of the trunk. They all have a sound system the size of a suitcase. This is not people with junky cars doing silly things. They are very serious about this. Each car sports a metal logo that says "Together."

Tom Martinez joined a gang at the age of twelve and did ten years for robbery and murder before he decided to quit. His nickname was "*Cholo*." He says almost everyone he's met in the lowrider culture belongs to a gang. When he got out of prison he felt like he met his mother for the first time. She got him a job and passed away a year later. He has committed himself to stopping the gang culture ever since. He owns a house today and says he runs a company with 120 employees that provides security for the movie industry.

"Things have turned out for me. I thank God that somewhere along the line I had the opportunity to do this," he says.

I get into a giant blue four-door car with a bunch of these guys. I don't know cars so I have no idea what kind it is. It jumps about a foot off the ground and I have to hold on to the window frame so I don't slam into the ceiling. It's funny. We're in this gang vehicle but everyone has to wear their seat belt. The whole thing is hilarious and I have a great time. At the end our still photographer motions for me to get into a picture with one of the guys and suddenly I'm surrounded by all of Together, wives and children included. It feels like we're taking a picture at some bizarre family reunion. There is barbecue and families and laughter. Everyone jumps in and shows off their black shirts or Together tattoos. You can get how this works. The next time one of those lowriders bounces by I'm going to see it as a work of art.

On the edge someplace between the Pico that's emerging and the one that almost sank are kids like Erica Sparks. Erica is thirteen. She's one of the kids in the PRIDE program and she is supposed to be graduating this month. But things are uncertain. Erica lives on a typical Pico street with one-story stucco houses and lawns ferociously edged by trimmers. But her story is not at all typical of Pico. Her mom has been in and out of prison and her father has long since disappeared. She's mostly been raised by her stepfather, Eric Barrientos, who moved her here because he thought Pico was a better place to raise children than the tough neighborhood where Erica was born. Eric is on his third major relationship and has several other kids, including a new baby with Ebony, his current girlfriend.

Erica was caught tagging her middle school with graffiti and was facing the possiblity of jail time as a juvenile when we met her. Pico considers spray-painting a pathway crime so there is every possibility they would come down hard. But it's clear when you enter her house that this is not some rotten-to-the-core gang girl who can't be saved. Eric clearly loves her and gets very defensive when you refer to her as his stepdaughter. "I'm her father," he says firmly. "I love her."

On their wall is an honor roll certificate from June 14, 2006, when Erica got between a 3.5 and 4.0 GPA. Her bedroom is decorated with soccer trophies and other accolades. "That was a long time ago," says this girl who hasn't been alive long enough for anything to be a long time ago. She is wearing black clothes with a long string of white rosary beads around her neck and black Adidas tennis shoes. She is beautiful. Her long, wispy hair has highlights and her eyebrows have been plucked razor thin. Her eyeliner brings out her large, oval eyes. She has a French manicure and looks like she carefully chose her look to greet me. We walk up and down her quiet street, which, she says, is a much nicer place than anywhere she's ever lived. Eric had wanted a neighborhood like this for her, yet she's chosen to use this setting to get into trouble.

"So you got in trouble for tagging, for doing graffiti? Was it like a group of people, a crew, of taggers, basically?"

"It was a party crew."

"What's that?"

"Where you go out to parties, and it's just a crew. And like, you ever heard of flyer?"

I laugh. "Erica, I'm five hundred years older than you. So no, anything cool that you've ever heard of, I have no idea what you're talking about, so you're going to have to do like a 101 for me."

"Flyer is like a party," she says, laughing back. "Like a house party with a whole bunch of people. And a party crew, and you bring like a whole bunch of other party crews and you have like a necklace that will say what crew you're from. And that's pretty much all it is. And it was me and two other girls went to school that was in it. They were like, 'Oh, you know how to do some pretty cool stuff, so why don't you let it be known,' and of course I had a great idea. 'Oh, let's do it at school.' So I had a spray can and it was around six at night and I just tagged in two big spots."

"So in other words, if you hadn't done it, then the girls probably wouldn't want you in their crew. It was like a test?"

"I kind of had that idea, too, so it was on me, too."

While I'm interviewing her, Eric and Ebony are watching their other children and worrying about whether it's a good idea for her to be talking with a reporter. They have built a nice home for themselves and they are frustrated that Erica has threatened it. Ebony is into Mexican art and she has woodblocks with color prints on them hanging from her wall. *"Vive. Ríe. Ama,"* one says. Live, laugh, love. Another one says, *"Fe. Familia. Amigos."* Faith. Family. Friends.

Erica tells me she has a tattoo and she's quick to drop her waistband to show it to me.

"What's 187 that you have tattooed on your hip mean?"

"It means murder, homicide."

"That's a sweet thing to have tattooed on your hip when you're thirteen. Why would you put homicide on your hip? What's that, the police code?"

"My mom had it on her back."

"Of all the things—some people get butterflies!"

"I got it because my mom has it on her back and people say, like my dad, my stepdad will say, 'Oh, it's stupid,' because for one, my age, and I agree with that, but my mom has a tattoo on her back, and I never get to see her. She comes around every once in a blue moon so I figured why not get something of her? Out of all her, I don't know why, but she has like ten tattoos . . . I don't know why that stuck out to me, but it did."

Erica's behavior is so adolescent you want to strangle her, but at the same time it's all very sad. It's obvious she misses her mother. Her counselors tell me that, as does her stepfather and even his new girlfriend, who admits she doesn't know Erica well. They are all afraid that she's trying to be closer to her mother by emulating her.

"Do you ever think that you're destined to be a bad kid?"

"I don't think so. People say it's in my blood."

"What does that mean?"

"My dad is in a prison, all the time, so is Mom. They say I've just got bad genes. Along with the drugs and stuff."

"People tell you that? Who tells you that?"

"I don't wanna say."

Erica has been out of trouble for a month and says she would test clean for drugs if she were tested. She wants to go back to her regular school and stop being in a special program for at-risk kids. She feels like she is under pressure to join a gang, but could also go back to being the kid she once was.

"How come it's so hard for you to pick the side that's the achiever side? And not the side that's the bad girl side? It's like both sides are pulling for Erica, and you're kind of going to the bad girl side. And you have a shelf full of trophies."

"Those are my brother's."

"You're obviously an achiever."

"I only have like three," she says, acknowledging some of the trophies are hers.

"You only have three? Oh, sorry, my bad. Only three, guys!" I shout to my photographers.

"I don't want to be placed as the nerd or the one that's like 'what the heck.'"

"What do you mean?"

"I'm used to being bad already. It's gonna be hard to change. But I'll do it to avoid a year in jail. I think I could hold out till July, I hope so."

"So for the folks who pressure you to join a gang, you think you're gonna join one?"

"I don't think so."

"What would be the thing that would make you decide one way or the other?"

"I'm not ready to die yet."

"I'm glad to hear that. . . . You think joining a gang means you're dead?"

"You're definitely on that road, I mean, somebody asks you where you're from, they don't get along with you, there's like an eighty percent chance you're gonna die right there. If you're not strapped."

"Strapped means . . . carrying a weapon?"

"Yeah . . . So yeah . . ."

The funny thing about Erica is she talks with just as much conviction about someday owning a big house and having her own car as she does about joining a gang. As her stepfather points out, she has the choice to go backward, emulate her mother and her old neighborhood, where gang bangers used to tease her for not being Latina enough.

"Do kids think you're Latina?"

"No. They think I'm white."

"Do you consider yourself Latina?"

"Yeah. I am."

"Do you speak Spanish?"

"Yeah, some. I'm Cuban, Italian, and Mexican. But people think I'm white."

"Does it bother you?"

"Yeah, because they always put them down. And they're like, 'Oh, you're white,' this, that. I mean, I'm used to it already . . . I wouldn't think I'm brown either, 'cause I'm light."

"So people put white people down because this town is pretty much Latino?"

"Yeah."

"So you don't count, you're too light-skinned."

"It used to, I mean, in Torrance that was bad, like, everybody knew me as *Huera*."

"What's that mean? *Huera*?"

"White girl."

Eric looks as frustrated as a parent can be. He listens intently to our interview but keeps walking around his living room taking deep breaths. He has known her since she was born. Eric wanted Erica to live in a place where she would fit in and they could make a home. She has a choice to become a part of her new environment in Pico, a stable family-oriented community where being Latino is taken for granted, he says. But he also worries that she cannot outrun the anger and resentment she feels toward her mother and he is very concerned.

"The day I discovered Erica's tattoo I just lost it," he tells me. "I've always told her, told 'em all, we don't get tattoos. Not even when you're older. I don't want any tattoos on you. So when we saw that tattoo I was just very upset. Especially since I thought, 'What is this?' It looks gang-related, it's all hidden and this is not anything that I wanted for her."

"How worried are you about her?"

"I'm very worried. I know she's on a better path, but I'd say that the path she had been on was the path to disaster. She was really headed down the wrong way."

Eric sees her decline as a reflection of what can happen when people lose sight of their dreams and the dreams of the people that came before them. He sees that in Erica's family and in his own. They are the children of immigrants who took a great leap forward, but then as they became more Americanized, they got lost somehow.

"You know what it is, people come to the country with hopes, dreams, and drive. They want to be a part of this. They push really hard and they succeed. They really do," says Eric. "Especially Latino people, I've seen them working their butts off to get ahead. And they do. They get a piece of the pie. Their kids benefit from it. And they seem to go a little farther, but then their kids seem to fall back and they lose their drive and settle for mediocrity."

"Why is that?"

"I couldn't tell you why."

"But you see it."

"I see it a lot."

"Do you see it in Erica?"

"Possibly. Yeah, I do. Possibly."

The day after our interview, Erica runs away. She just vanishes. Eric is beside himself. I have left town but our producer goes to visit him and observes the search. Everyone is talking about how she must have run off with her best friend, the one who dared her to tag the school so she could fit in with her crew. She is not far from graduating from the PRIDE program and the counselors there expect she will show up even without her parents. She does. Eric does not go. She is in a place where she just doesn't want his help. He is exhausted. He says he can't fill in for her mother, can't make her into someone she's not. All he can do is change the place settings for her. That's why he's come to Pico.

"Do you feel that having come to Pico Rivera, you've sort of gotten your chunk of the American Dream here?"

"I did. Yeah, I did," he says.

"What makes you feel that this is the American Dream?"

"You get like these nice neighborhoods—for us, it's home. It's our

Latino Mayberry, if you will. Everybody's outside doing their thing. It's a quiet community, it's safer. And we just feel at home here. It's home for us."

"What do you think of the American Dream for Erica?"

"I'll tell you what Erica thinks. She wants to settle down, get married, and have a kid. And be normal. That's what she tells me. I think that's what she wants."

"Is she a bad girl or a good girl?"

"She likes to think that she is bad. She's not. She likes to pretend, she's not."

8

the graduation of cindy garcia

ARRIVING AT JAMES A. Garfield High School in East L.A., I feel like I'm walking into a run-down garden house. The buds on the tall jacaranda trees outside the entrance have exploded into pale violets cups, marking the oncoming of spring from Southern California down through Mexico and parts south. White and red roses burst from thorny long stems along the school walkway. The building is a creamy white with crimson and blue trim, reflecting the school colors. A flag flaps enthusiastically from on high. You can feel spring in the air. The sun is hot and the air is cool. It's a lovely day and teenagers are sitting quietly in the bright green grass devouring the contents of their lunch boxes. Some kids don't seem to notice how pretty the flowering jacarandas look set against a crisp blue California sky, but they put a punctuation mark on the place that announces something special is about to begin.

Garfield is a place rich with history in the Latino community. On one wall of the lobby is a plaque from the 1950s proudly listing the names of students who gave their lives in World War II, right from Acosta to Zepeda. Another wall has a bronze plaque emblazoned with a replica of the Constitution and the Bill of Rights, which was given to the school by the teacher Jaime Escalante, whose exploits were memorialized by Edward James Olmos in the movie *Stand and Deliver*. Jaime built an advanced placement program for the school in an effort to escape its reputation for churning out failure two decades after having gone from being mostly white to mostly Latino. There was a rubber-hits-the-road moment for him in 1982 when eighteen of his students—poor Latinos from a community beset by drugs and

Meeting Cindy Garcia to discuss her hopes of graduating from Fremont High School.

gangs—passed the advanced placement calculus test. The College Board accused them of cheating and made them retake the test. The moment the kids pass it again is a Hollywood heart-stopper.

But Garfield is no longer a place of unexpected results. In a country where Latinos already have the highest dropout rate of any ethnic group, 22 percent versus 6 percent for whites, Garfield is doing even worse. The student body is 99 percent Latino and 65 percent will drop out. Most years, they start with classes of fifteen hundred and end up with seven hundred graduates if they're lucky. That's even worse than the performance of students around the state of California, which is in last place in educational achievement. L.A. County has 680,000 students and 73 percent are Latinos. The dropout rate for Latinos is 36 percent and 35 percent for kids of other races or ethnicities. But the stats are punctuated in schools like Garfield, where so many students are poor and so much is at stake.

I have come to interview Monica Garcia, the president of the Board of Education of the Los Angeles Unified School Board. But she hasn't arrived. So the principal has lent me his office to recover from the cross-country flight and change from New York black to L.A. white. The office has books on Aztec warfare and the history of Chiapas alongside California Law Relating to Minors. It's clear a lot has changed since this place opened in 1923. I emerge to inquire about the L.A. public schools, passing walls with murals celebrating the Mexican Revolution and Aztec myth and toothy bulldogs in Mexican dress. Sharply dressed faculty members are on the go. The plan is to walk the halls with Monica with two cameras, one still photographer, two producers, one associate producer, and her PR person, as if this was a casual stroll through a public school.

When Monica arrives she sweeps into the building like a force of nature looking like a woman ready for battle. She is a large, imposing woman wearing a tailored black pantsuit and a bold red blouse. Faculty members rush up to kiss her cheek and say warm words. Monica is the daughter of poor Mexican immigrants who grew up in East L.A. going to Catholic schools. We immediately connect. Her mom also came to this country as a teenager. She didn't speak English and met her father, another Mexican immigrant, in a foreign student program. She was one of six kids just like I am, also one of four girls and two boys. Monica's parents were poor but very active in the schools and were determined that their children would learn.

Monica's parents became citizens in 1996, two years after California passed Proposition 187, which prohibited illegal immigrants from using social services, public health care, or going to school. Millions of new Latino voters were registered following Proposition 187's passing in 1994, and Monica believes it's one of the reasons she has had a successful political career. (The proposition was declared unconstitutional in 1997.) Monica is a political animal by nature and she was president of both her middle and high school classes. She tried being a social worker and even a stand-up comedian, but she was a natural leader and kept running for things. She is only the third Latino on the school board and she enjoys huge popularity.

Our walk through the hallway reveals a total contradiction of the depressing statistics unfolding before me. The classrooms look tidy and not overly crowded. The halls are clean and quiet, with barely a smidge of graffiti. The floors glow as if they are swabbed more than daily and everything smells of an institutional cleanser. The students look attentive and the teachers alert. A sign in one hallway declares: "15 Days Absent = No Prom. No Grad Night. No Grad Ceremony." In fact, the attendance of both students and teachers is officially over 90 percent. But what I'm seeing is an obvious case of doing something with nothing, Monica tells me. The L.A. system didn't build any schools for thirty-nine years while the schools exploded with students. Of the top five largest high schools in America, three are in East L.A. and one of them is Garfield. Of the 680,000 students in L.A. Unified Schools, 200,000 are going to schools in portable classrooms.

In the 1960s, Garfield began erecting their portable mini-classrooms in the parking lots and service roads around the high school. They are so orderly and regimented they resemble army barracks. Every corner you turn there is another row of them, painted in white and blue. There are so many portable classrooms at Garfield that the portable classrooms sit alongside portable storage rooms to make room for all the portable furniture. And the portables are not even portable anymore; they have concrete bases. But all the portables weren't enough to accommodate all the kids. So Garfield imposed a year-round schedule with three sessions of school. No one has a normal summer break or even a normal school day. Everyone is going to school seventeen days less than they're supposed to and class hours are staggered so there are students there twelve hours a day just to keep the classrooms from overflowing. A school that was built for fifteen hundred students at most is trying to educate forty-eight hundred. They may have found room for all of them but that doesn't mean they've found the money. California is number one in the country in funding prisons and dead last in funding schools.

Monica Garcia was spared this experience. She lived in the Garfield High School zone but her parents sent her to the Catholic school, St. Alphonsus, instead. She used to come over to use the impressive Garfield track. She knows these kids and they are good, smart kids. She doesn't see the dismal graduation statistics as a reflection of their potential but as a sign that they have been given unbeatable odds.

"For decades, our students have lived in very, very overcrowded conditions. Beyond severely overcrowded," she told me.

"How does severely overcrowded affect the dropout rate?"

"It explains a lot of why students don't feel a personal connection to a school, don't feel like they could get help, don't feel like there's a place for them. Some students will graduate. We'll graduate twenty thousand kids in L.A. Unified this June. If we didn't have a dropout rate, it should be forty thousand."

Of every two students I see in the hallways, one won't get a high school degree. One of two.

"How difficult is that to fix?" I ask. "How big is this challenge?"

"It's the challenge of the nation. It is *the* issue . . . because every challenge that we have relates to education. And our decisions to invest in education are decisions to make sure that we want one hundred percent graduation. That our workforce is ready, college-ready, career prepared. This is what's going to matter. The United States used to be the leader in high school graduation. Today we're number nineteen. It's a problem that affects national security, the economy, the well-being of our communities and families."

A few weeks earlier I had called Roberto Suro to ask him to be a part of our documentary. Roberto is a walking, talking encyclopedia of all things Latino. He is a professor at the Annenberg School of Communications at USC and a nonresident fellow at the Brookings Institution in Washington, D.C. Suro had an impressive career as a journalist, reporting for the *New York Times* and the *Washington Post* before directing the Pew Hispanic Center, a nonpartisan Hispanic think tank. Pew churns out these extensive analyses that paint a graphic picture of where Latinos stand. By 2050, more than half of all students in all schools in the United States will be Latino, and 84 percent of those will have been born in the United States. About 69 percent of all Latinos now are of Mexican origin. There are twenty-two states, including California, where Latinos are already the majority minority, according to Pew. They already look like what a lot of America might look like in just forty years.

Garfield High School is very much the future of this country. The Pew Hispanic Center research determined that Latinos are most likely to attend schools with the most poor students, the worst student-teacher ratios, and the most crowding. More than half of all Latinos are attending the largest public high schools in the nation with the poorest students. In California, 40 percent of Latinos go to large high schools full of economically disadvantaged people. What makes their study different is that rather than focus on the students, they have focused on the quality of the schools they attend. Places like Garfield.

"Every year there are four hundred thousand Latinos turning eighteen," Roberto told me. "If you want to give your documentary a forward spin then build a sense of the unknown around this generation of Latinos who are the future students of this country, the future labor force, the future voters."

Roberto worries about what's going on in the heads of these young people who've experienced the United States as a place of limited opportunities and great suffering. They are mostly U.S.-born but not so distant from immigration that they have not felt the sting of the ongoing national debate on the subject. What will our country look like if a large portion of its youth is struggling and disaffected, having experienced the demonization of their parents and lacking the education or the resources to cope?

"If they don't get educated," Roberto said, "we're all done." I've kept that thought in my head as I've reported the documentary and written this book.

The National Council of La Raza released a wide-ranging report in 2007 looking at "Hispanic Education in the U.S.," which found that in just ten years, from 1993 to 2002, the proportion of Hispanic students in public elementary and secondary schools rose from 12.7 percent to 19 percent, while the proportion of white students fell from 66 percent to 58 percent. Hispanic children account for more than one in five children of preschool age, but they are attending preschool in smaller numbers than black or white children. They are also missing in Head Start. So, long before they get to high school, they are already at an enormous disadvantage.

Once in high school the warning signs are evident. Hispanic students are absent from advanced math and science classes if they are even offered in their schools and are not likely to be admitted into gifted and talented programs. Perhaps the most pronounced issues are among the 45 percent of Latinos considered English-language learners. Most of them were born here or have parents born here, yet they are struggling with the language in school. And that number is growing. From 1995 to 2005, the population of English-language learners jumped by 56 percent to 5.1 million public school children.

"I feel as you mention all those things that I want to say, 'Or what?'" I ask Monica. "If we don't deal with the problems, what happens?"

"Well, when a student doesn't reach graduation, when a child can't read or write, they are limited in what they can do in this society. They're isolated. They're marginalized. They have to figure out something else. So when our dominant culture is built on inclusiveness, that is built on being a part of something. Right, when we're limiting what people can participate in because they're not getting access to basic skills, that's a problem that should be everyone's concern. Because then it makes more sense to be outside the mainstream, to be outside the mainframe. But what we know is that everyone wants to fit in. Everybody wants a chance to have a job, to be self-sustaining. And I'm very, very concerned that tolerating this reality in education for much longer will further divide, further tear apart and really put the United States in a place where it hasn't been."

A loud school bell interrupts Monica and students pour into the hallways. Monica scans the crowds. The moment the classroom doors are open the hallways fill with the scent of gum and construction paper. The kids talk low, often in Spanish, and politely weave around us without the usual antics you expect of teenagers when they see television cameras and lights.

"We have to accept that the child in our classroom is not the same child that was there ten years ago, twenty years ago, thirty years ago. And I think more than that, our world is changing. And so the school system hasn't changed fast enough to meet the kids of today. So indeed, we've got a technological revolution, we've got a green revolution, we struggle with the basics, literacy and numeracy. And now we've got a diversity of cultures," she says.

"School has to be a place that draws from it, builds the strength of it, grows it. We know that when any child gets a chance to read and write, life changes. And so for Latinos, for children of poverty, for children of color, that's the chance they need. But you can't give them the same thing that we know is not working everywhere."

Monica boldly tells me she doesn't think it's unreasonable for her to expect 100 percent of these students to graduate. We both smile at the improbability of that but her eyes have this inspiring determination. She would very much like to be a part of the solution to this problem.

An aide pulls us away to meet a group of students staging strikes all over the district in support of teachers who have been dismissed because of budget cuts. They are very angry and they'd like a word with Monica. The students have taken over a portion of the football stands and are refusing to go back to class. This is just the sort of thing that drives school officials to call in police officers and drag teenagers off to class or parents or worse. But that's not Monica. She tells me to give her a sec and marches over to the football stands to talk to the strikers.

The stadium is something to behold for a school that has the kind of issues Garfield faces. It looks like it belongs to a college with its long, shiny metal bleachers and towering stadium lights. Enormous bulldog murals stare down on a perfectly lined green. The bulldog is surrounded by the school saying: "A clear head. A true heart. A strong arm." The same dirt track where Monica Garcia used to run releases puffs of dust into the warm air. The strikers sit clutching posters and wearing shirts embracing different forms of revolution with logos of raised fists or Che Guevara's face. Hector Flores, an adult who organizes students for a group called Inner City Struggle, raises a fist and leads a chant.

"When I say, 'All power,' you say, 'To the students.' Power . . .," he yells.

"To the students!"

"All power!"

"To the students!"

Monica walks up and immediately invites the students to talk to her. A young girl in the front explains: "We sat in because they wouldn't [let] the teachers strike. So we felt the need to help our teachers. Because our teachers are like our second parents. Everyone knows that. First, it's our parents, and then our teachers. And we need our teachers. And the higher class sizes. That's going to affect us dramatically. Like, we need as much attention from teachers as we can get in order for us to work well and in order for us to do better."

Monica listens intently—not that she's hearing anything that surprises her. "So I got it," she responds after hearing out a few more strikers. "You don't want to keep class-size increases. You don't want to lose your teachers, and you're absolutely working hard because all of this affects you. I heard you. Got it? So I gotta tell you two things. One. I absolutely respect your decision to get involved with the decisions that this school district makes. Your voices are important and they matter. Two. We need you in the long fight. I know I talked to a lot of you and you know our mission is graduation. So this movement can't happen without you. We need you to graduate. So Hector is absolutely right. We need to make sure you are in the classroom."

The students know Monica agrees with them but she is president of the school board. "She represents an institution that has historically marginalized and disenfranchised students of color in L.A. So the students are skeptical," says Hector later. "She's trying to do good work but she represents an institution that has disinvested in students."

I ask Monica to give me some concrete examples of how she can improve things. She points to a bond program where $27 billion of local and state money has been invested in building schools. The district has already built seventy-six new schools and has fifty more to go. By this fall, Roosevelt, Garfield's rival school, will have its first class ever with a normal summer vacation. Two new schools are about to open that, Monica hopes, will relieve enough pressure on both schools to give them a normal classroom situation.

The names of the new schools speak volumes about where the population is going. Felícitas and Gonzalo Méndez Learning Center is named after a Mexican couple who signed up their children for their local elementary school in Westminster in the early 1940s. But the all-white school refused to take them because California segregated their schools by race. The Méndezes and a group of families sued Orange County with the support of the League of United Latin American Citizens in 1945. The families were supported by Jewish, black, and Japanese civil rights organizations and won a victory that is considered a precursor to *Brown v. Board of Education.*

The second school will be named Esteban E. Torres High School, after the former U.S. Representative who graduated from Garfield. Esteban was the son of an Arizona miner who was deported back to Mexico despite being a U.S. citizen. Esteban fought in Korea, became a prominent labor organizer, and founded one of the nation's largest antipoverty agencies, the East Los Angeles Community Union, before representing the 34th District of California in Congress, an area that includes East L.A. and Pico Rivera. Monica's hope is that these new schools will tip their hats to the historic names they carry and deliver a culturally sensitive education to the children who enter. That would mean teaching to the children who are in our schools now, children who are showing up without English skills.

"I learned Spanish as my first language. It doesn't need to be a permanent showstopper," Monica says, using herself as an example of why bilingualism can be good, not a detriment. "Poverty's not permanent, not being able to speak English is not permanent. All those things can change. And I think that's the biggest belief system that I want to offer Los Angeles United School District and anyone interested in changing our graduation rate. Children want to be successful. Families want them to be successful. In urban Los Angeles, where some of our neighborhoods are not safe, where we don't have access for families, and families rely on their children or siblings, this is a challenge. Families need to survive. Latino culture is built around families. But I think it can be a strength as well. Can we help families get the help they need?"

Monica believes they can, but the schools have to start by treating bilingualism as a good thing, not a stumbling block. They need to see that family-centered cultures can encourage education. Realistically, she says, there is no real option. Nearly half of all Latino children in U.S. public schools are learning English for the first time. Seventy percent of all Latino schoolchildren are speaking Spanish at home. She sees plenty of students whose parents want them to learn but frequently pull them out of school to work, to care for small children, to translate for them, to deal with adult issues they cannot navigate on their own because of language barriers. She wants to see the schools offering more social service resources to entire families so that children are freed up to learn.

All of these ideas take money. But right now, California is not spending enough money on their students, much less their families.

"We are at about eight thousand dollars a student. And teachers are being laid off, and class sizes are going up, and students are angry and are expressing their disapproval of this action. And students are also taking the responsibility of saying—this is what they can do—they're sitting in, they're doing a protest, they're expressing themselves. And we will say we heard you. We invite you to be a part of the solution. I certainly didn't come to this school board to lay off teachers and to increase class size. We have a financial challenge in Los Angeles. We're looking at 1.4 billion dollars cut over the next two years. And this is very difficult. We are a part of a global recession right now. This is not just happening in education."

So instead of bringing about the changes she desperately wants, Monica is looking at English teachers facing forty-three needy and challenged kids in one class, PE classes with seventy students, and guidance counselors "guiding" six hundred and fifty students. When you hear numbers like that, it's hard not to be deflated. But I feel a burning anger on behalf of every kid walking the halls clutching a stack of books. This place does not feel dangerous or disorganized. It's not even loud. The kids look like really good kids. But half of them will not make it out of here. One of two.

We walk through the maze of portable classrooms to complete our tour just as teenagers are spilling outside to eat their lunch, subsidized food for most of them. It's amazing how regular they look, full of teenage energy. Monica's aide tells me the school has its share of violence and disruption, but on this day every kid seems to have a smile and a hello to distribute. A group of boys in jerseys is diligently following the commands of a man who is unmistakably a coach. Girls are combing each other's hair in the stands. Most kids have a book cracked even as they eat their sandwiches. They could be the teenagers of any Latino I know.

There are a few students at Garfield who have beaten the odds and then some, including kids involved with the protest group Inner City Struggle. Monica's staff referred us to Jaime Vega. Jaime is a senior at Garfield High who is waiting to hear on college admissions. His parents came from Mexico in 1984, but his father has been in and out of the picture. His older brothers and he were born in the United States but his mother took them all back to Mexico because she was so desperately homesick, and his sister was born there. But soon his mother realized they had no future in Mexico and she crossed back into the United States illegally. She jumped the fence with a coyote and the two kids she had who were born in Mexico. She is still undocumented, unemployed, and raising them off welfare and money that his older brothers earn.

Jaime will be the first in his family to attend a four-year college if he goes. He applied to all the Ivy League schools but his 3.86 grade point average wasn't enough. His plan is to attend UC Santa Barbara. His older brothers dropped out of Garfield and ended up in low-wage jobs. His sister was the only one to graduate. But she is undocumented and ended up in a community college. A private organization is giving her money so she can transfer to UCLA. Jaime has a brother about to enter Garfield and another right behind him. He worries how they will do without their older siblings around to guide them. Jaime spent the first two years of high school homeless, shuttling between hotels and the homes of relatives. Yet he got straight As. He is living, breathing proof that there are some very hardworking kids walking these halls.

One of the things that turned him around was Inner City Struggle. His sister was involved with the first chapter at Garfield. He went to a rally like the one today and saw five hundred students in front of the school demanding a better education.

"Being there, feeling emotion, excitement, I knew I could participate for the next four years," he said. "I don't know how I would be without Inner City Struggle. I have no computer at home, it's difficult for me to even do homework, so them letting me use their resources . . . they've driven me to interviews since my mom can't drive, my brothers don't drive. I live quite a distance from Garfield—commute on public transportation—live on the border of East L.A. and Boyle Heights. I know the most challenging aspect of Garfield is the severe overcrowding. We have the track schedule, we go year-round, that makes it even harder to get enrolled in courses you wanna take. If I want to take an AP course in another track, that will change my schedule in school. That's difficult for a student who wants to achieve. If you're involved in other things that takes time. There's only about five counselors per track—so about fifteen counselors to schedule forty-five hundred students' classes. . . .

"I've known a couple of people that just decided—my cousin decided to drop out, didn't think Garfield was a good fit for him, now he's going to a technical school to be a computer administrator . . . he dropped out as a sophomore. I know other people that just don't get that attention that keeps them going. I had the support of my sister and my mother but some kids don't have that at home or at school, that just puts a great burden on them."

Jaime finds Garfield a pretty rough place to go to school. It's in East L.A. after all and the gang violence, graffiti, and what he calls the "negative attention" can be overwhelming. This very pleasant-looking campus I visited still sits in a very rough neighborhood.

"I think I was able to excel, I guess because of my dedication. I knew since middle school I would be a college student, my teachers told me you are gonna succeed, I was like, 'Wow, if they believe in me I can do it.' In ninth grade I enrolled in honors classes, then AP courses, five AP courses in eleventh grade. If students want to do well at Garfield they need to take initiative, I've had so many clubs. I'm in a program called College Match that helps underprivileged students. I'm also in the Berkeley program. I was able to succeed with the help of others' generosity."

At Garfield Jaime says there are measures in place to fight off the forces outside its doors. No gang attire is allowed, not even hats. He has had friends who found the military an escape from Garfield. He talked one friend into going to Cal State rather than see him become a marine.

Kids like Jaime encourage Monica to believe that her dream of a 100 percent graduation rate might someday be within reach. But Jaime is clear that he has done an exceptionally good job of navigating a tough situation. A study done by the same university he plans to attend tried to identify which obstacles present the biggest barriers to success in L.A. Unified School District. Why, the study asked, do kids have just a fifty-fifty chance of graduating? What they found was that the quality of education had more to do with whether you learned than your race, ethnicity, gender, language, or socioeconomic status. The dropout research done by David Silver, Marisa Saunders, and Estela Zarate showed that 25 percent of students began failing in ninth grade. It was particularly bad in schools with a lot of teens learning English. When a student attended a magnet school, his chances of graduating were doubled.

When you read reports like that, it all sounds less complicated. Algebra is a "gateway" to advanced math. Students who pass algebra by the end of their freshman year of high school are twice as likely to graduate. But 65 percent don't. The first level of geometry, biology, and world history are failed by nearly half those who take them. There is a clear place where student performance lags. It makes it clear that good schools can graduate more kids, regardless of whether the kids face a lot of challenges.

Their report says: "More than three-quarters of the difference in on-time graduation in this study were attributable to schools, meaning that *school* [italics theirs] factors were stronger predictors of graduation at LAUSD than *student* factors. Three school characteristics—the percentage of qualified teachers at school, percentage of English learners, and magnet school status—accounted for nearly half of the differences in graduation rates between schools."

We look for a typical student, someone who faces typical obstacles and is being educated in one of the district's tough schools. Monica introduced us to Cindy Garcia, a seventeen-year-old senior at John C. Fremont High School, which is near Garfield. Cindy is one of those students who could go in either direction, and the day we meet her she has approximately four weeks to go before she either graduates or doesn't make it. She is this small, curvy little thing with catlike green-brown eyes that have tiny specs of yellow. Her skin is a honey color and she has brown hair tinted with light blond streaks that's swept back in a thrown-together ponytail. Cindy is pretty and smiles every time I ask a question, but she looks sad overall. She looks her age, wearing no makeup but eyeliner. What is it with young Latinas and eyeliner?

We sit in the courtyard. The flight path for LAX runs above our heads, so we get interrupted a lot. I can only imagine how annoying that sound is when you are trying to study. It is a beautiful day, a tad chilly in the shade. Cindy has added a lip ring to her getup and I ask her if it hurts, which elicits a smile as response. Cindy describes her life as a disaster, separated from hope by just thirty credits of high school. She is in school twelve hours a day plus Saturdays trying to catch up to graduate.

Her troubles began in the ninth grade when she began hanging out with her sister's friends, seniors who skipped class. "What happened your ninth-grade year?" I ask her.

"I guess I didn't find it important," she says with regret.

"Did you go?"

"To school? No."

"Every day?"

"Kind of, yeah. I was kind of hanging out with the wrong kind of people. People that didn't care, and I guess if they didn't care, I didn't care."

"What happened to those people? Where are they now?"

"Oh, they didn't graduate. They're long gone."

"Do you run into them?"

"Yeah, I do. And they work at Target or, like, McDonald's. And they're like nineteen years old already. They were people that were seniors when I was in ninth grade."

Seeing her former friends in these jobs scared her. Was this what she'd be doing all her life? Her sister had gotten pregnant at fifteen but graduated and had become a bit of a role model for her. But Cindy's biggest problems are not her own lack of direction. At Fremont just 29 percent of the students graduate in four or five years. A national study once called Fremont a dropout factory. Like Garfield, the school was built for a smaller population of no more than two thousand and its tall brick buildings now explode with students. There are five thousand attending in three tracks that run the course of the year. Even the kids who reach graduation have little to smile about. An estimated fifth of them are receiving a certificate of completion rather than a diploma because they failed the state exit exam.

The campus at 76th and San Pedro is a bit of a dump, sitting in one of L.A.'s toughest neighborhoods. Like the rest of California, it was enjoying the spring bloom when I visited, but the school is a mirror of the community around it with all the problems of a ghetto—high rates of drug use, gang membership, teen pregnancy, and poverty. To Cindy and the kids inside, it's just the place they go to school.

"Did you know how bad the graduation rate was at Fremont when you went there?"

"No. No, I didn't."

"When did you figure it out?"

"Recently, not that long ago."

"Did you think Freemont was considered a good school?"

"Well, when I tell people I go to Fremont, they go, 'Ooh, you go to Fremont?' Like, 'Ooh.'"

"What does that mean?"

"I don't know. That's what I say sometimes, like, what does that mean? Like, I guess some people don't consider Fremont a good school."

Yet Fremont is the place Cindy turns to escape her numerous problems at home. Her mother is from Guatemala and her father, who vanished years ago, is from Mexico. She doesn't give their names and says she doesn't know her mother's immigration status. Her stepfather is in detention facing criminal charges. There is a lot on this girl. She is surprisingly open with me, answering every question with the maturity of an adult, someone used to handling a lot. As difficult as the answers are, she never drops the sad smile. Cindy is exhausted from studying and her life is wearing her down. So many things are happening all at once. The family is about to lose their home. Her mother has lupus and needs Cindy to come to doctors' appointments to translate. Her mother's business is struggling, and if Mom is not at work, her only option other than closing the store is Cindy. The stepfather's car is about to be repossessed and she has to deal with that, too.

Cindy is a strong kid but there is something fragile about her. There are days she says she just doesn't want to get up. Yet she has signed up for additional weekend classes because school is coming down to the wire.

"I'm taking two classes in the afternoon, three fifteen to five and six to eight thirty. I'm taking a class on Saturdays in downtown—depending on how many hours I put in, that's how many credits I get. If I follow my plan, I'll graduate on time," she says.

This girl is anything but lazy. The classes she is missing are all electives, art and health.

"Last week I was so tired. I didn't want to stay the night. It was just getting so frustrating." I ask what her day looks like.

"In the morning I get up at six, six fifteen, take a shower. I try and be out of there by seven ten. I get to school; don't get out of school until eight thirty, eight forty-five sometimes. My sister picks me up, I come home. All I wanna do is sleep. But, I can't just get home and sleep. There is always something to do. Like I have to pick up something or my little brother or my niece and I always have to take part and like play with them. My little brother especially. Because he's always at the store with my mom. She doesn't play with him much so we always try to. And then I sleep with him, sometimes he cries, I have to deal with that. My day is short, it just flies by. There have been days when I'm just, uh [sighs] I can't. I can't."

My producer, Catherine Mitchell, is only able to talk to Cindy's mother once, briefly. Her mother says she wants Cindy to graduate but needs her at home. Her own mother didn't think she should go to school. That was something for men. But she wishes Cindy would do better. It's just that they are truly losing their home and there are so many other pressing issues she needs help to address.

Cindy feels the pressure. "Some days, like you would think that on Saturday and Sunday it's just my resting days, I can just chill but it's not like that. It's just sometimes I'm like, 'Oh, god, I can't.' I just wanna stay home. But I can't afford to. I have missed too much. I have missed too much school. And that's one of my problems, as well my attendance just isn't that great."

A few weeks earlier, Cindy was in a panic because she faced

one-hour finals in both economics and American literature. If she didn't pass those exams, graduation would drift out of reach. She had stayed up until midnight the night before and walked into the building saying she was rooting for herself.

"I'm thinking I am going to pass my test. The only one I am really worried about is economics. Because the only thing I am worried about is economics. Because it's a lot. It's a lot. It's like everything just put together in one big exam."

She has already started fantasizing about passing the tests and walking down the aisle at graduation. "*If* I don't walk in June I still have until December to get my diploma. So I'm going to get it. High school graduate."

As Cindy was taking the test, Catherine Mitchell, my producer, talked with Cindy's counselor, Marquis Jones. He is hopeful that Cindy is going to pass. She is smart and she is trying hard. Marquis is a "diploma project advisor," a program started a few years ago that is currently threatened by the budget cuts. His job is to make sure kids like Cindy don't drop out. He zeroed in on Cindy and has become her number-one cheerleader, guiding her through the process of how the impossible can actually be done.

"We know for sure that she is not passing one class. A science class. So we already met about a month ago, we set up for her to take that class during her off time. Pretty much she has four classes to do. She is going to be doing two adult school programs, one at our Fremont Adult school over on 65th and Avalon and one at our adult school here on campus. So by how we set it up if she's on task, which she has pretty much been on it lately, she should definitely finish by the time in June," Marquis says optimistically.

It's that kind of focus that teenagers like her seem to need. Someone to yank them out of the well they've fallen into.

"I think she is going to make it, like I said, if she stays consistent like she has been doing for the past three or four months, she should definitely. Because she has the ability, it's just up to her to make it happen," he says, as if he's talking about his own daughter.

"She is going to be taking classes, no break, she has no vacation. She is going to still be in class from eight to twelve thirty and three to five thirty, but our plan was since she lives a little far from the school walking-wise she is going to be going to in the morning—Fremont

Adult is about ten blocks from here—once she finishes there she is just going to walk over to school, bring her work to my office, work on that until three o'clock and then go to school from three thirty to five thirty in the evening." He is so matter-of-fact that you can almost forget how brutal that day is for someone who is seventeen.

Cindy says that her family believes in her but they just don't have the resources to support her. Marquis has those resources and he can see much further into the future than this teenage girl who lives the stress of her life in the here and now. It is critically important that she has someone in her life that can see past today's problems.

"A lot of the students over here, even if they have the ability to go to a four-year university, their mind is set on going to a junior college or going straight to work," he says. "One force is the Latino culture. A lot of the parents are like, 'If you're not going to go to school, you are going to start working.' So that's what happens with a lot of kids and the dropout rates. If you're not going to go to school you are going to have to start working so they start sixteen, seventeen years old, leave school, and she ends up in that type of job that's going to end up with no benefits. If you're fired, you're fired. Nothing to fall back on.

"I just tell them, college was easier than high school because it's a subject, everything you're doing, you want to do it, you're into it. So when you're into a subject, it makes you try harder, it's easier and more important to you."

Can Cindy really be one of those kids who push past this? "Oh, yeah, definitely. Definitely get into college," he says like a proud parent. "With her current situation, she'll probably want to go part-time first or do a junior college first, and then as things get better go ahead and transfer somewhere else. But she definitely has the knowledge and ability to go to a four-year college."

Debra Duardo created the Diploma Advisors Project that pays Marquis. She is the chief administrator charged with preventing dropouts in the L.A. schools. She was a high school dropout herself. Her father was Mexican, very strict, and didn't allow her to date. She eloped with her boyfriend to get away from him, traveled to Las Vegas and was pregnant at sixteen. She found herself the mother of a baby with spina bifida. She started dealing with doctors she didn't understand. Debra realized she was going to have to get a good education and enrolled in a community college, eventually transferring to UCLA and getting a master's in social welfare while raising four children.

"I'm working to get more people who are traditionally denied access to services to understand there are resources out there," she says. "So people understand you can do it. That's the message we're trying to get out in L.A. by using the Internet, MySpace, ads, finding things students find interesting and truly trying to think what it's like for today's students."

The idea behind the diploma advisors is they are supposed to seek out kids with poor attendance, failing math and English scores or behavioral problems. They assess the students to figure out what stands in their way and do workshops with the parents. They found that parents don't even understand that finishing school is not the same as graduating. If you don't pass the California exit exam, you haven't graduated, you're just done. And students who are done don't necessarily go to work. Their research has shown that one in five youths between the ages of sixteen and twenty-four is doing absolutely nothing.

"Most really want to come back and find a way to feel successful," Debra says. "So they're looking for them, bringing them back, and really trying to work with the administration at the school to change the culture—make it more personalized. Some teachers would prefer not to have students there who are problems. We have to help them understand why students act out, why they have attendance problems."

Marquis took Catherine Mitchell on home visits so she could see what they are up against. Catherine is used to meeting poor and desperate people as part of her job. By her measure, these were some very tough neighborhoods. As Marquis went out to corral children who don't show up for school, she found many houses where nobody was home. One kid who was home reported he was in a gang and had to navigate five rival gang territories to get to school. So he doesn't go because he's afraid he'll get jumped or killed. At another house, the kid and his mother are home but the kid slams the door on Marquis and Catherine, locking his own mother out, too. He had told his mother he was on break and since she didn't know English, she believed the lie. Marquis says that happens a lot in houses where the parents don't speak English. When kids go bad, they begin to run the place.

That is not how Marquis describes Cindy. He has hope for her because he sees the best of her intentions.

"It is going to be close, but I think she can finish the classes in about six weeks," he said. "She's one of the kids, you know, that is pretty typical of the area. They have a lot of different things going on at home. You have the issues of just living in the area, the gangs, and, you know, financial situations that people are dealing with but just a little more hard hit in this area. You have her culture, which is really strong, family-oriented. She just has a lot of obligations at home as well as at school. So that's a lot of the reason why she's been missing a lot of school. She has different obligations to take care of at home and she has [things] expected of her that wouldn't be expected of other students. . . .

"In 2012, without a high school diploma, you aren't even going to get a fast-food job, if you've not got a high school permit or are already working there. As far as her wanting to make something better for herself, if she wants to get out of the area or even if she wants to stay over here and she just wants to live better than she is now, you have to take care of your education and school first."

It's clear that Marquis is the only person who's ever really focused on whether Cindy studies and gets a degree. He believes in her and feels for her. He is constantly saying, "You can do it. You can do it." He thinks her sisters and her mother are behind her, too.

"They just are all carrying a lot as a family as far as taking care of their family and taking care of their own business at the same time," he says. "When people have these things thrown at them like pebbles, I say, 'Are they going to use them as stepping-stones or stumbling blocks?'"

But in Cindy's life, even the support of Marquis Jones is tenuous. As part of an effort to reduce its $6 billion budget, two months before Cindy's graduation, the L.A. Unified School District cut the $10 million Diploma Project, laying off nine thousand employees and depriving thousands of at-risk teenagers of counselors like Marquis Jones. He is still waiting to hear whether he will be one of the nine thousand. He may not make it to Cindy's graduation.

The new schools superintendent, Ramon Cortines, is a veteran educator who has served in big districts before, like New York. He is using the cuts as an opportunity to trim the central bureaucracy and shift resources to the schools. But the three-year-old program, which assigned counselors to forty-nine high schools and thirty-one middle schools, had been launched to combat shocking graduation rates. Without the Diploma Project there is no one left to seek out the kids who simply fall off the cliff. High school counselors are already working with an average of 500 students and the loss of the Diploma Project people combined with other cuts means they could be "counseling" as many as 650 students each, if such a thing is possible. When we last saw Marquis, he was holding out hope he would attend Cindy's graduation.

We drive over with Cindy to her mom's store and walk up and down the street with a trail of cameras. Her neighborhood reminds me a bit of where Francisca lives except it's quieter. Her mother owns a shoe store with shoes in bright colors and platform heels stacked high on the walls. On the floor she sells clothing, the typical L.A. summer stuff, strapless dresses, ruffled blouses. This is their livelihood and the store is empty. That's another reason Cindy needs to graduate. Her family needs her to work.

"Has it been difficult to try to make up those credits?" I ask.

"It has."

"How hard?"

"Very. Because it's like dealing with your extra classes, and then dealing with those, and then your social life, your house life, your family life is a lot of things."

"Your mom's not well?"

"My mom. My stepdad. My brother. My sister."

"You've got a lot of pressure on you."

"Yeah," she says and laughs that laugh teenagers use when they can't believe their situation.

"Does your mom speak English?"

"Not really. Well, she understands some of it, but . . ."

"One of your jobs is to translate?"

"Yeah, but I don't mind. Like, it's okay. Yeah, because it takes part of my day, like on Wednesday of last week, she needed to go see a lawyer. And he—I don't know how he didn't have an interpreter for her, but I had to go and—and then it gets kind of frustrating. Sometimes I understand and I don't know how to explain. There's certain words I don't know how to say in Spanish, and then there are certain words that are Spanish that I don't know how to say in English, but yeah."

"So at seventeen, you're kind of learning how to navigate lawyers, and doctors."

"Yeah."

That translation assignment cost Cindy a valuable day at school. But this is her mother's husband who is in jail. This is not a translation her mother can trust to anyone but a professional, which the lawyer did not provide. So Cindy is the next best thing.

"Have you missed school from that?"

"Yeah. Well, because I'm the only one that my mom can actually, like—my sister, she gets frustrated. My mom wants you to explain word by word and explain everything. Whatever you say, whatever she says, she wants you to say. And my sister's really high-tempered so she'll get frustrated. So I'm the only one that can explain stuff to her. And I'm the only one that can go with her to visit my stepdad because I'm the only one that has an ID."

Cindy cares a lot about her stepfather even though he is in jail facing charges of armed robbery. He told her his friends were armed and he was in the wrong place at the wrong time. Every time her mother goes to visit him it's more time from school and her mother is torn about pulling her away. But someone has to watch her little brother while her mother is in there, so even if she doesn't come along, she has to be home.

"It's a long process. You have to get in, make line, fill out papers, then you have to get in, get checked, then you get in another line, fill out another paper, then you wait for the bus."

"Takes hours, doesn't it?"

"Yeah. You're only in there for thirty minutes, but it takes your whole day. Because just the whole process of getting there and getting back."

"How often do you have to do that?"

"To go see him, not often. But to go to lawyers, I've missed a lot. Because I have to go with her. I miss the day before court, and the day of court. And then sometimes court's only fifteen minutes, but there goes my whole day, you know?"

"Do you ever want to say to her, 'I need to be in school!'?"

"Yeah. I do."

"And do you say that?"

"No," she says and shakes her head sadly.

"No. Why not?"

"Because. Because, I'm the only one that can help her. You know? If it was something else, like go to the store with me, then okay, but, like, this is very important. I kind of have to be there."

Cindy walks me through the store and introduces me to her boyfriend, Javier, who reminds me of Xavier, Francisca's boyfriend in the Bronx. He is slightly heavyset with brown eyes and dark short hair. He is very attractive with prominent black eyebrows and brown eyes. You can see why Cindy would be into him. He is playing with her ten-month-old brother, Brendan, on a hammock out back. Brendan has just woken up and has beautiful sleepy eyes. He is wearing only his diaper, and they put him down in one of those rolling bouncy things to roll around the store. Javier, just like Xavier, is great with babies. He is making Brendan smile. I'm relieved the baby doesn't belong to Cindy and Javier. But it's nice to see a seemingly nice, responsible twenty-five-year-old hanging out helping these people.

Cindy's take on her boyfriend fluctuates. They broke up once because she thought he was holding her back, but now she says he encourages her. He definitely handles things in her mom's store. This is Watts and it's not exactly overrun with great businesses. Someone has to be in charge of this thing. The stores are mostly small and run-down. There are three hair places in two blocks, a liquor store, another clothing store. There is no street traffic and the homes are these run-down, typical California bungalows. Not the best place for customers.

"Do people think you can do it?"

"No."

"They don't think you can graduate?"

"No. I think a lot of people don't. Sometimes I don't. Like, there's some days where I wake up and I'm like, 'Ooh, god.'"

"Does it feel like no one's rooting for you?"

"Well, kind of."

"Mr. [Marquis] Jones and that's it?"

"Yeah. Pretty much. I mean, it's nice to hear when someone actually says stuff. That's the thing I like about talking to Mr. Jones. He goes, 'I think you can do it,' and that's what he'll tell me. He's like, 'It's up to you. I don't care what they think, I know that you can do it.' It's even like the way he says it. You know when somebody's being honest with you, you know? I had a teacher like the last week of school who was trying to, like, convince me to go to continuation school. And I was, like, I don't want to go to continuation school. I want to at least try. I want to at least know I tried. I'd rather be, like, two credits short than forty. I want to at least say, 'You know what, at least I tried, you know.'"

She walks me the three blocks to her home, a basic beige color with a mango tree in the front that has failed to provide fruit beyond the first summer they lived there. The squawk of a bird can be heard from inside. I meet Cindy's thirteen-year-old sister, who has the same sweet smile. I ask Cindy if she thinks her school is terrible since her sister is going there, too.

"I mean, I don't want my little sister to come here," she says, looking over at her.

"Why not?"

"Because my little sister's very smart. She's very, very, very smart. I just don't want her to come here, and fall off track."

"Like you did?"

"Kind of."

It's the first time I've heard her even allude to her school situation being anything but a reflection on her. She has not said a single bad thing about the schools, the teachers. It's all on her, except that she wouldn't send her sister to Fremont.

She doesn't take me inside her house. We just park inside the gates, but in the yard is a bright blue truck. Cindy says that is the car that's going to be repossessed any day now because her stepfather hasn't made payments on it since he went to jail some five months ago. They can't afford his bail. They even ran out of money for his lawyer. So now he has a public defender. His incarceration has put the family's already fragile economic situation into dire straits. Cindy says they are behind on the mortgage. It's a three-bedroom house and they have not paid the mortgage in a year. Her mother is trying to rent out the bedrooms and have them sleep in the living room.

Cindy's mother works some days and makes nothing. On a good day her mother brings home $300 in sales. Her sister was going to El Camino Community College but dropped out to help care for

Brendan and her own two-year-old, Jacelle. Cindy was working at a shop called Glamour Girls but quit because her cousin's children needed a sitter. Her cousin was in the United States illegally and was filing for work papers when he was deported back to Guatemala. So Cindy is helping his wife with three daughters. Now she's considering applying for another job but there are not enough hours in the day for her to work.

Cindy herself is an entrepreneur. She noticed a graduation at the small school at the end of her street and ran back to the store to grab teddy bears to sell. And candy bouquets. The candy sold out and netted her thirty bucks. The bears were labeled for Mother's Day and they didn't sell. Cindy is a hard worker. She is always looking to do anything to make a buck. She's trying to get a dress for prom, and the senior fees, which are over $200, and she can't afford any of it. She's thrilled about the thirty bucks, though, because it brings her closer to her goal for the prom. I leave her in her yard.

Catherine hands Cindy a cell phone we are lending her so we can keep in touch because her situation seems so tenuous and no one around her has a phone. She smiles her beautiful smile but her sad and gorgeous cat eyes give her away. She keeps telling me how hard her mother has worked and how she is about to lose it all, everything, her house, her car, her store. She says she wants to graduate for herself, but about 50 percent is for her mother. She wants to accomplish it for her, even though she's the one pulling her out of school to go to the doctor. She understands her mother is doing what she can to survive, that the urgency of staying afloat takes precedence.

Hours earlier I had told Monica that Cindy seemed kind of like an accordion in the family, pulled in every direction.

"The service provider," she called her. "I don't know if it's so much the Latino culture as much as it's an immigrant experience, or it's the culture of poverty." What she does know is that Cindy is typical. There are a lot of kids like her in this vast school system and Monica does not believe they can be helped if the community cannot help the entire family. "Creating the community connections so that Cindy's mom can get help somewhere else other than Cindy," Monica tells me. "Cindy is absolutely a trailblazer. She's a trailblazer, she's a pioneer. She'll be the first one in her family to graduate. And she's facing a world that her other brothers and sisters didn't. Because if Cindy doesn't have a graduation diploma, she is less behind in another way. Because our world is just changing so fast. So Cindy's working real hard. And what Cindy needs to be able to build Cindy is to say Cindy comes first, which is a challenge.

"Well, especially when you have a tight family, a tight Latino family that values the family first and foremost, saying, 'We agree, but I need to pull you out so you can translate, I need you to come to this doctor's appointment, we need you to be a part of this. You are the family helper.

"She is the family helper. If I was Cindy's counselor, as I had been to many children, I would go and talk to Mom. I would say, don't we both agree that Cindy needs to graduate and Cindy can't make the appointment? Who else can do this? Sometimes there are habits and maybe Cindy is the best one to help Mom. Maybe Cindy is the one to get along with Mom best. But maybe there is a neighbor or extended family member. For Cindy, between now and June thirtieth, time is precious. So we need to help the family understand. If no one has graduated, we need to help them understand that here is her window. And I bet the family would get behind Cindy."

⎯⎯⎯◦

Days after I met Cindy, the U.S. Census Bureau reported that the minority population reached an estimated 104.6 million, or 34 percent of the nation's total population. They counted 46.9 million Latinos, one of six Americans. More significantly, the median age of Latinos was 27.7 years, compared to 36.8 for everyone else. A quarter of all live births are Latinos.

Our nation is changing. Not just because Argentines or Brazilians or Guatemalans or Mexicans have crossed the long border into the United States but because a new culture called Latino was born here and has given America a new face and sensibility. While these new families debate whether to assimilate or integrate into traditional U.S. culture, U.S. culture is changing with them. How that process happens will determine much of the future of this country.

I have had a chance to explore our community and witness how we stand in the world and I have every reason to believe that future can be bright if we decide to embrace this change for the better. Latinos face tremendous odds and some of us pay a very high price for being here. But just like my mother who pushed us to simply forge ahead, study hard, work hard, have faith, and embrace family, there are millions of Latino mothers and fathers out there devoted to that same ethic. We are like the conspicuous large panicles of violet flowers on the jacaranda trees that bloom everywhere from Queensland to Mexico to high above the entrance to Garfield High. We can flower and be lovely and announce each spring, or you can pass us by unnoticed until our moment is gone.

Cindy Garcia's moment was just a few weeks away when I met her, so I asked her to try to imagine for me what it might be like.

"Do you imagine what graduation day is going to be like?" I said.

"Yes. I think about it all the time. And I don't know how it's going to be if I don't graduate. But I think it's going to be bad."

I'm surprised that her first response is to consider how painful it will be if she fails. But this is a kid who, like many in our community, has become accustomed to taking her lumps.

"I'm not going to even come and see nobody graduate. I mean, I know that's selfish because my friend Amy's graduating, but I don't think I can stand being there and hear other people get their name called and not me."

"And how about the vision where you do graduate?" I ask.

"Well, that one's great. I can imagine me and my mom basically," she says, zeroing in on the most important part of the image. The two of them standing there on the football field. She is dressed in cap and gown. And on this one day her mother is not working. The car is not being repossessed or the house lost. There are no lawyers or doctors to visit or needy children to babysit. It's all about her and her future and the future of her family.

"I know my mom's going to be crying," she says, thinking about how it will feel for the two of them when she reaches the end of this uphill journey. "That would make me really happy. I know I'll be crying, too."

At that moment, I find myself rooting for this girl because it's not just about this girl. I think of the journey I have taken reporting this story and how important it is for our country to invest in this generation. I know that the Latino population is exploding and that the average age of Latinos is in the teens. More than half the 16 million Latino children are second generation and another 37 percent are third generation or higher. These young Latinos are mostly U.S.-born and U.S.-bred, and if they are our future, our future will only be as strong as our commitment to them. All around this country there are teenagers like Cindy trying to decide where they fit in, trying to figure out their place in U.S. society. We can choose to embrace their Latin culture and Spanish language or we can choose to demonize it and marginalize generations of Americans. I agree with Monica Garcia—being Latino shouldn't be a showstopper. Not when you have a culture capable of surmounting enormous obstacles and one whose success is essential to the well-being of our entire nation.

For her but also for all of us, I desperately want Cindy Garcia to graduate.

BY THE TIME CNN airs the *Latino in America* documentary for the first time on October 21, 2009, a lot of these characters' lives will have changed dramatically.

"Los Garcias" continue to search for their place in this new Latino America. In July, Bill and Betty Garcia will take their boys to a big family reunion in New York so they can spend time with their Spanish-speaking relatives and not lose touch with their Made in the USA, Latino roots.

Noelle Garcia has recovered from her bout with depression to be counseling teenagers. She gets married on August 29.

Francisca Abreu is still fighting off depression but was strong enough to speak at the Puerto Rican Family Institute annual event. She credited her mother's support with helping her overcome her suicidal thoughts.

Isabel Garcia's client, Araceli Torres Ruiz from the Panda Express case, will go to court in Arizona on September 15, where a judge will be trying to decide whether she will officially join the American family or be deported to a country she has not seen since childhood.

I am still rooting for Cindy Garcia. who is fighting off a new set of obstacles. She got pregnant, and severe morning sickness kept her from the classes she needed to walk with her classmates at graduation. But she hasn't stopped studying and is determined to complete her work over the summer and get that degree. By the time the documentary airs, we should know whether she makes it. Her struggle, like the struggles of all our Garcias, is about so much more than her.

Life presses on for the Latinos chasing their dreams in our four communities: Pico Rivera, California; Shenandoah, Pennsylvania; and Miami and Orlando, Florida. Pico lost Bob Spencer, its Australian Public Information officer to a bigger job, but this town needs no cheerleader as it sprawls into the lovely hills around it. The specter of the gang days does remain. Melinda Wall moved to England to get away from the place where her mother died. Erica Sparks ended up in Juvenile Detention for tagging her middle school. She will spend her fourteenth birthday behind bars but will likely come home to Pico Rivera, where her counselors believe a good environment will be stronger than the pull of the gangs. Pico's most famous resident continues to thrive. Lupe Ontiveros is playing second fiddle once again in her upcoming movie, *American Wedding*, but this time the star is another Latina, America Ferrera, whose character is marrying an African-American, creating family tensions over race. Lupe gets to film nearby at Frank Sinatra's house in L.A. so she can go home every night and tend to her flower garden in Pico.

After failing the sheriff's exam, Carlos got a second wind, signed up for more classes, and asked to take the test again. His fiancée, Keila, is expecting a girl in November.

The young Shenandoah men convicted of Simple Assault in the beating death of Luis Ramirez were scheduled to report to jail in mid-July, but it was unclear if they might remain free pending any possible appeals. Many expect they will face federal charges. Brandon Pierkarsky was sentenced to six to twenty-three months and Derrick Donchak was sentenced to seven to twenty-three months.

Perhaps the most dramatic turn of events happened in the story of Marta, the child in immigration detention at Boystown/Children's Village. On July 2, a Florida Circuit Court judge declared that she had been "abused, abandoned and neglected" and paved the way for her to ask the U.S. to grant her a visa. She was saddened because the ruling also meant she would be barred from seeing the mother she had come to this country to join. The next week a very nervous Marta walked into a Florida Juvenile Court to hear what would happen next. She wrung her hands and her face looked sweaty from the stress. Michelle Abarca from the Florida Immigrant Advocacy Council represented Marta for free with the help of some Florida International University law students. Miami Judge George Sarduy, a Cuban-American refugee himself, asked her what she wanted from him.

"I wanna get out of Boystown." she replied.

"That's what you're asking me to do?" he said.

Marta nodded her head vigorously.

"If I could do that for you, you're gonna promise you're gonna do good in school?" he asked.

"Yes," she answered clearly.

"Real good?"

Another nod.

"Ok. Guess what. Your motion is granted."

Marta's face widened into the first genuine smile we had photographed as we have recorded her story. "Thank you. Thank you," she repeated.

The Cuban-American judge picked up the phone and called the Cuban-American head of a local foster care agency, who got a Cuban-American case manager to assign this Central American refugee girl to a Cuban-American foster family by the next day. A year earlier she'd been denied her *Quinceañera* by her angry stepfather. But the day after her release, I was there to see her celebrate her American Sweet Sixteen. She still faces court hearings on her immigration status, and she spent her birthday surrounded by strangers: the foster family she had just joined; Lissette Alvarez, who came to meet her and sing "Happy Birthday"; and a collection of lawyers and social workers and our photographers. But she announced to the small crowd, "Thank you. I am free!" Her life as a Latina in Miami's America was about to begin.

acknowledgments

THERE IS THIS great saying that Latinos like to use: *"Pa'trás ni pa'coger impulso"* "Not going backward, not even to gather speed."

That's how I feel about this book. It was a great opportunity to blend my identity as a black Latina with my work as a journalist. Now that I have done it, I have nowhere to go but forward.

So many people in the Latino community embraced this project and gave me support. All they asked was that I be fair in my reporting and treat the story of our people with care and kindness. If I have not let them down, it is because of the contributions of Rosanna Rosado, the publisher of *El Diario La Prensa*, Maite Junco, the editor of *Viva* Magazine, Janet Murguía of La Raza, Elaine Rivera, Christy Haubegger, Linda Villarosa, Cheryl Little, Michelle Abarca, Gladys Limon, Gustavo Godoy, Emilio Perez, and Lupe Ontiveros. I also am thankful to all the Latinos whose homes and lives I entered to tell the story of our community.

When you work for a place as fast-paced as CNN, you steal so much time from your friends and family already. This book stole even more time. So thanks to my friend Kim for keeping me sane and Ed for answering my insane two a.m. e-mails promptly and Wendy, who never says no to a Cosmo and can do hair! My assistant, Robert, literally does it all for me and never breaks a sweat. Those are good friends.

This book stole even more time from my family, particularly from my husband, Brad, who is the best friend and husband a girl could have. And he's a great father to boot! A special thanks to my daughter, Sofia, for telling me, "I'm fine with travel if it's important, but if it's for a stupid meeting, then forget it." I hear ya! I am grateful to Cecilia, Jackson and Charlie for telling me I'm "the best mommy ever," even when I'm not. Thank you also to the teachers, administrators, staff and moms and dads at my children's schools for helping me get it all done, and for loving my kids as much as I do.

My siblings—Maria, Cecilia, Tony, Estela and Orestes—deserve a million thanks for helping every step of the way. I even forgive those of you who threatened litigation for any photos that were unflattering! Ah, to grow up in a family of lawyers!

The greatest thanks—added to that long list of what I already owe more than forty-plus years—go to my mother and father, my lifelong cheerleaders, supporters, helpers. And especially to my mother, who still believes that one day I can learn to make black beans as good as hers—if I would just PAY ATTENTION and TRY.

I am equally grateful to all the people at CNN who have worked to make *Latino in America* and all the documentaries we are producing come to air, particularly Jim Walton, Jon Klein and Johnita Due for having the vision to embrace coverage of racial and ethnic minorities. Particularly I'm grateful to Jon, who fired me and promoted me on the same day, giving me the chance to tell stories about people whose voices rarely get heard. I am indebted to Mark Nelson, Kathy Slobogin, Bart Feder, Jay Kernis and Marianna Joslyn for their support and to Carolyn Disbrow, our champion from the get-go, who met insane deadlines, without batting an eyelash!

The reporting of the CNN Presents team is what makes this book possible, particularly that of Catherine, Courtney, Alyse, and Kimberly, who is as smart as she is beautiful. The photography of Leon, Dominic, Greg, Ferre and so many others contributes immeasurably to the work I do.

This book would not exist without my literary agent, Lisa Queen, my facile and patient editor, Ian Jackman and my enthusiastic publisher, Ray Garcia. My coauthor, Rose, is a genius and a wonderful friend whose e-mails will kill my BlackBerry limit! She shares my love of diversity of all kinds in all people, and after six years of working together, this is Special Project Number One of many for us.

The book would not have been written had it not been for all the Latino journalists who paved the way. I am donating the proceeds from this book to the Soledad O'Brien and Brad Raymond Family Foundation, which funds educational scholarships and will give generously to the National Association of Hispanic Journalists.